Carnegie Commission on Higher Education
Sponsored Research Studies

A STATISTICAL PORTRAIT OF HIGHER
EDUCATION
Seymour E. Harris

THE HOME OF SCIENCE:
THE ROLE OF THE UNIVERSITY
Dael Wolfle

EDUCATION AND EVANGELISM:
A PROFILE OF PROTESTANT COLLEGES
C. Robert Pace

PROFESSIONAL EDUCATION:
SOME NEW DIRECTIONS
Edgar H. Schein

THE NONPROFIT RESEARCH INSTITUTE:
ITS ORIGIN, OPERATION, PROBLEMS, AND
PROSPECTS
Harold Orlans

THE INVISIBLE COLLEGES:
A PROFILE OF SMALL, PRIVATE COLLEGES
WITH LIMITED RESOURCES
Alexander W. Astin and Calvin B. T. Lee

AMERICAN HIGHER EDUCATION:
DIRECTIONS OLD AND NEW
Joseph Ben-David

A DEGREE AND WHAT ELSE?:
CORRELATES AND CONSEQUENCES OF A
COLLEGE EDUCATION
*Stephen B. Withey, Jo Anne Coble, Gerald
Gurin, John P. Robinson, Burkhard Strumpel,
Elizabeth Keogh Taylor, and Arthur C. Wolfe*

THE MULTICAMPUS UNIVERSITY:
A STUDY OF ACADEMIC GOVERNANCE
Eugene C. Lee and Frank M. Bowen

INSTITUTIONS IN TRANSITION:
A PROFILE OF CHANGE IN HIGHER
EDUCATION
(INCORPORATING THE 1970 STATISTICAL
REPORT)
Harold L. Hodgkinson

EFFICIENCY IN LIBERAL EDUCATION:
A STUDY OF COMPARATIVE INSTRUCTIONAL
COSTS FOR DIFFERENT WAYS OF ORGANIZ-
ING TEACHING-LEARNING IN A LIBERAL ARTS
COLLEGE
Howard R. Bowen and Gordon K. Douglass

CREDIT FOR COLLEGE:
PUBLIC POLICY FOR STUDENT LOANS
Robert W. Hartman

MODELS AND MAVERICKS:
A PROFILE OF PRIVATE LIBERAL ARTS
COLLEGES
Morris T. Keeton

BETWEEN TWO WORLDS:
A PROFILE OF NEGRO HIGHER EDUCATION
Frank Bowles and Frank A. DeCosta

BREAKING THE ACCESS BARRIERS:
A PROFILE OF TWO-YEAR COLLEGES
Leland L. Medsker and Dale Tillery

ANY PERSON, ANY STUDY:
AN ESSAY ON HIGHER EDUCATION IN THE
UNITED STATES
Eric Ashby

THE NEW DEPRESSION IN HIGHER
EDUCATION:
A STUDY OF FINANCIAL CONDITIONS AT 41
COLLEGES AND UNIVERSITIES
Earl F. Cheit

FINANCING MEDICAL EDUCATION:
AN ANALYSIS OF ALTERNATIVE POLICIES
AND MECHANISMS
Rashi Fein and Gerald I. Weber

HIGHER EDUCATION IN NINE COUNTRIES:
A COMPARATIVE STUDY OF COLLEGES AND
UNIVERSITIES ABROAD
*Barbara B. Burn, Philip G. Altbach, Clark Kerr,
and James A. Perkins*

BRIDGES TO UNDERSTANDING:
INTERNATIONAL PROGRAMS OF AMERICAN
COLLEGES AND UNIVERSITIES
Irwin T. Sanders and Jennifer C. Ward

GRADUATE AND PROFESSIONAL EDUCATION, 1980:
A SURVEY OF INSTITUTIONAL PLANS
Lewis B. Mayhew

THE AMERICAN COLLEGE AND AMERICAN CULTURE:
SOCIALIZATION AS A FUNCTION OF HIGHER EDUCATION
Oscar Handlin and Mary F. Handlin

RECENT ALUMNI AND HIGHER EDUCATION:
A SURVEY OF COLLEGE GRADUATES
Joe L. Spaeth and Andrew M. Greeley

CHANGE IN EDUCATIONAL POLICY:
SELF-STUDIES IN SELECTED COLLEGES AND UNIVERSITIES
Dwight R. Ladd

STATE OFFICIALS AND HIGHER EDUCATION:
A SURVEY OF THE OPINIONS AND EXPECTATIONS OF POLICY MAKERS IN NINE STATES
Heinz Eulau and Harold Quinley

ACADEMIC DEGREE STRUCTURES:
INNOVATIVE APPROACHES
PRINCIPLES OF REFORM IN DEGREE STRUCTURES IN THE UNITED STATES
Stephen H. Spurr

COLLEGES OF THE FORGOTTEN AMERICANS:
A PROFILE OF STATE COLLEGES AND REGIONAL UNIVERSITIES
E. Alden Dunham

FROM BACKWATER TO MAINSTREAM:
A PROFILE OF CATHOLIC HIGHER EDUCATION
Andrew M. Greeley

THE ECONOMICS OF THE MAJOR PRIVATE UNIVERSITIES
William G. Bowen
(Out of print, but available from University Microfilms.)

THE FINANCE OF HIGHER EDUCATION
Howard R. Bowen
(Out of print, but available from University Microfilms.)

ALTERNATIVE METHODS OF FEDERAL FUNDING FOR HIGHER EDUCATION
Ron Wolk
(Out of print, but available from University Microfilms.)

INVENTORY OF CURRENT RESEARCH ON HIGHER EDUCATION 1968
Dale M. Heckman and Warren Bryan Martin
(Out of print, but available from University Microfilms.)

The following technical reports are available from the Carnegie Commission on Higher Education, 2150 Shattuck Avenue, Berkeley, California 94704.

RESOURCE USE IN HIGHER EDUCATION:
TRENDS IN OUTPUT AND INPUTS, 1930–1967
June O'Neill

TRENDS AND PROJECTIONS OF PHYSICIANS IN THE UNITED STATES 1967–2002
Mark S. Blumberg

MAY 1970:
THE CAMPUS AFTERMATH OF CAMBODIA AND KENT STATE
Richard E. Peterson and John A. Bilorusky

MENTAL ABILITY AND HIGHER EDUCATIONAL ATTAINMENT IN THE 20TH CENTURY
Paul Taubman and Terence Wales

AMERICAN COLLEGE AND UNIVERSITY ENROLLMENT TRENDS IN 1971
Richard E. Peterson
(Out of print, but available from University Microfilms.)

PAPERS ON EFFICIENCY IN THE MANAGEMENT OF HIGHER EDUCATION
Alexander M. Mood, Colin Bell,
Lawrence Bogard, Helen Brownlee,
and Joseph McCloskey

AN INVENTORY OF ACADEMIC INNOVATION AND REFORM
Ann Heiss

ESTIMATING THE RETURNS TO EDUCATION:
A DISAGGREGATED APPROACH
Richard S. Eckaus

SOURCES OF FUNDS TO COLLEGES AND
UNIVERSITIES
June O'Neill

NEW DEPRESSION IN HIGHER
EDUCATION—TWO YEARS LATER
Earl F. Cheit

PROFESSORS, UNIONS, AND AMERICAN
HIGHER EDUCATION
Everett C. Ladd, Jr. and
Seymour Martin Lipset

A CLASSIFICATION OF INSTITUTIONS
OF HIGHER EDUCATION

POLITICAL IDEOLOGIES OF
GRADUATE STUDENTS:
CRYSTALLIZATION, CONSISTENCY, AND
CONTEXTUAL EFFECT
Margaret Fay and Jeff Weintraub

FLYING A LEARNING CENTER:
DESIGN AND COSTS OF AN OFF-CAMPUS
SPACE FOR LEARNING
Thomas J. Karwin

THE DEMISE OF DIVERSITY?:
A COMPARATIVE PROFILE OF EIGHT TYPES
OF INSTITUTIONS
C. Robert Pace

The following reprints are available from the Carnegie Commission on Higher Education, 2150 Shattuck Avenue, Berkeley, California 94704.

ACCELERATED PROGRAMS OF MEDICAL EDUCATION, *by Mark S. Blumberg, reprinted from* JOURNAL OF MEDICAL EDUCATION, *vol. 46, no. 8, August 1971.**

SCIENTIFIC MANPOWER FOR 1970–1985, *by Allan M. Cartter, reprinted from* SCIENCE, *vol. 172, no. 3979, pp. 132–140, April 9, 1971.*

A NEW METHOD OF MEASURING STATES' HIGHER EDUCATION BURDEN, *by Neil Timm, reprinted from* THE JOURNAL OF HIGHER EDUCATION, *vol. 42, no. 1, pp. 27–33, January 1971.**

REGENT WATCHING, *by Earl F. Cheit, reprinted from* AGB REPORTS, *vol. 13, no. 6, pp. 4–13, March 1971.*

COLLEGE GENERATIONS—FROM THE 1930s TO THE 1960s, *by Seymour M. Lipset and Everett C. Ladd, Jr., reprinted from* THE PUBLIC INTEREST, *no. 25, Summer 1971.*

AMERICAN SOCIAL SCIENTISTS AND THE GROWTH OF CAMPUS POLITICAL ACTIVISM IN THE 1960s, *by Everett C. Ladd, Jr., and Seymour M. Lipset, reprinted from* SOCIAL SCIENCES INFORMATION, *vol. 10, no. 2, April 1971.*

THE POLITICS OF AMERICAN POLITICAL SCIENTISTS, *by Everett C. Ladd, Jr., and Seymour M. Lipset, reprinted from* PS, *vol. 4, no. 2, Spring 1971.**

THE DIVIDED PROFESSORIATE, *by Seymour M. Lipset and Everett C. Ladd, Jr., reprinted from* CHANGE, *vol. 3, no. 3, pp. 54–60, May 1971.**

JEWISH ACADEMICS IN THE UNITED STATES: THEIR ACHIEVEMENTS, CULTURE AND POLITICS, *by Seymour M. Lipset and Everett C. Ladd, Jr., reprinted from* AMERICAN JEWISH YEAR BOOK, *1971.*

THE UNHOLY ALLIANCE AGAINST THE CAMPUS, *by Kenneth Keniston and Michael Lerner, reprinted from* NEW YORK TIMES MAGAZINE, *November 8, 1970 .*

PRECARIOUS PROFESSORS: NEW PATTERNS OF REPRESENTATION, *by Joseph W. Garbarino, reprinted from* INDUSTRIAL RELATIONS, *vol. 10, no. 1, February 1971.**

. . . AND WHAT PROFESSORS THINK: ABOUT STUDENT PROTEST AND MANNERS, MORALS, POLITICS, AND CHAOS ON THE CAMPUS, *by Seymour Martin Lipset and Everett C. Ladd, Jr., reprinted from* PSYCHOLOGY TODAY, *November 1970.**

DEMAND AND SUPPLY IN U.S. HIGHER EDUCATION: A PROGRESS REPORT, *by Roy Radner and Leonard S. Miller, reprinted from* AMERICAN ECONOMIC REVIEW, *May 1970.**

RESOURCES FOR HIGHER EDUCATION: AN ECONOMIST'S VIEW, *by Theodore W. Schultz, reprinted from* JOURNAL OF POLITICAL ECONOMY, *vol. 76, no. 3, University of Chicago, May/June 1968.**

INDUSTRIAL RELATIONS AND UNIVERSITY RELATIONS, *by Clark Kerr, reprinted from* PROCEEDINGS OF THE 21ST ANNUAL WINTER MEETING OF THE INDUSTRIAL RELATIONS RESEARCH ASSOCIATION, *pp. 15–25.**

NEW CHALLENGES TO THE COLLEGE AND UNIVERSITY, *by Clark Kerr, reprinted from Kermit Gordon (ed.),* AGENDA FOR THE NATION, *The Brookings Institution, Washington, D.C., 1968.**

PRESIDENTIAL DISCONTENT, *by Clark Kerr, reprinted from David C. Nichols (ed.),* PERSPECTIVES ON CAMPUS TENSIONS: PAPERS PREPARED FOR THE SPECIAL COMMITTEE ON CAMPUS TENSIONS, *American Council on Education, Washington, D.C., September 1970.**

STUDENT PROTEST—AN INSTITUTIONAL AND NATIONAL PROFILE, *by Harold Hodgkinson, reprinted from* THE RECORD, *vol. 71, no. 4, May 1970.**

WHAT'S BUGGING THE STUDENTS?, *by Kenneth Keniston, reprinted from* EDUCATIONAL RECORD, *American Council on Education, Washington, D.C., Spring 1970.**

THE POLITICS OF ACADEMIA, *by Seymour Martin Lipset, reprinted from David C. Nichols (ed.),* PERSPECTIVES ON CAMPUS TENSIONS: PAPERS PREPARED FOR THE SPECIAL COMMITTEE ON CAMPUS TENSIONS, *American Council on Education, Washington, D.C., September 1970.**

INTERNATIONAL PROGRAMS OF U.S. COLLEGES AND UNIVERSITIES: PRIORITIES FOR THE SEVENTIES, *by James A. Perkins, reprinted by permission of the International Council for Educational Development, Occasional Paper no. 1, July 1971.*

FACULTY UNIONISM: FROM THEORY TO PRACTICE, *by Joseph W. Garbarino, reprinted from* INDUSTRIAL RELATIONS, *vol. 11, no. 1, pp. 1–17, February 1972.*

MORE FOR LESS: HIGHER EDUCATION'S NEW PRIORITY, *by Virginia B. Smith, reprinted from* UNIVERSAL HIGHER EDUCATION: COSTS AND BENEFITS, *American Council on Education, Washington, D.C., 1971.*

ACADEMIA AND POLITICS IN AMERICA, *by Seymour M. Lipset, reprinted from Thomas J. Nossiter (ed.),* IMAGINATION AND PRECISION IN THE SOCIAL SCIENCES, *pp. 211–289, Faber and Faber, London, 1972.*

POLITICS OF ACADEMIC NATURAL SCIENTISTS AND ENGINEERS, *by Everett C. Ladd, Jr., and Seymour M. Lipset, reprinted from* SCIENCE, *vol. 176, no. 4039, pp. 1091–1100, June 9, 1972.*

THE INTELLECTUAL AS CRITIC AND REBEL: WITH SPECIAL REFERENCE TO THE UNITED STATES AND THE SOVIET UNION, *by Seymour M. Lipset and Richard B. Dobson, reprinted from* DAEDALUS, *vol. 101, no. 3, pp. 137–198, Summer 1972.*

COMING OF MIDDLE AGE IN HIGHER EDUCATION, *by Earl F. Cheit, address delivered to American Association of State Colleges and Universities and National Association of State Universities and Land-Grant Colleges, Nov. 13, 1972.*

THE NATURE AND ORIGINS OF THE CARNEGIE COMMISSION ON HIGHER EDUCATION, *by Alan Pifer, reprinted by permission of The Carnegie Commission for the Advancement of Teaching, speech delivered Oct. 16, 1972.*

THE DISTRIBUTION OF ACADEMIC TENURE IN AMERICAN HIGHER EDUCATION, *by Martin Trow, reprinted from* THE TENURE DEBATE, *Bardwell Smith (ed.), Jossey-Bass, San Francisco, 1972.*

THE POLITICS OF AMERICAN SOCIOLOGISTS, *by Seymour M. Lipset and Everett C. Ladd, Jr., reprinted from* THE AMERICAN JOURNAL OF SOCIOLOGY, *vol. 78, no. 1, July 1972.*

MEASURING FACULTY UNIONISM: QUANTITY AND QUALITY, *by Bill Aussieker and J. W. Garbarino, reprinted from* INDUSTRIAL RELATIONS, *vol. 12, no. 2, May 1973.*

PROBLEMS IN THE TRANSITION FROM ELITE TO MASS HIGHER EDUCATION, *by Martin Trow, paper presented at an Organization for Economic Cooperation and Development conference on mass higher education, June 1973.*

*The Commission's stock of this reprint has been exhausted.

*Changes in
University
Organization,
1964-1971*

Changes in University Organization, 1964-1971

by *Edward Gross*

Professor of Sociology
University of Washington

and *Paul V. Grambsch*

Professor of Management
University of Minnesota, Minneapolis

A Report Prepared for
The Carnegie Commission on Higher Education

MCGRAW-HILL BOOK COMPANY

New York St. Louis San Francisco Düsseldorf

London Sydney Toronto Mexico Panama

Johannesburg Kuala Lumpur Montreal

New Delhi São Paulo Singapore

The Carnegie Commission on Higher Education,
2150 Shattuck Avenue, Berkeley, California 94704,
has sponsored preparation of this volume as a
part of a continuing effort to obtain and present
significant information for public discussion.
The views expressed are those of the authors.

CHANGES IN UNIVERSITY ORGANIZATION, 1964–1971

Library of Congress Cataloging in Publication Data
Gross, Edward.
Changes in university organization, 1964–1971.
"A report prepared for the Carnegie Commission on
Higher Education."
Bibliography: p.
1.   Universities and colleges—United States—
Administration.   I.   Grambsch, Paul V., date,
joint author.   II.   Carnegie Commission on Higher
Education.   IIID   Title.
IB2341. G74 1974   378. 73   73-13634
ISBN 0–07–010066–7

123456789MAMM798765 4

Contents

68611

List of Figures

List of Tables

Foreword

In 1964, Professors Edward Gross and Paul V. Grambsch surveyed administrators and faculty about the goals and power structures of 68 universities in the United States. Their report on that survey proved to be a significant and useful one for serious students of American higher education. The 1964 survey did not, however, anticipate the major upheavals on many campuses that began that year. In 1971, Professors Gross and Grambsch surveyed these 68 universities again to find out if the events of the late sixties had significantly altered their organizational structure, their goals, and the distribution of decision-making power within the university community. This resulting study is an analysis of the data compiled from these two surveys, and the Carnegie Commission is pleased to be able to include it in its series of research reports.

The university could hardly escape being caught up in the events of the past decade. What is surprising, the authors find, is not that the university has changed because of those events, but that it has changed so little and in ways that often were unexpected. For example, the rank ordering of goals and goal preferences did not change at all from 1964 to 1971. What did change was the emphasis on goal attainment. In 1971, universities were no longer trying to be all things to all people, but were surrendering some of their functions to other institutions of higher education, such as community and comprehensive colleges. Disputes within the universities, as another example, have not always been resolved, but universities have begun to develop dispute-settlement mechanisms that offer alternatives to direct confrontation. Understanding more clearly their functions in the national society and in their local communities, and preparing themselves better to manage controversies, the universities have become more stable, not less.

This reshaping of the university identity, has, however, created new areas of potential difficulty. Internal power holders (faculty, administrators, and students), who are beginning to see eye-to-eye on the university's goals, are grouping together to face opposition from outside power holders (regents, legislators, and the general public). The divisions are now less inside the campus and more inside versus outside.

These are among the many interesting findings of this authoritative study. This analytical work by two experienced students of the organizational and power structure of the university gives those concerned with higher education fresh insights into the inner workings and underlying stability of this major educational institution.

Clark Kerr

Chairman
Carnegie Commission
on Higher Education

July 1973

Preface

This volume analyzes changes in the organization and power structure of American universities between 1964 and 1971. It is based on replies to a lengthy questionnaire from 7,200 persons in 1964 and 4,500 persons in 1971 in 68 universities. Such a replication would, we felt, shed light on whether the major events of the 1960s had merely shaken American universities, or whether they had led to structural change. Our findings tend to support the latter supposition: there are signs of genuine changes, some startling, all worth examining closely.

Carrying on a work of such magnitude generates many obligations. For assistance in the analysis of the huge amounts of data we accumulated, we are especially indebted to Dr. Thomas Steinburne, Betsy Morton, and Bruce Morton. Important help was also contributed by Marilyn Harren, Victor Grambsch, and David P. Gross. For a particularly painstaking job of typing the manuscript, we wish to thank Janet Heineman and Jean Warner, and to recognize as well the many tasks undertaken by Beulah Reddaway. And for general, all-round work, as well as careful proofreading of a document unavoidably filled with statistics, we are grateful to Ann Montague.

The 1964 study was made possible by a grant from the Office of Education of the U.S. Department of Health, Education and Welfare. The 1971 study was financed by the Ford Foundation. We offer this book as our expression of appreciation for that assistance.

> *Edward Gross and Paul V. Grambsch*
> *Seattle, Washington*

May 1973

*Changes in
University
Organization,
1964-1971*

1. Studying Universities: 1964-1971

The distinctive features of American institutions of higher learning—their magnitude, range of quality, diversity, and high degree of autonomy—have gained increased research attention in recent years (Burn et al., 1971; Ben-David, 1968, 1972; Ashby, 1971). Such institutions encompass a broad range of types, including liberal arts colleges (from the most prestigious to those struggling to stay alive), state colleges, community colleges serving a specified geographical clientele, evening schools of law, military academies, and universities. Though universities make up a scant 6 percent of such institutions, our study is wholly concerned with them. This limitation turns out to be less restrictive than might appear, for universities contain within them much of the variety offered by the remaining institutions. For example, whereas most liberal arts and comprehensive colleges give no more than a B.A. and an M.A., universities also give those degrees, the Ph.D. degree as well, and many also give the associate in arts that community colleges offer. Ben-David (1972) describes three strategies that institutions of higher learning employ to attract students: the cultivation of prestige (as employed by Ivy League colleges), the establishment of a service tradition (as exemplified by most comprehensive colleges and by community colleges), and the emphasis on research (observable in some institutes for applied research and in some independent professional institutions). Universities seek to employ all three of these strategies. In an important paper, Trow (1970) identified three types of students: those with strong academic interest, those who are oriented to occupational careers, and the collegiate (fun-loving) students. To those one might add the group who have come to an institution of higher learning to "find themselves." Each of these types may be found in different kinds of institutions—the academic student in a liberal arts college, the vocational student in a community college, the collegiate student in a state college, and those searching for personal identity anywhere. But one is sure to find all four in a university. So too, though community colleges are celebrated as "open-door" institutions which admit anyone, it is surely in the university that the openness of the American institutions to the higher education of racial and ethnic minorities is most strongly observable, and where the resources allow for the program variety necessary to assist persons to realize their potentialities. In all these senses, then, universities are a microcosm of the large set of institutions of which they are only one type. In any case, though they make up only 6 percent of all institutions of higher learning, they enroll about 30 percent of all students. We are, then, describing the setting in which a large proportion of all students spend their lives, and which includes some of the best and worst of such places. They include most of the celebrated centers of student unrest and train most of the scientists and a very high proportion of all professionals in the society. They include most of the places "where the action is" and can be counted upon to shed light, therefore, on the broader category of all institutions from which we have selected them.

In spite of their obvious importance, universities were strangely neglected as serious objects of study until the outbreak of the student "troubles" in 1964. Historians had written biographies of the more lustrous universities, and there was a considerable number of biographies of presidents (e.g., Dodds, 1962; Stoke, 1959; and Wriston, 1959; see also Eells & Hollis, 1961), and a small number of general histories (Rudolph, 1962; Veysey, 1965). Such neglect may be attributed to the lack of public attention paid to universities until World War II, when government turned to universities for assistance in designing the weapons of war. The large growth in student enrollments and the consequent expansion of facilities after the war led to increased attention, as did the ability of social and behavioral scientists to study the development of organizations. Hence, only recently has there been both the interest and the methodology with which to study universities empirically.

Such considerations led us to undertake a study of some 80 universities (reduced to 68, as explained below) in 1964. At that time we had no idea of the great crises that were about to convulse those institutions. Our interests were largely scientific, seeking to describe the social structure of universities in a way that would add one more type—the university—to the already large literature on formal organizations that included factories, hospitals, businesses, schools, government bureaus, and prisons. The events since then led to a decision to replicate the study in 1971, in order to see whether those events had led to significant changes in social structure.

The findings make up the substance of our report in this book. In brief, we found that there had been very little change in the goals or values of universities and persons in them. Universities remained in 1971 what they had been in 1964: institutions oriented to research and scholarly production, set up to provide comfortable homes for professors and administrators, and according students and their needs a distinctly secondary position. But important changes had also taken place. Professors and administrators both felt a stronger congruence between the actual emphases in their universities and the kind of emphases they felt proper. Universities had grown more stratified to the point of fragmentation. Private universities—already differing from public universities in 1964—were even more distinctive in goals; highly "productive" universities were increasingly differentiating themselves from less productive universities, and the more prestigious universities were even more distinctive from the others than they had been in 1964. In essence, distinct "leagues" were being carved out, with decreasing competition between them.

We found little change since 1964 in the university power structure: higher administration was dominant, with professors occupying a middle position, and students and various "outsiders" (parents, alumni, citizens of the state) at the bottom. Yet, with the exception of department chairmen, all felt they had more power than ever, reflecting a growing confidence in their ability to take charge of their own professional lives. But an ominous cleavage had grown up between outside power holders (regents, legislators, state government, citizens) and "insiders" (chairmen, deans, faculty, students), which very much affected the goals of universities. That power struggle showed evidence of a shift from the national to the local level, with strong implications for the internal structure of universities. Partly as a consequence of this battle, administrators and faculty formed an increasingly cohesive group, having resolved much of their traditional antagonism and suspicion. We concluded that the accusation that universities change only at a glacial pace was inaccurate and unfair. Given that we were looking at a scant seven years, and given some powerful forces that would be expected to resist change, the results offer impressive evidence of the adaptive and robust character of universities.

We turn, in the balance of this chapter, to a description of our approach to the study of the university.

SCIENTIFIC MODELS OF THE UNIVERSITY In order to subject the university to scientific study, we had to develop a model of universities which enabled us to identify the key variables to be subjected to research attention. Two main alternatives were available—the university as a community or the university as a bureaucracy. The concept of community is very popular, particularly among those who are concerned about impersonality and those students and faculty who come to the campus to search for identities (Goodman, 1962). As Baldridge (1971*a*) notes, such a model lays stress on the democratic values by which the community of scholars shall govern itself and on the extent to which the importance of professional values means that the expert faculty cannot take orders from any "superior" in the official sense of the term. Quite apart from the special problems presented by the model as a basis for the formulation of research hypotheses, we felt that it had only limited value as a picture of reality. It has, perhaps, more utility in studies of the liberal arts college (Clark, 1970). But for universities, the assumptions in the model of common values give grave trouble. The enormous turnover among faculty, students, and administrators, together with variation in programs and goals on the average university campus, suggests that the model applies in only limited ways. The model also fails to take account of the increasing importance of central administration and other pressures on the university that shift the focus of government away from the scholars.

On the other hand, a bureaucratic model (Stroup, 1966) tends to exaggerate the picture in an equally misleading direction. There is no question that the university exhibits bureaucratic elements, such as the employment of competence as a major standard for evaluating both staff and students or the payment of fixed salaries (see Baldridge, 1971*a*, p. 10). Yet those elements tell us very little about the structure of universities. Relationships among teaching and research staff, though stratified, are not hierarchical to any appreciable extent—full professors do not give orders to associate professors. And for that matter, much of the work of administration is carried on by the faculty in committee or on temporary assignment. Nor does the university exhibit the degree of centralization of control that the bureaucratic model implies.

Neither of these models, then, seemed to offer us much help in our plan to study a large number of American universities. One difficulty in applying these models is that the university resists classification in terms of *any* model.[1] The reason seems to be that, so far as organization is concerned, the university has a very *loose* structure. Some portions of the university are highly organized, even bureaucratic. One could argue this to be the case in some of the professional schools, when contrasted to the college of arts and sciences, for example. In those portions of the university in which there is a conception of the student as a "product," in the sense that he begins as an apprentice and ends up with an M.D., bachelor of accounting, or Ph.D. in mathematics, then those who design curricula may feel that there are certain experiences and skills that the individual must have and that steps can be taken to be sure that he does have them. In that sense, the student may be regarded as someone to whom things are done as he is processed on his way to some fairly clear goal. By contrast, in the arts and sciences, at least in the undergraduate period, a much looser conception may be operating which assumes the goal of helping the student to become autonomous, which goal, by its very nature, argues against any processing model or any notion of any peculiar product.

A second kind of looseness is exhibited in the varying definitions and differential emphasis placed on the value of research in different parts of the university. In psychology, the Ph.D. is felt to be essential to a professional career, even should the holder of the Ph.D. want to be a psychotherapist. Research concerned with applied areas may well be different from research in fundamental subject-matter areas. In the arts, research may take the form of creative output of paintings or pieces of music. As is

[1] Baldridge (1971*a; b*, pp. 11–16), after expressing, as we have, criticism of both the bureaucratic and community (which he calls "collegial") models, advances a model which he calls a "political model," based on conflict theory, community-power studies, and interest-group theory. It seems a highly attractive one which Baldridge uses with great effectiveness in his study of New York University. In its present form, it calls for intensive study at a particular institution and hence would be difficult to apply simultaneously to a large number of universities, as was our wish.

well known, in these areas the Ph.D. is rarely given, and training at a special center or under a recognized leader is felt to be more important.

Finally, in speaking of the structure as loose, we are not implying that it is anomic or that the various parts of it are entirely without relationship to one another. Some parts of it may well be connected into meaningful or distinguishable clusters. The various departments concerned with physical health, for example, express their unity in their proximate physical location. Such is quite possibly the case with other clusters identified by having buildings of their own, such as those associated with engineering. We think, on the other hand, one may come relatively close to complete *anomie* in the case of arts and sciences wherein the department is the fundamental unit of instruction and research. But even within arts and sciences, some departments are closer to one another than are other departments and feel sensitive to one another's needs.

What is often spoken of as "central administration" occupies an anomalous position in the university. Such concerns as student affairs, business and finance, and university relations are felt by some to be service functions enabling the departments and the professional schools to perform better. On the other hand, such administrative units may be important agencies of social change by providing leadership, since the various other parts of the university are often so caught up in their own concerns that they are unable to see the university as a whole.

Such considerations alert us to the possibility that a loose structure, in the overall sense, may yet exhibit some very tightly organized parts which are completely bureaucratic, while at the same time retaining communities of self-governing scholars. This seems indeed to be the case at most American universities. But having called attention to such looseness, and having thus been reluctant to classify the university as either a community or a bureaucracy, we must now point out that events are occurring which make the choice of a model less problematic. That is, because of vast societal changes, the loose structure of the university is becoming a good deal tighter and more centrally coordinated than it has been. The societal changes are familiar. The increased professionalization of occupations and the expansion of demand for educated persons has sent ever larger proportions of the expanding population into the universities. In addition, international competition has generated pressures for the training of scientists and engineers. The arms and space race has led to heavy university involvement in contract research with governmental authorities, often upsetting traditional status relations on campus and forcing departments or parts of departments into becoming "productive organizations" for paying clients.

Such changes have inevitably led to shifts in the administrative structure of the university in response to demands by state legislatures, private foundations, and governmental agencies for an accounting of how such monies are being spent and how efficiently the organization is being administered. The growth of student unrest, and the pressures from minority groups for changes toward open enrollment and new programs on campuses have accelerated the involvement of outside agencies in university affairs. With these changes, central administration has found itself, often reluctantly, being driven into a position of seeking tighter control over the functioning of the university, of insisting on regular reports on faculty teaching and research, of establishing common accounting practices, of forcing on all departments common hiring practices (in the face of legal requirements on affirmative action for minority hiring, for example), or insistence on legal protection for volunteers in scientific experiments. Research itself, though carried on by professors who think of themselves as entrepreneurs, now requires heavy support from the university—in the form, for example, of a computer—which can be operated efficiently only if centrally controlled.

In sum, we felt that though neither the community nor the bureaucratic model was directly applicable, the university was beginning to move toward the bureaucratic model, at least in the sense of greater coordination. Although the university is not likely to conform to the traditional bureaucratic model with its emphasis on hierarchy, fixed positions, and uniformity of behavior, we think that the university may nevertheless be viewed as a complex organization.

The idea of a complex organization (or "organization," for short) may be most easily understood if we contrast it with the concept of a community. When one speaks of a community, one thinks of a body of persons bound together by affectional or personal ties who value their relationship with one another intrinsically. We may call such ties "communal" (MacIver, 1936), and observe them in a variety of settings, such as in a closely knit family, a group of friends, the members of an adolescent gang, the neighborhood of a traditional small town, or in the contemporary "urban villages" dominated by an ethnic group (see Gans, 1962). Such groups or communities may occasionally set goals for themselves— a family may decide to take a camping trip; a gang may set out to claim a turf for itself; and an ethnic group may develop enough cohesiveness to elect one of its own to public office. But though communal groups may be capable of acting as a unit in the pursuit of a common aim, the members do not usually evaluate the group in terms of such aims or their success in attaining them. Rather, the significant factor for most is their liking for one another and for the group, their sense of being at home in it, and the expressive value that the group or community has for them.

In organizations, by contrast, the problem of goals and goal attainment has priority over all other problems (Parsons, 1960, Ch. 1; 1961, pp. 38–41). The ties that bind members may be called "associational" (MacIver, 1936) in the sense that persons associate themselves with one another in order to attain some end or goal which cannot be attained without such association, or which is attained more efficiently through such association. Of course, such persons may develop attachments to one another, and occasionally an associational relationship may shift altogether and become communal. It is even possible that associational relationships are more efficient if there are some minimal communal relationships as well.[2] Yet, it remains true that the organization was not formed nor does it continue to exist in order to provide persons with such intrinsically satisfying interpersonal relationships. Rather, its existence is justified primarily by its orientation to a set of goals, and it is continually judged by how successfully it attains those goals. It is the presence of such goals and the consequent organization of effort to attain them which characterizes modern industrial society. Such goals might include the production of a high standard of living, success in healing the sick, defending a society from military attack, incarcerating criminals, organizing governmental affairs, or any other activities requiring large-scale coordination of men and resources.

In spite of the very great amount of research and theoretical attention which has been given to formal organizations, surpris-

---

[2] Such, at least, was the belief of human relations theorists who saw themselves as helping break down the atomism and impersonality of work relations. No better illustration is available than the classic statement in Mayo (1933).

ingly little attention has been paid to developing a clear definition of what is meant by a goal in the first place (Simon, 1964). The concept seems to be taken for granted in most studies, yet the specific goal of a particular organization is an empirical matter which can be ascertained.

Etzioni (1964, p. 6) defines an organizational goal as "a desired state of affairs which the organization attempts to realize." But this definition immediately raises the question, pointed to by many, of *whose* state of affairs is to be desired. Theoretically, there could be as many desired states for the organization as there are persons in it, if not more. What appear to be goals from the point of view of the top administrators may not be goals at all from the point of view of those further down.

Even before one can talk about different perceptions of organizational goals, however, it is essential to distinguish private from organizational goals. A private goal consists of a future state that the individual desires for himself. Such a notion comes close to the psychologist's conception of a motive. This meaning may be distinguished from what a particular person desires *for the organization as a whole* (Cartwright & Zander, 1953, pp. 308–311). The latter comes closer to the notion of an organizational goal, although it still consists of something that the particular person wishes and may not at all correspond to the organization's goals. Further, it still leaves open the question of how one is to determine an organization's goals when there are differences of opinion. In a small organization there may not be much difficulty, for the top man's personal goals for the organization *are* the organization's goals. It is this simplification which made it possible for classical economics to develop the theory of the firm without being much concerned about developing a precise definition of organizational goal that differs from the goal of the entrepreneur. The firms discussed by the classical economists were in the main small ones with no greater problem to solve than decisions about the selling price of its product and the number of units to produce for the market. Once organizations grow large, the possibility exists that there will be many persons in a position to influence the goals of the organization (Cyert & March, 1963, Ch. 3). In the case of ideological organizations, where personal values are similar to each other, there may be a close correspondence between private goals for the organization and group goals. Yet one cannot assume that private and group goals will coincide, and it is safe to say that typically they will not. It is consequently necessary to offer a person an inducement to participate (March & Simon, 1958, Ch. 4), so that he attains his personal goal through the group goal of the organization. Persons must be motivated to participate to the extent that they will give up their personal goals for the organization as a whole should those personal goals differ from those of the organization. Nevertheless, in order to avoid any reification of the concept, it is necessary to emphasize that goals will always exist in the minds of certain persons. That is to say, although an organizational goal is not the same thing as a personal goal nor is it necessarily the same as the goal that a particular person desires for an organization (as distinct from what he desires for himself), it certainly would seem that one kind of evidence on the nature of organization goals would consist of the statements of particular persons attesting what they thought the organization's goals were.

Thompson and McEwen (1958) and Parsons (1960) have attempted to define goals in terms of system linkages. Both have seen a goal as involving some type of output to a larger society. In this sense organizations are always subsystems of larger systems, the goal of one subsystem being a means or input of a different subsystem. In the simplest case, the production of automobile batteries is a goal to the firm that manufactures them but will be a means or input to an automobile manufacturing firm. Such an approach has the great value of emphasizing the need to relate organizations to one another and to the surrounding society. When goals are defined in this manner, it becomes clear that those within organizations have only a limited amount of freedom to set the goals of the organization. They will be constrained by what outsiders can be persuaded to accept. Such an emphasis may tend to underestimate the role that rational decision makers within organizations play in choosing the goals of organizations (Gouldner, 1959). A more serious limitation of the output approach is that organizations have a great many outputs, both intended and unintended, many of which will' be no different than functions or consequences. It becomes a problem to single out certain kinds of outputs as *the* goals of the organization. The importance of by-products in industrial organizations should alert the investigator to the danger here.

In spite of the strictures we have suggested, there is no doubt that these elements all bear upon a definition of goals. Goals will exist in someone's mind, and they will involve the relationship between an organization and the situation in which it is implicated.

An important contribution has been made by Etzioni (1964, pp. 16–19) in a work criticizing the goal approach to the study of organizations as being too limited. To define an organization solely in terms of its goal and therefore to judge its effectiveness in terms of its degree of success in obtaining that goal is to doom the investigator to disappointment. The "metaphysical pathos" to which Gouldner (1961) has called attention—namely the pessimism of those who see men doomed forever to disappointment in their organizational hopes—Etzioni attributes to expecting too much. One typically must settle for a good deal less than one hopes, and the leaders of organizations, their hopes high, would seem to be always expecting more than they will ever receive. Rather than seeing these limited results as a consequence of man's inherent limitations or as the basis for a sad romantic lament on man's smallness in the face of his large goals, Etzioni takes the view that the definition itself may be at fault. He compares organizations to electric lights and other types of mechanical equipment which may have very low efficiencies. Much of the energy may be lost in heat. Nevertheless, no one expresses great concern but rather compares one mechanical gadget to another, and discovers that one may be twice as efficient as another even though it is only 10 percent efficient, compared to the other which is 5 percent efficient. Still, despite lowered goal expectations, goals retain their importance in organizations.

THE BUREAUCRATIC PERSONALITY One of the classic texts in organizational analysis is Merton's (1957) discussion of the tendencies of some persons to make ends of means in organizations. The relevance of this discussion for organizational goals has not been given explicit attention in the literature, although it has important implications for an understanding of the problem. Merton pointed to a possible dysfunction in formal organizations. For an organization to accomplish its goals, a person must be required to conform to explicitly laid down rules. Only by this means can the organization's special advantages of precision and predictability be enjoyed. In order to ensure that such precision and predictability in fact result, it is necessary to insist upon rule compliance. Yet that very insistence may lead a person to forget that rules exist, after all, only in order to facilitate goal attainment. Some persons then may be carried away by the very rules and insist on compliance with them even at the expense of organizational goals. Merton's examples include the requirement in the early part of World War II that navy officers should carry calling cards, even though they were destined for the service in the battles of the South Pacific, or an instance of an explorer being denied citizenship on the grounds that he had been out of the United States for a period of time, in spite of the fact that his absence had involved service on a United States expedition exploring Antarctica. It is such overemphasis that has led to the association between bureaucracy and red tape and has helped make the bureaucrat into a synonym for the haughty, unapproachable agent.

For our purposes, the most important implication of Merton's discussion is the assumption which seems to underlie it. The assumption may be stated briefly as follows: The great danger in formal organizations is that persons, in their interest in taking care of certain means, will lose sight of the end to which these means are meant to contribute. What we wish to point out is that there is a clear assumption that *any activity other than one which is directed toward the overall goal or goals of the organization does not by that token make a contribution to those goals.* Persons who get caught up in their work or excited about the particular activity in which they are engaged are warned to be careful lest they forget what the organization is about, after all.

We do not imply, of course, that only those whose activity contributes directly to goal attainment in an organization may be said to be making a contribution to that goal. It is freely conceded in any organization that all persons who are given specific assignments in the division of labor of the organization are making a contribution. It is nevertheless felt that the activities of several participants in the organization, insofar as they are broken down into departments or other units each of which has subgoals or targets, are to be conceived of essentially as halfway stations on the road to the overall organizational goals. Their behavior therefore is organizationally meaningful only insofar as it makes a contribution either directly or indirectly to those goals. The particular arrangements are goal relevant only insofar as they may be interpreted as making some kind of a contribution to a set of overall goals.

THE PROBLEM OF SUPPORT AND MAINTENANCE

Much recent research on organization goals emphasizes that no organization can spend all its participants' time on goal attainment. Some of the time, and perhaps a great deal of it, must be spent on activities which in no sense make even an indirect contribution to goal attainment.

Bales (1958) recognized this point in his studies of task-oriented small groups under laboratory conditions. He found two major sets of processes operating in these groups. The groups, on being assigned a particular task or goal, would typically begin by giving their attention to the most efficient way of moving toward that goal. It was discovered, however,' that other kinds of activities began to make their appearance. When someone made a proposal that a given approach be tried, others had to agree, disagree, or take no stand, and this activity began to divide the group on the basis of differing estimates of the most worthwhile procedures. The consequence of such cleavage was the development of feelings toward one another or toward the solutions proposed, irritation at not having one's own views taken properly into account, as well as ordinary fatigue. It became necessary, Bales found, for the group to stop its goal-directed activity and give some attention to repairing the social damage that was being done as the group attempted to move toward the solution of the problem. A kind of "maintenance" activity was necessary, with certain persons assuming the role of "maintenance engineers," as it were, in giving attention to what Bales came to speak of as "social-emotional" needs. Such needs might be taken care of in a phase manner, or in other ways. It has of course been the experience of persons who have worked with conference groups and other kinds of task-oriented groups that some time must always be given to such maintenance activities. For example, all have noticed the tendency of many meetings to begin with informal chatter and to end with laughter or other kinds of activities which are related to solidarity or to satisfaction of various kinds of personal needs.

The paradox may be stated as follows: An organization must do more than give attention to goal attainment in order to attain its goals. A useful approach is that suggested by the Parsonian functional imperatives (Parsons, 1961, pp. 38–41). Whether or not one is prepared to agree that only these and no other imperatives exist, they do represent an attempt, based on Bales's work, as a matter of fact, to state a set of conditions necessary for system survival. As such, they apply directly to organizations. It is noteworthy that only one of the system imperatives is goal attainment. The names given to the other imperatives are adaptation, integration, pattern maintenance, and tension management. The import of these categories is that a good part of any system's energies must be given over to activities that do not contribute in any direct sense to goal attainment but rather are concerned essentially with maintaining the system itself.

Such considerations lead directly into the general problem of what economists speak of as *suboptimization*. This term refers to the tendency of the various units in an organization to exaggerate the importance of their own contribution and to begin to think of the whole organization in terms of the goals of the particular unit with which they are associated. Thus, in a large firm, the head of a section which is concerned with providing rivets which are used in a manufacturing operation in the firm begins to think of the making of rivets as an end in itself. Such an attitude can come very close to the notion of bureaucratic personality. A person then may become so concerned with the importance of making rivets that he can easily forget that rivets are essentially a means for making some product which requires rivets. Yet it is absolutely essential that persons who are given the responsibility of making rivets should begin to believe that rivets are the most important thing in the world. It is essential that they give their full attention to making rivets rather than to the question of what rivets contribute to the overall organization. We come here to something close to a craft or professional orientation. One of the functions of providing the craftsman or professional with independence is to free him from the necessity of having to be concerned with the uses to which his skills are put so that he can give his full attention to the maximum development of those skills themselves. Only in this manner is it felt that he makes his major contribution.

In other words an organization *must* insulate its units from attention to goals other than the particular concerns of those units. This is not to say, of course, that each unit is to be given its head and that the purposes of an organization are well served if all members of it are bureaucratic personalities. However, a great deal of attention must be given to activities which may only be directly related or even unrelated to organizational goals. We go further in our argument and insist that the same reasoning applies to activities which are wholly of a maintenance character, that is, to those activities that are concerned with adaptation, integration, pattern maintenance, and tension management. It is important that persons who are concerned with activities that fall in any of these areas should give their whole attention to them so that those activities are carried out as effectively as possible. There is only one way that one can be sure that persons will do a job as well as it can possibly be done and that is to insist that they make ends of such "means" activities. When a means has been made into an end, it has then become a goal of the organization.

We are suggesting that there are at least two different kinds of goals in organizations: those goals which are reflected in an output of some kind, which we call *output goals,* and the goals of those who are charged with responsibility for the maintenance activities, which we will call *support goals.* For our convenience we subdivided the support goals using the general categories that Parsons has suggested for the functional imperatives.

IDENTIFYING UNIVERSITY GOALS The studies undertaken in both 1964 and 1971 involved questionnaire surveys of some 80 universities in the United States. The breadth sought and the obvious geographical scatter of our respondents required that we should develop an instrument which was self-administered but which would provide us data on university goals. We were then faced with the problem of how to secure reliable data on organizational goals. Further, we wished to include not only output but also support goals in accordance with the rationale just outlined: In any organization, activities concerned with support may be regarded as goals, since they are essential to the functioning of the organization, clearly involve an intention or aim of the organization as a whole, and receive a great deal of attention from many participants who deliberately engage in activities that will move the organization toward them. With respect to the situation in which means become ends, we have claimed that the success of the organization depends on that process taking place. It represents a dysfunction or problem only when support goals are *substituted* for output goals to such an extent that the output goals are neglected. Such would illustrate the celebrated bureaucratic personality or bureaucratic ritualism. But our way of conceptualizing this process immediately suggests that the opposite process is quite possible, that is, output goals may be substituted for support goals, a process usually referred to as one in which the organization is too "ivory-towerish." Examples often are found in situations in which persons in organizations have strong ideological motivations and become impatient with the support necessary to move toward the goals of the organization. The phenomenon is, of course, common enough in universities (which provided the name "ivory tower") as in the case of many faculty who regard administrative activities as a waste of time. It is by no means confined to universities.[3]

We were faced with the problem, then, of devising a way of asking questions about both output and support goals so that persons could give reliable responses in written form. How is one to know whether a given goal is present, and how is one to measure its importance? Two kinds of evidence are necessary before one can claim a goal is present: intentions and activities. By *intentions,* we refer to what participants see the organization as trying to do or what direction they perceive it to be taking. Such intentions are revealed by verbal statements or by inferences made from symbolic acts, gestures, and other meaningful behavior. By *activities,* we refer to what persons in the organizations are in fact observed to be doing: how they spend their time, how resources are allotted. Such an approach derives from a simple model that may be illustrated with an analogy of an automobile that is stopped at an intersection, waiting for the light to change to green. Ignoring lane indications, what information is needed to conclude that the goal of the driver is either to go straight ahead or turn? One may first ask the driver, but his statements are only clues, for he may change his mind; he may not be paying attention (either to our question or to the car as he presses the accelerator); or he may be drunk and in poor control of the car. Hence, we will also step back and watch what happens when the light changes to green. If the car begins to move in a direction consistent with the driver's stated intentions, we can conclude that the goal was in fact what the driver said it was.

Both intentions and activities must be distinguished from outputs, which the organization produces or distributes to persons or systems outside itself. In the case of the university, there may be strong consensus that a major goal is preparing students for

---

[3] An interesting illustration is provided in Berliner's (1956) study of the problem of "storming" in Soviet factories. Production to meet a given month's quota may involve completing 5 percent of the target in the first week, 15 percent in the second, 30 percent in the third, and a hectic 50 percent in the last week. This occurs because, as the deadline approaches, maintenance is increasingly neglected, and even dropped in the last period, while the gained time is used to try to meet the quota. To some extent, the sheer neglect of maintenance in the service of speed up, must, sooner or later, be paid for in the form of machine breakdown, which lowers production and thus further accentuates its unevenness.

careers as scientists (an intention), but members of the faculty may be observed to be spending much of their time in consulting with business firms on practical problems, and a high proportion of the students may end with terminal master's degrees. Thus the three variables need not correspond. There does have to be some consistency between intentions and activities. For example, if the car moves in a different direction from that stated by the driver, we are no longer sure what his goal is. We cannot conclude that it corresponds to where he is actually going, for as we stated, the driver may not be paying attention; there may be something wrong with the car; or for that matter, our own observation may be biased. We need both intentions and activities, and there must be some consistency.

But data on outputs refer not to goals as such, but to the degree of success in attaining goals. Goals are targets, in this sense, and the output measures how well one meets the target. The automobile driver who says he intends to turn right and then later begins to twist the wheel in the direction that would likely move him right may be said to have a goal of turning right. If he later actually does turn right, we can conclude that he has reached his goal and perhaps pay tribute to his skill and control of himself and the good running condition of the car. Similarly, data on organizational outputs tell us how well the organization is running. It may, of course, also provide symbolic data on what the goals might have been. But it is not necessarily reliable, as is evidenced by the importance of by-products in factories.

Since we desired to study goals and not outputs, we did not employ the obvious measures of outputs, such as the proportion of students graduating from professional schools as compared to the number getting Ph.D.'s, the publication output of faculty, or the relative volume of contract research.[4] Instead we sought measures of goal intention and activities. On activities, ideally we might have sought data on time allotted to teaching requirements, policy of the institution on allowing the faculty time off to do research, the proportion of persons on the staff with extension responsibility, average outside speeches per month, proportion of total enrollment in graduate school, and other such measures. However, for two rea-

---

[4] We did not, of course, hesitate to use such measures as *control* variables. For example, we related the goal structure to the volume of contract research, where the latter might be a measure of productivity.

sons we elected not to employ those measures. First, such data are difficult to obtain in comparable form from all universities. Second, and more important, they are very gross measures which do not correspond to the detailed goals that we felt were necessary to be able to describe the goal structure of universities. As we show below, we ended up with 47 goals, many of which are highly subtle and correspond to no simple, objective measure that would be available from university records. Further, to get data on how people spend their time on campus would demand extensive and very expensive contacts, requiring that persons keep diaries or be subject to personal interview. Since we desired to survey all administrators and a sample of faculty, such an approach would have been prohibitive in both time and money.

Hence we were faced with the problem of securing data on both goal intentions and activities by asking questions that respondents could reply to briefly and in measurable form. Such questions should have two features: (1) they should be reliable in the sense of being subject to check by many observers; (2) they should present the respondent with a statement to which he is asked to respond, rather than inviting him to make a statement. The difficulty about invited statements is that they are likely to take the form of what Perrow (1961, p. 855) calls an "official goal," which he describes as follows:

Official goals are the general purposes of the organization as put forth in the charter, annual reports, public statements by key executives and other authoritative pronouncements. For example, the goal of an employment agency may be to place job seekers in contact with firms seeking workers. The official goal of a hospital may be to promote the health of the community through curing the ill, and sometimes through preventing illness, teaching and conducting research. Similar organizations may emphasize different publicly acceptable goals. A business corporation, for example, may state that its goal is to make a profit or adequate return on investment, or provide a customer service, or produce goods.

Such statements may more properly be regarded as legitimations rather than goals. They do not describe what organizations actually do but rather provide a public justification for what they are doing. For example, a hospital may emphasize its curative functions as a way of justifying the heavy attention it gives to research (which may contribute more to basic physiology than to medicine). So too a public university will insist that its "sons and daughters" benefit the state, even though those with Ph.D.'s leave the state, never to return. In fact, a good deal of waste lies in the attempt of journalists and reformers to debunk such statements by "proving" the organizations do other things. Thus, the prison which proclaims its "goal" of rehabilitation will be found to spend most of its energies in custodial activities, and the university will spend much of its energies not in teaching, research, or direct service, but in cultivating alumni and seeking to maintain its reputation. These activities are legitimate and make up the very stuff of organizational goals, but only certain ones will be emphasized in public efforts to seek support.

Even when statements of official goals do include activities of importance in the everyday running of the organization, they tend to be too vague to measure. The best way of avoiding such vagueness, we felt, was to present the respondent with a statement corresponding to a sector of behavior which he was likely to have observed as a member. We did not ask for opinions — which persons are likely to offer when given the chance to volunteer a "goal." We stated, in effect: "We wish to discover what the goals of your university are. Since we cannot come there and observe activities ourselves, we are asking you to serve as our eyes and ears. We are asking you what you *perceive* to be the importance of each of the following goals." Hence we sought to catch, in a written statement, both the intentions and activities that are essential to identifying a goal.

Moreover, the goal statement had to be specific. Not only are "official goals" vague, but as Perrow writes, they exclude the "host of decisions that must be made among alternative ways of achieving official goals, the priority of multiple goals, and the many unofficial goals pursued by groups within the organization" (ibid.). In this sense, the analogy we drew above with the individual automobile driver is flawed because humans cannot pursue contradictory goals simultaneously without some type of neurotic breakdown. The automobile cannot go straight ahead and turn right at the same time. But organizations not only can pursue contradictory goals, they usually do (Cyert & March, 1963, p. 28). The term *goals* simply refers to the way the organization allocates resources to various intended activities. In a business organization, production and sales involve contradictory goals in a given decision in that money committed by that decision to improving production facilities is not then available for sales promotion. Similarly, universities may, at the same meeting of the Board of Regents, make decisions to commit money to encouraging disadvantaged persons to enroll, while committing other money to strengthen an elitist, restricted graduate program. Such divisions of resources may reflect divergent interests, or, as Perrow (1970, pp. 134–135) puts it:

> . . . our main reason for distinguishing types of goals is to deal with the question of whose point of view is being recognized—society, the customer, the investor, the top executives, or others. For society, the justification of a steel company's existence may be to produce needed goods; for customers, the goal of a firm may be to produce certain kinds of steel and deliver them on time; for the investors, the aim may be to pay out large dividends; for top executives, the purpose may be to run a stable, secure organization where life is fairly predictable and not too stressful; for a division manager the goal may be to make the best damn steel around. From the manager's point of view, delivery, price, profits and stability all take a back seat, just as all goals except dividends may be secondary to investors.

All these points of view represent organizational goals, and they are all being pursued at the same time, which may be why none of these interests is ever wholly happy. We expected that there would be many goals in a university, and that they would all be pursued, but with varying degrees of emphasis.

The form which we eventually devised for asking about degree of emphasis on organization goals may be illustrated by the sample question which we gave our respondents on the questionnaire. It was as follows:

One of the great issues in American education has to do with the proper aims or goals of the university. The question is: What are we trying to accomplish? Are we trying to prepare people for jobs, to broaden them intellectually, or what? Below we have listed a large number of the more commonly claimed aims, intentions or goals of a university. We should like you to react to each of these in two different ways:

(1) How important *is* each aim at this university?

(2) How important *should* the aim be at this university?

EXAMPLE— To serve as substitute parents:	Of absolutely top importance	Of great importance	Of medium importance	Of little importance	Of no importance	Don't know or can't say
Is	___	___	_X_	___	___	___
Should be	___	___	___	___	_X_	___

A person who had checked the alternatives in the manner shown by X's would be expressing his perception that the aim, intention, or goal "to serve as substitute parents" *is* of medium importance at his university but that he believes it *should be* of no importance as an aim, intention, or goal of his university.

It was hoped that this way of asking questions about goals would provide both the measurability we were seeking and the specificity.[5] The question could be easily scored, and we could secure an average for any given group (for instance, the faculty in business schools, or university presidents), or we could secure weighted or other averages at a given university. We thought it particularly important to put the "is" and "should be" response categories right next to each other in order to guard against the tendency of persons to confuse organizational goals with their own desires for those goals. It was hoped this location of questions would remind respondents to keep these things separate. When we identified goals, we used only the "is" statements, regarding the "should be" statements as revealing personal or organizational values, rather than goals.

GOAL STATEMENTS FOR UNIVERSITIES

We classified the goals broadly, as we have stated, into two major groups—output and support goals. We further subdivided output goals into four subgroups: student-expressive (changing the student's identity), student-instrumental (changing the student's skills or capabilities), research, and direct service (other than to students). For all these there was some identifiable output that the university contributed to its environment. Support goals were subdivided into subgroups that correspond to the Parsonian functional imperatives (as we noted above). These included adaptation, management, motivation, and position.[6] The actual goals were each put into the form of the sample question above and placed in a random order on the questionnaire, but not identified as to category. The goals are as follows.

---

[5] Because we wished to be able to measure and compare organizations with one another, we were not able to use such common ways of characterizing goals as growth, stability, emphasis on uniqueness of product, and the like. Although it can be claimed, with complete objectivity, that an organization is, at a given time, pursuing a policy of emphasizing growth, we would want to be able to say how much it is emphasizing growth and how much in comparison to another organization which might also be emphasizing growth.

[6] Perrow (1970, pp. 134–135) classifies organizational goals into a list broader than ours: societal, output, system, product, and derived. Ours would cut across the last four.

Output Goals Output goals are those goals of the university which, immediately or in the future, are reflected in some product, service, skill, or orientation which will affect (and is intended to affect) society.

Student-Expressive goals involve the attempt to change the student's identity or character in some fundamental way.

1 Produce a student who, whatever else may be done to him, has had his intellect cultivated to the maximum.

2 Produce a well-rounded student, that is, one whose physical, social, moral, intellectual, and aesthetic potentialities have all been cultivated.

3 Make sure the student is permanently affected (in mind and spirit) by the great ideas of the great minds of history.

4 Assist students to develop objectivity about themselves and their beliefs and hence examine those beliefs critically.

5 Develop the inner character of students so that they can make sound, correct moral choices.

Student-Instrumental goals involve equipping the student to do something specific for the society into which he will be entering or to operate in a specific way in that society.

6 Prepare students specifically for useful careers.

7 Provide the student with skills, attitudes, contacts, and experiences which maximize the likelihood of his occupying a high status in life and a position of leadership in society.

8 Train students in methods of scholarship and/or scientific research and/or creative endeavor.

9 Make a good consumer of the student—a person who is elevated culturally, has good taste, and can make good consumer choices.

10 Produce a student who is able to perform his citizenship responsibilities effectively.

Research goals involve the production of new knowledge or the solution of problems.

11 Carry on pure research.

12 Carry on applied research.

Direct Service goals involve the direct and continuing provision of services to the population outside the university (that is, not faculty, full-time students, or staff). These services are provided because the university, as an organization, is better equipped than any other organization to provide them.

13 Provide special training for part-time adult students, through extension courses, special short courses, correspondence courses, etc.

14 Assist citizens directly, through extension programs, advice, consultation, and the provision of useful or needed facilities and services other than teaching.

15 Provide cultural leadership for the community through university-sponsored programs in the arts, public lectures by distinguished persons, athletic events, and other performances, displays, or celebrations which present the best of culture, popular or not.

16 Serve as a center for the dissemination of new ideas that will change the society, whether those ideas are in science, literature, the arts, or politics.

17 Serve as a center for the preservation of the cultural heritage.

Support Goals *Adaptation* goals reflect the need for the university as an organization to come to terms with the environment in which it is located: to attract students and staff, to finance the enterprise, to secure needed resources, and to validate the activities of the university with those persons or agencies in a position to affect them.

18 Ensure the continued confidence and hence support of those who contribute substantially (other than students and recipients of services) to the finances and other material resource needs of the university.

19 Ensure the favorable appraisal of those who validate the quality of the programs we offer (validating groups include accrediting bodies, professional societies, scholarly peers at other universities, and respected persons in intellectual or artistic circles).

20 Educate to his utmost capacities every high school graduate who meets basic legal requirements for admission.

21 Accommodate only students of high potential in terms of the specific strengths and emphases of this university.

22 Orient ourselves to the satisfaction of the special needs and problems of the immediate geographical region.

23 Keep costs down as low as possible, through more efficient utilization of time and space, reduction of course duplication, etc.

24 Hold our staff in the face of inducements offered by other universities.

Management goals involve decisions on who should run the university, the need to handle conflict, and the establishment of priorities as to which output goals should be given maximum attention.

25 Make sure that salaries, teaching assignments, perquisites, and privileges always reflect the contribution that the person involved is making to his own profession or discipline.

26 Involve faculty in the government of the university.

27 Involve students in the government of the university.

28 Make sure the university is run democratically insofar as that is feasible.

29 Keep harmony between departments or divisions of the university when such departments or divisions do not see eye to eye on important matters.

30 Make sure that salaries, teaching assignments, perquisites, and privileges always reflect the contribution that the person involved is making to the functioning of this university.

31 Emphasize undergraduate instruction even at the expense of the graduate program.

32 Encourage students to go into graduate work.

33 Make sure the university is run by those selected according to their ability to attain the goals of the university in the most efficient manner possible.

34 Make sure that on *all* important issues (not only curriculum), the will of the full time faculty shall prevail.

Motivation goals seek to ensure a high level of satisfaction on the part of staff and students and emphasize loyalty to the university as a whole.

35 Protect the faculty's right to academic freedom.

36 Make this a place in which faculty have maximum opportunity to pursue their careers in a manner satisfactory to them by their own criteria.

37 Provide a full round of student activities.

38 Protect and facilitate the students' right to inquire into, investigate, and examine critically any idea or program that they might get interested in.

39 Protect and facilitate the students' right to advocate direct action of a political or social kind and any attempts on their part to organize efforts to attain political or social goals.

40 Develop loyalty on the part of the faculty and staff to the university, rather than only to their own jobs or professional concerns.

41 Develop greater pride on the part of faculty, staff, and students in their university and the things it stands for.

Position goals help to maintain the position of the university in terms of the kind of place it is compared with other universities and in the face of trends which could change its position.

42 Maintain top quality in all programs we engage in.

43 Maintain top quality in those programs we feel to be especially important (other programs being, of course, up to acceptable standards).

44 Maintain a balanced level of quality across the whole range of programs we engage in.

45 Keep up to date and responsive.

46 Increase the prestige of the university or, if you believe it is already extremely high, ensure the maintenance of that prestige.

47 Keep this place from becoming something different from what it is now, that is, preserve its peculiar emphases and point of view, its "character."

The goal statements themselves were drawn up by the investigators and their research staff, based on a reading of available literature on universities, informal interviews with administrators, faculty, and students, and our own experience with universities. In addition, both authors were faculty members, one a professor and one a dean, at the University of Minnesota at the time. We used that university for pretest purposes, as well as to secure goal statements and modifications of proposed goals. In the end, we employed 47 goals, shortened from an original list of close to 70.

Far from apologizing for the length of the list, we assert that the study of organizations has suffered from a restricted focus on too small a list of goals. In fact, usually only one goal is identified.[7] It was our belief that a list of variety of goals, each charac-

---

[7] For example, a considerable literature on prisons examines shifts from a custodial to a rehabilitation goal, when it is highly likely that both goals (and many others) are present at all times in all prisons, though varying in emphasis. A famous study of the polio foundation (Sills, 1957) is frequently cited as an example of "goal succession," by which is meant the problem of shifting from a goal which has been achieved (presumably the discovery of the polio vaccine) to a new goal (presumably a new disease or set of diseases). Yet the Sills study itself provides strong evidence that the existence of multiple goals, especially revolving about the "support" (in our sense) of some of the professional staffs was part of what made the goal succession so stressful. Perrow (1961) is one of the few who is keenly aware of this phenomenon, even seeing goal succession as a normal part of the history of organization.

terized by a certain degree of emphasis, might provide a richer picture of the directions in which universities were moving. And for a given university, the relative positions of goals would provide, not simply a statement of *the* goal or goals, but a picture of the goal structure.

From the list it can be seen that less than half of the goals are related to the outputs of the university. Of course, it is such outputs that most persons have in mind when they use the word "goal," and it is the Mertonian emphasis which would suggest that activities are suspect unless they have something to do with output goals in some manner. But we claim that the goals called adaptation, management, motivation, and positional *are* goals in the same sense in which output goals may be so categorized. They clearly involve an intention or aim for the university as a whole, and their presence is reflected in clearly observable activities. For example, take Goal 26: Involve Faculty in the Government of the University. This statement would likely not have been volunteered as a "goal" if we had asked our respondents, though some faculty would probably have mentioned it as something they personally would like to see increased. But when we asked our respondents to treat it as a goal and tell us how important it actually was, as they saw it, they had no difficulty in doing so. On the average, it jumped from being ranked 25th in 1964 to 9th in 1971 (being tied in average score with Do Pure Research). Its movement as a value, that is, as a personal reference—indicated by the "should be" reply—was in the same direction, but a good deal less in magnitude, from 19th to 12th in rank. What were our respondents thinking of when they thought of it as a goal? We can only guess, but it is not so difficult to treat as a goal. Respondents (including, of course, administrators) might note that there was a good deal more attention being given on the campus in 1971 than in 1964 to involving faculty in the government of the university. Presidents made public statements about it, faculty and administrators found themselves working together on problems of governance, and both faced problems of how to increase the role of the faculty in the face of frequent resistance from legislatures and the general public. To make such participation possible, faculty were given released time from teaching, and resources were shifted around in other ways. Further, these were clearly activities not confined to one department or intended to provide new career lines for professors. They were universitywide activities affecting the direction in which the university was seen to be going.

Yet, some may insist, these are merely "means." Increasing the role of the faculty in university government is only a means toward enabling the university to do its job of teaching, research, and community service better, or differently. With faculty running the place, the argument goes, the university will be able to resist the blandishments of government funds and the students will be better served. This is questionable, to put it mildly, but it may be offered as an argument. Even if this were true, we see no particular point in insisting on it. It is no less a goal for all that. Goals feed into each other, some being helpful and some getting in the way of others. Faculty control may contribute to emphasis on, say, applied research, but then applied research contributes to faculty control. Each may be regarded as a means to the other. Examine another of our support goals, Goal 23: Keep Costs Down. This goal can be (and usually is) the focus of energies: persons are reminded of its importance, and behavior is controlled to make it relevant. But are not costs just a "means" so that we may have enough money left over to do a better job of, say, Goal 6: Prepare Students for Useful Careers? Of course, but it is still a goal. And may it not be equally true that we emphasize preparing students for useful careers (as opposed to, say, Goal 37: Provide a Full Round of Student Activities) because it is a way of keeping costs down?

RESEARCH OBJECTIVES, 1964 AND 1971 To sum up the discussion thus far, we had decided to study American universities as organizations. An organization, in contrast to a community, is a social system which is going somewhere; that is, it is goal directed and can therefore be judged in terms of the way it utilizes resources in moving toward its goals. Like any theoretical stance, this one involved obvious costs, the most obvious being that we would not shed light on the multitude of communal activities that go on within the university, nor on the details of internal and face-to-face encounters which make up the stuff of everyday life on campus. Instead, we would focus on the direction in which the university was moving and ask what might shed light on that direction, either as cause or effect.

Our first task would be the delineation of the goals themselves. We would want to know if all universities could be characterized in terms of their goals. This could be determined by the degree of agreement of respondents, including an expressed inability to respond to the goal questions (by checking "don't know or can't say," for example). Assuming that there was sufficient agreement to make possible a goals analysis (and there was), our next task was that of describing what the major goals of American universities were in both 1964 and 1971, together with an analysis of any shifts that had occurred.

It will be recalled that each goal question included a "should be" component that provided information on persons' values, or goal preferences. Whatever the goals were, it was important to know whether persons felt that these goals received the emphasis they thought proper. We would, therefore, compare perceived goals with preferred goals in order to discover if there were significant amounts of congruence or incongruence between them. Such congruence or incongruence might be exhibited as either overemphasis ("is" greater than "should be") or underemphasis ("should be" greater than "is"). We would want to examine these goal phenomena for both 1964 and 1971.

An overall picture of goals and goal preferences tells us little of the variety of universities, so we set out to discover distinctive organizational forms by examining patterns of differentiation among universities. We decided to see whether there was significant goal variation by type of control, prestige, productivity, and graduate emphasis. For example, we would seek answers to the questions: Do private and public universities exhibit differences in their goal structures? Are the prestigious institutions pursuing goals different from those of low prestige? Do highly productive universities and those that have a heavy emphasis on graduate study have different goal structures from the less productive and less graduate-oriented? Finally, given that the major event (and the motivation for the 1971 study) was the student unrest in the period between 1964 and 1971, we would ask if goals shed any light on such student unrest. In other words, is student unrest more intense in universities with certain goal structures than in others?

Goals obviously do not form by themselves. Inherent in the study of universities as organizations is the assumption that they are being directed by persons who play critical roles in influencing those directions. Our attention turned next to the key power holders in universities. We would first want to identify them and then relate the power structure to the goal structure. Here we would want to discover whether there was a stable relationship; for example, were universities in which the administration was powerful, characterized by a distinctive goal structure? If so, could we infer that the administrators, by their power, created that goal structure, or perhaps, might universities with a certain goal structure be those in which administrators found it easy to seize power?

We would also want to examine the power structures themselves. We wanted to know whether power in universities was a zero-sum phenomenon or not. For example, in universities where the administration was perceived as powerful, was the faculty perceived as weak?

Lastly, we wanted to ask if the convulsions of the 1964–1971 period had affected the relationship between administrators and faculty. First, do such role groups see the university differently (that is, are they so divided that their perceptions of university goals are different?), and do they exhibit differences in their beliefs of what the goals should be? Do such groups vary in their perceptions of the power structure? Do they vary in their commitment to the university and in the feelings about their ability to get their work done? We wanted to see whether faculty and administration still exhibited sufficient unity to work together on attaining commonly desired ends. If they did not, then the university could indeed be said to be in serious trouble. If they did, they still might have difficulties working together, but at least there would be hope for the future of the organization itself.

PROBLEMS OF RESEARCH METHODOLOGY We have discussed in detail the problem of goal measurement and the steps that led to our development of the goal question. Through this means we were able to attach a score to each person's response, indicating the relative emphasis which he perceives his university attaches to that goal. In estimating the strength of a goal on a campus, our practice was to take an average of the scores assigned by all respondents.

Two questions might be raised about such averages — the number of cases on which they are based and the dispersion. In our 1964 study, we sent out questionnaires to approximately 9,000 administrators and 7,000 faculty. This was 100 percent of the administrators and approximately 10 percent of the faculty. In 1971, we sent out questionnaires to approximately 5,700 administrators and 3,500 faculty, representing approximately 60 percent of administrators and about $3\frac{1}{2}$ percent of the faculty. In both cases, the number of returns on a given campus for all but denominational institutions (which are not reported in this study) practically never fell below 50 (the lowest being 46) and in most cases was closer to 100 than 50. Hence an unweighted mean was based on at least 50 scores, and usually around 75, thus providing assurance of a stable mean. In addition, the standard deviation around the mean was typically low. We decided that if the dispersion of individual responses at a given campus was high on the perception of a goal, we would conclude that the goal statement was *not* a goal. Note that we are talking about goal statements, not preferences. It is, of course, entirely possible for there to be high dispersion about a goal value, with some thinking it should be highly emphasized and others disagreeing strongly. But we felt that disagreement about the actual emphasis being given to a goal must be due to totally different points of view or the fact that they were simply talking about different things. The goal statement, as may be seen above, dealt only with a matter of campuswide interest on which, it was felt, every person had some opportunity to provide valid information. If there were strong differences, persons must have different sources of information or else, as we said, the goal statement was no goal. We deal in Chapter 5 with the question of differences in perceptions and values, but at this point we can say that the standard deviations were low, practically never exceeding one standard deviation. We feel some confidence, then, that the means are stable and that what we are calling goals are in fact goals.

Without anticipating the analysis of varied goal perceptions by role groups, we can state here that we tried a number of different weights (e.g., weighting top administration more highly, weighting various levels equally, weighting academic divisions such as social sciences or physical sciences equally) only to discover that any variation was slight and usually a good deal less than the variation within categories. Nor would we have been much concerned if there had been more variation for, as we have said, we were seeking to have respondents act not as subjects but as informants. We were asking persons to serve as agent observers on our behalf, so that any substantial variation would have been cause for concern that the statement to which they were responding was simply no goal at all. Since our goal list was based on extensive search and followed a pretest in which academicians in a major university had a chance to judge precisely whether the statements were goals or not (and if not, to amend them), we felt some confidence in the list.

Lastly, it should be mentioned that we rarely made use of raw scores in analysis. Our practice was to divide a given distribution into thirds, with the assumption that such very broad ranks corresponded realistically to the precision of the data. We were usually content merely to state that a given goal was as important or more important than some other goal (if one level above) or quite a bit more important (comparing a goal from the bottom third with one from the top third). We think that being so conservative in establishing measured differences has the effect of tipping the scales against ourselves, of forcing us to deal only with large differences in the data.

MEASURING ORGANIZATIONAL POWER

A university campus provides a potentially revealing locus for the study of power (Baldridge, 1971a). One might look at the whole system and examine the questions raised by theorists of elitism and pluralism (Bottomore, 1964; Dahl, 1961; Schumpeter, 1956; Rose, 1967) of whether, for example, university administrators form a single elite that rules American universities, or whether there are several elites who form a loose association with one another (e.g., limited to land-grant colleges, or state colleges, or confined to professional groups such as personnel officers, or certain deans of professional schools). The evidence seems clear that administrators form neither single nor multiple elites, even though a small number of presidents and former presidents, plus occasional others, serve on the panels of commissions dealing with issues of national policy, or influence educational policy through the foundations, or advise the Congress or the White House. Within the university it would be difficult to make a case for the elite status of administrators since they simply do not exhibit sufficient cohesiveness to act as a group. For example, it would be meaningless to claim that "deans wield a lot of power" on any campus. Of course, some deans do, but the variations are more impressive. The dean of arts and sciences exhibits relatively little cohesiveness with the deans of the professional schools, and the latter rarely make common cause with one another. Each may act more like a feudal lord, with strong local loyalties but only vague feelings of affinity with other deans. Further, deans are in competition with each other for budget funds. Similarly, chairmen appear to exhibit no solidarity with other chairmen, even when they are under the same dean. The chairmen compete for the same resources (Demerath, Stephens, & Taylor, 1967, Chs. 9–11) and have differing academic orientations. Perhaps the chairmen under the dean of a professional school feel more cohesiveness.

Apart from their degree of cohesiveness, the power of administrators or faculty would have to be evaluated differently in each area of its exercise. Power over the budget would be important. Administrators are evaluated by how successful they are in getting support from the legislature, rich alumni, and administrators higher than themselves. Moreover, the question of success is posed not merely "in general" but "right now," as compared with, say, last year. Important also is power expressed as the ability of faculty or students to hamstring or limit power exercised by other role groups. A relevant consideration is whether faculty members can become independent entrepreneurs with their own institutes or have sufficient prestige to be able to consider (or threaten) alternative employment if they do not get their way (Veysey, 1965, Ch. 7).

The scope of power needs to be taken into account: A person may have practically dictatorial power over his own research institute but have little influence on universitywide decisions — say, whether the university shall take on a new function, such as a school of social work, or merge with another university. Recently, a significant form of power has come to attention as the ability to negotiate or compromise with students, especially blacks and women. The possibility of potential disruption has strengthened the hand of administrators who can create conditions for peaceful coexistence through equal opportunity and women's studies programs which siphon off discontent and enable teaching and research to go on. A new power threat comes from cost-cutting legislatures and citizen vigilantes. Yet such threats may also strengthen the hand of central administration since it may include the only persons able to protect the faculty and the students from such attacks.

A study of organizational power should also take account of the various dimensions of power (Parry, 1969). The power of a president as compared to that of a dean cannot be discussed apart from the question of what areas or topics are involved, how many persons are influenced, and how much influence each has over the persons influenced. There is, in addition, the question of potential versus actually exercised power; a chairman might be able, through his control of the agenda (see Bachrach and Baratz, 1962) at departmental meetings, to influence the outcome of faculty votes but refrain from doing so because he considers such behavior improper, whereas another will use such tactics deliberately (ibid.). Another chairman may make use of what Friedrich (1963, Ch. 11) calls the "rule of anticipated reactions," e.g., ending discussion on some matter by informing the staff that "the dean won't sit still for this kind of thing." However, the examination of the workings of power at this level would require intensive case study and observation. Persons are often not even conscious of employing these devices or do not do so deliberately.

A final point worth noting is that universities are, after all, professional organizations (Etzioni, 1964, Ch. 8) in which administrators function to facilitate basic processes—teaching and research, the latter being the concern of the professionals. If so, then the lack of participation of faculty in the government of the university, as noted by Eckert (1959) *inter alia,* is not necessarily proof that the administration "rules" the faculty, but rather a matter of professors sticking to what they are hired to do and do best— teach and carry out research.

In approaching the problem of gathering data on the concept of power in universities, we reviewed the three major methods for studying power developed in the study of communities: the reputational method (knowledgeable persons are asked to identify key leaders or decision makers, as they perceive them), the functional method (observing which persons or groups play decisive roles in settling a variety of controversies), or the positional method (identifying power groups by official position). Unfortunately, selecting a method is more complicated than simply choosing the one best suited to one's data, for disputes among protagonists of each of the methods are strong, and their views ideologically based, or the favorites of persons in various disciplines (Aiken & Mott, 1970).[8]

We finally decided on an approach which represents a compromise among the various approaches. We decided not to "create" the major power holders by limiting attention only to those at the top of the organization (presidents and regents, for examples), but to include all persons or groups which, from the literature, from informal interviews, and from our own experience, *might* play some significant role in wielding power on campus. Hence, there was no question that the president belonged, as did high officials, in central administration. But we decided to include the faculty,

---

[8] Functional theorists attack the reputational theorists as failing to take account of the area in which power is exerted. That is, simply to ask who the "leaders" are in a community is begging the question, since one is bound to come out with a "list" and conclude there is a single power elite. Instead, they say, one must examine who actually play key roles in a variety of situations. Reputational theorists, in turn, claim that observing who actually play roles often means observing only the front men or flunkeys who do the work, while "real" power holders operate behind the scenes. Both theorists are critical of those who identify power with the holders of official positions, claiming such a method is excessively naïve or else merely "creates" elites by defining them as those who are at the official top of institutional orders (the heads of corporations, military generals, etc.). Since all organizations have someone at the head, one is bound to come up with an elite.

students, parents, alumni, and the citizens of the state. We felt that it would not be feasible to include a variety of issue areas since there would likely be different areas at issue on different campuses. Further, we were not interested in power as such, but in the relationship of power to goals. Since goals are a universitywide phenomenon (as we used the term), we felt we should limit ourselves to power over universitywide matters only. We borrowed the language of Tannenbaum (1968) in devising a question which asks "how much say" persons are observed to have as a way of getting at power over decisions or outcomes. But we did decide to ask persons to give us their perception of how much say persons had, using the reputational approach for that aspect of the problem. And we did specify the issue area to some extent—namely, only power to affect the major goals of the university. The final form of the question can be seen in Table 1.

As in the case of the goal questions, this approach enabled us to generate averages for particular role groups, for a whole campus, or for all universities, and to relate such averages to the power structure.

THE USES OF THE QUES-TIONNAIRE   A question raised by some of our respondents in volunteered comments was whether questions, such as those on power and goals, would catch the depth of feelings and complexity of these issues on a given campus. Our answer, surely, is that they would not—nor could any research technique. We are, after all, not novelists or journalists who hope to convey the "spirit" of a campus in order to give the reader a vicarious sense of participation in its affairs. We saw ourselves as researchers, seeking to develop generalizations, and generalizations are, by definition, simplifications of the reality of existence.

Use of a questionnaire, then, involves inevitable sacrifices of possible richness of detail as well as the ability to describe process or how a given set of decision makers goes about the work of making policy. But in exchange for these sacrifices, we felt the questionnaire approach had great advantages over that of making a detailed study on a small number of campuses, or taking personal interviews. First, it enabled us to survey a large population in a short period of time. We sought responses from all administrators in 1964 and from most in 1971. This helped guard against the obvious bias of refusals or a selection of a small number of respondents (such as interviewing presidents only, or a small select group). Hence, with the approximately 50 percent response rate (as de-

TABLE 1 *Who makes the big decisions?*

Think again [this question followed the goal question] of the kind of place this university is; that is, what its major goals or distinctive emphases are. Below are listed a number of positions and agencies. In each case, indicate by a check mark in the appropriate place *how much say* you believe persons in those positions have in affecting the major goals of the *university as a whole.* A man might have a lot of say in his own department, but not in the university as a whole.

	A great deal of say	Quite a bit of say	Some say	Very little say	No say at all
The regents (or trustees)					
Legislators					
Sources of large private grants or endowments					
Federal government agencies or offices					
State government agencies or offices					
The president					
The vice-presidents (or provosts)					
Dean of the graduate school					
Dean of liberal arts					
Deans of professional schools as a group					
Chairmen of departments, considered as group					
The faculty, as a group					
The students, as a group					
Parents of students, as a group					
The citizens of the state, as a group					
Alumni, as a group					

scribed below), we were still left with numbers large enough for statistical analysis.

The questionnaire enabled us not only to survey large numbers of persons, but a large number of universities—some 80, of which the responses from 68 (excluding mainly the denominational universities) are described here. Although that may not, at first glance, look like a large number, it is very much larger than the number employed in most studies of universities thus far. Many are case studies of single universities, while those seeking comparative data must settle for eight or nine. With such a large number we were able to make what we think are reliable comparisons between a variety of types (public and private universities, and universities at four prestige levels, with various levels of productivity, and with various types of goal structure), and we therefore believe our generalizations have relatively wide applicability. Some part of the test of the value of our approach lies in the large number of statistically significant findings that we report. Since we made use of a printed instrument, others may check our study in order to verify or disconfirm our claims.

The questionnaire has also proven to be a flexible instrument. Since we concluded our own research, adaptations of it have been used to study denominational colleges, colleges dominated by blacks, small liberal arts colleges, community colleges, and special parts of universities (e.g., schools of social work and other professional schools at a variety of universities). Some researchers have said that they are applying the goal approach to other kinds of organizations, including business organizations (Grambsch, 1966, 1970). Such developments will help in generating the sort of cumulative research from which understanding of organizations can grow.

Some readers (and some of our respondents) are, we recognize, questionnaire-shy. The president of a major university returned our questionnaire with the comment that he "can't stand questionnaires," though he added that he wanted a copy of the results when they came out. The little boxes in which persons are asked to give their "replies" are offensive, particularly when so many questionnaires are sent out these days. In an attempt to reduce the stress of this factor, we included a space at the close of the questionnaire where persons might volunteer any comments or qualifications they chose. To our great pleasure, approximately one person in four wrote comments, some extending to several pages in length. We endeavored to analyze these volunteered comments and shall report on them in future publications. They often sensitized us to variant interpretations of findings, and we have drawn upon them in ways the writers will recognize as they read through this book. We comment on some of them in Appendix A.

RESEARCH PROCEDURES In 1964 our universe was restricted to those institutions which we felt could be fairly described as "full universities" in the sense that they were not dominated by a particular value system (as is the case in many denominational institutions) nor by a narrow definition of goals (as is the case in many teacher training or technical institutions).[9] We selected universities that met the following criteria:

- The Ph.D. degree (or equivalent) is granted in at least three of the four major disciplinary areas (humanities, biological sciences, physical sciences, and social sciences).

- The degrees granted in the two least emphasized disciplinary areas must come to 10 percent or more of total degrees conferred. Through this criterion and the previous one we felt we would ensure a broad representation of areas.

- The institution has an undergraduate liberal arts school, as well as three or more professional schools. This criterion helped eliminate institutions that were strongly committed to a vocational area.

- The institution conferred 10 or more Ph.D.'s or other doctoral degrees during the year preceding the survey. This criterion helped eliminate several institutions that offer a very small number of doctoral degrees but which concentrate overwhelmingly on their lower degree programs.

Seventy-nine universities were found to meet these criteria,[10] including nine denominational (mostly Catholic) universities. Early in our analysis we found these nine fell continuously at the upper or lower ends of given distributions, hence imparting the impact of extreme cases to analysis. For that reason we decided to handle

[9] Our usage appears similar to that of Parsons and Platt, who say, in their own research on six departments at eight universities: "The continued cohesion of teaching and research, of graduate and undergraduate teaching, of the whole range of intellectual disciplines and of the liberal arts and the more technical and professional faculties, constitutes a major feature of the full university" (Parsons & Platt, 1968, p. 522). Note however, that Shils (1963) appears to differ in claiming that there is an emphasis on research at the most prestigious universities, which are, in turn, imitated by the rest. Although this claim seems to be true (more so in 1964 than 1971 according to our data), the "full university" includes a good deal more than research emphasis.

[10] This number is obviously smaller than the approximate number of 150 institutions which make up the membership of the American Association of Graduate Schools. In that connection, Kaysen's comments are relevant: "If the distinguishing characteristic of the pure university is taken to be the training of scientists and scholars and the production of serious work in science and scholarship, then their number is much smaller than the total of 150 which offers some kind of advanced professional training and graduate work. Indeed, no more than three dozen institutions, currently accounting for nearly two-thirds of the total output of Ph.D. degrees, constitute the body of American universities. . ." (Kaysen, 1969, p. 15). Hence, our number of 79 is midway between the highly restrictive definition of Kaysen and the loose criterion for membership of the American Association of Graduate Schools.

them separately, and they are not reported here, either for 1964 or 1971. The result was 70 universities, but the final number was reduced to 68 by the elimination of the University of Minnesota and the University of Washington, the home institutions of the investigators.[11]

We found that a small number of universities, which had not done so in 1964, now met our criteria for 1971. Nevertheless, we felt that since we were interested primarily in comparing 1971 with 1964, we had to hold the population of universities constant. It would be difficult to justify comparing two different sets of universities with one another because some of the special features of the newly included universities would have unpredictable effects. Hence, we restricted our attention to the same group of 68 universities in both years.

Because we were more limited in funds for the 1971 study than we were in 1964, we had to draw a smaller sample. Nevertheless, we attempted to be as faithful as possible to the idea of replication. Because of the small number of presidents, vice-presidents, and deans, any sampling of this population, even allowing for a good response rate, could easily result in very small returns from some universities. In both 1964 and 1971 we therefore decided to send questionnaires to all of them. In 1964 available funds permitted us to send questionnaires to all academic directors and department chairmen as well. In 1971 we sampled them randomly, but in such a way as to provide a minimum number on each campus of 20 academic directors and 25 department chairmen. This procedure resulted in a sampling ratio of between 25 and 100 percent for directors and chairmen. Finally, for faculty, we sampled 10 percent in 1964, and sought a minimum of 50 persons per campus in 1971. This latter resulted in a percentage never lower than 3 percent. In sum, in 1964 we sampled 100 percent of presidents, vice-presidents, deans, chairmen, and directors, plus 10 percent of the faculty. In 1971 we sampled 100 percent of presidents, vice-presidents, and deans, approximately $33\frac{1}{3}$ percent of academic

---

[11] Our reason was simply that we felt that our own presence (and the fact that our study rapidly became widely known) would seriously bias the results. We made use of the University of Minnesota for pretest and general advice, but did not survey it or the University of Washington. In 1971 we decided to include them partly to test the validity of our concerns for bias. Preliminary analysis suggests that the main effect is to push the response rate up with little evidence to support the hypothesis of bias. Nevertheless, they are not included in any of the analyses presented in this book, unless specifically mentioned.

directors and chairmen, and around 3 percent of the faculty. Following these criteria, we ended with a total population from the 68 universities of 15,584 in 1964 and 9,130 in 1971.

Each individual received a covering letter and a self-addressed, stamped envelope. The preparation of the mailing list and the identification of individuals by title was a tedious and difficult task. While there generally appear to be comparable titles and offices, university directories are unique instruments encoded in ways which are fiendishly difficult to break.

Usual follow-up procedures were employed. In 1964 and 1971 postcards were mailed to nonrespondents after an appropriate waiting period. In 1964 these were simple reminders. In 1971 they took the form of double postcards, allowing the person to send for a fresh copy of the questionnaire if he had mislaid or lost his questionnaire. In 1964 the further device of mailing out new questionnaires to all nonrespondents—after a further waiting period—was also employed. This did not seem to increase the response rate over what we experienced in 1971 when we did not employ this procedure.

All mail questionnaires are plagued with the problem of adequate response, and ours is no exception. In both 1964 and 1971 our questionnaire was mailed rather late in the school year (March, April, and May). Possibly this time may be as good as any, but, in general, it would be our preference, if we could control the situation, to mail the questionnaire several months earlier. A second factor which we believe cut down our response rate was the length of the questionnaire. Even after we dropped a number of sections that appeared in the 1964 questionnaire, a substantial number of questions remained in 1971, and it is doubtful whether the questionnaire could be filled out in less than an hour and one half. Some respondents indicated that they spent much longer working on it. Although we are assuming the length to be a drawback, it may not have been as serious a flaw as we believe. As we stated earlier, in the 1971 questionnaire we invited written comments and allowed better than half the page for them. A large number of our respondents wrote short essays or generously extended comments, either about individual questions or about the education world in general and the administration of their schools in particular. To these people the length of the questionnaire evidently was not a major deterrent because they took time not only to answer the stated questions, but, in fact, went the "second mile" with us. On the other hand, we know from the nonrespondents who took the trouble to send the questionnaires back to us unanswered that the length was a factor in many cases.

While we are disappointed not to have had a larger response, our response rate was better than customary in national mailed surveys witz, & Madow, 1953, pp. 69–70; Parten, 1950, pp. 396 ff; and Moser, 1961, pp. 133–144.) This question must be of concern to us, slightly higher than in 1964. When we break down the response rate into administrators and faculty, we find that this improvement can be attributed to a substantial increase in the response rate of administrators. The response data are found in Table 2.

Is our respondent population representative? (Cf. Hansen, Hurwitz, & Madow, 1953, pp. 69–70; Parten, 1950, pp. 396ff; and Moser, 1961, pp. 133–144.) This question must be of concern to us, especially if we try to draw any inferences about universities as a whole. We know from our experience in 1964 that it is very difficult to collect any further information on a systematic basis from nonrespondents. In 1964, as we said, we tried the device of selecting a very small random sample from the nonrespondents, then making a special, personal appeal to them to respond ("to represent the nonrespondents," we wrote them). The result was practically identical with the response rate for the population as a whole.

The data we have do not support a hypothesis of response bias. First, we found a variation of response rates among the 68 universities from 40 percent to 75 percent. One source of this variation was the higher response rate in public universities, a situation that fit our predictions. Persons at state universities tend, as shown by their response to the goal questions, to be more strongly service-oriented and more likely to be responsive to requests for assistance from outside sources.

Another source of the variation of the response rate among institutions was due to certain "parameter effects." In general, most

TABLE 2
Response ratio: 1971 compared with 1964

	1971			1964		
	Administrators	*Faculty*	*Total*	*Administrators*	*Faculty*	*Total*
Respondents	3,155	1,417	4,572	4,494	2,730	7,224
Nonrespondents	2,512	2,046	4,558	4,334	4,026	8,360
TOTAL	5,667	3,463	9,130	8,828	6,756	15,584
Percentage response	55.6	40.9	50.1	50.9	40.4	46.4

surveys of universities use control variables such as size, type of control (public or private), and prestige. In a matrix drawn with these three variables, certain cells have many universities in them (e.g., large state universities of middle or low prestige). But some cells have few—e.g., large, public universities of high prestige (Michigan, and U. of California at Berkeley, for example), or large, private universities of high prestige (Harvard). We would infer that those universities are heavily questionnaired, to the point of over-saturation. Persons there would become weary of answering questionnaires and tend to exhibit low response rates. Such was our experience.

If we look at the internal variations in response rate among our several categories, we obtain the following results:

	1971	1964
Presidents and vice-presidents	44.8	49.0
Deans	60.4	52.0
Directors	55.2	49.5
Chairmen	67.7	51.1
Faculty	40.9	40.4

One would expect the presidents and vice-presidents—being very busy executives—to exhibit a lower response rate than other administrators. Similarly, it is hardly surprising that administrators, as a group, exhibit a higher response rate than does the faculty. The former have secretaries to assist them in answering questionnaires (especially on their backgrounds and job histories) and generally had greater interest in our study, their comments tell us, since it related directly to their own jobs. In addition, the accompanying letter was keyed more to administrators than to faculty. The higher response rate from administrators in 1971 is also quite understandable, for our report on the 1964 study (Gross & Grambsch, 1968) was made available to many of them freely or at very low cost by the American Council on Education. They were much more likely to have heard of our first study and to be interested in participating in the replication.

Taken together, there seems little in these variations of response rate that would suggest any special bias or that any important group was not represented. But there remains a possible source of response bias which may be described as follows. It is possible that among the nonrespondents who did not trouble to state their reasons for nonresponse, there were a small number opposed in principle to questionnaires as a way of gathering knowledge. We did receive a small number of letters from persons who asserted this feeling. It is conceivable that persons who are opposed to questionnaires as a way of gathering knowledge may also be persons who hold variant beliefs on the goals of the university. We do not know of any data to support this claim, but it is conceivable, for example, that persons who are opposed to questionnaires are also opposed to the study of human behavior because they do not believe it can be studied scientifically. If that is the case, they may have some feelings about the teaching of social sciences in universities, feeling that such studies may have some place in the humanities but should not be regarded as science. Although we did not state this particular point of view as one of the goals of the university, it is possible that this opinion may be correlated, for example, with ones that regard the university as a place which should spend its time in scientific matters or in attempting to emphasize intellectual matters rather than service to the community. This is possible although doubtful, but if there is a bias operating in our data, we speculated that it may be of this sort. Our results may not reflect as much as they might have the feelings of those who see the university as primarily a place in which "hard science" research and possibly what we have called student-expressive goals are important. On the other hand, as we shall point out in our discussion of findings, so many of our findings "make sense" and fit together with internal consistency that it is hard to believe there is any consistent bias operating.

2. Goals of American Universities

A main thrust of this study is an attempt to ascertain the relative importance which administrators and faculty place upon the goals of the university as we have described them in our questionnaire. In this chapter we start by developing our findings for the universities in the aggregate so that we can draw tentative conclusions regarding the perceptions of goals and the goal preferences as shown by respondents at all universities. We then proceed to analyze the differences in goal rankings and preferences. We have chosen to refer to these comparisons as the "sins of goal commission" and the "sins of goal omission." Next we compare 1971 findings with 1964 findings to note the differences in goal rankings as well as the similarities. Finally, we analyze the congruence between goals and goal preferences to try to gain some insight into the degree of stability in universities themselves.

HOW AMERICAN UNIVERSITIES RANK GOALS

In Table 3 we have listed the 1971 rankings of all 47 goals as well as the mean scores and the standard deviations. On each goal each respondent was asked to indicate how important he perceived the goal to be at his university. (See Appendix C for a duplicate of the actual questionnaire used.)

Before looking at the rankings themselves, it is worth recalling the meaning of the question. We asked each respondent to give us his perception of how important a goal is at his university. We were asking each respondent not to give us his personal opinion, but rather to act as an informant on our behalf. Take, for example, the goal ranked first: Protect Academic Freedom. We said, in effect, to each respondent:

How much emphasis is being given in your university to protecting academic freedom? We do not mean how much emphasis you think *should be* given to it (that is what we want to know in the next question we ask). Rather, as you can observe it from your location on campus, what *is* being done to protect academic freedom? Does your president make public statements about its importance? Has someone's academic freedom been abridged on your campus—if so, what was done about it? As you talk to your colleagues, does the subject of protecting academic freedom come up? If so, do people tend to feel it is important that the university do all it can about protecting it, or do they tend to downgrade its importance?

Based on his observations, we hoped he would then give us his considered perception of how important the goal was at his university. We utilized the following scale:

5   Of absolutely top importance
4   Of great importance
3   Of medium importance
2   Of little importance
1   Of no importance

We were asking around 70 persons (the average response rate) on each campus to look at the whole campus and report on the intentions and activities with reference to all 47 of our goal statements. We calculated the arithmetic mean of the respondents for a picture of the emphasis of each goal on the campus. This procedure, we hope, is not simply an aggregate of opinions, some of which might be more accurate than others. Each person's perception was, if answered honestly, a report on how things looked from his position. We anticipated that there would be some variation, since persons have different opportunities to observe a goal. A member of the faculty of agriculture might be more sensitive to the goal Satisfy Area Needs than would a member of the faculty of liberal arts. Still, we felt that each person could see a part of the picture on campus, and, when taken together, these perceptions would offer a reliable summary of the actual state of affairs.[1]

[1] What if there were disagreement? Disagreement on goal preferences (the "should be" replies in the next question) would, of course, be a social fact. On the other hand, strong disagreement on the question of goals themselves would surely mean that persons were not looking at the same thing, or else that it was *not clear* that the statement was a goal at all. To take an analogy. Suppose we ask a set of astronomical observers about a planet visible from different parts of the world. We could ask two kinds of questions: One: would you be interested in observing the planet? Two: would you tell us what you see? In answer to the first question, persons would, of course, show varying degrees of interest. A

The standard deviations in Table 3 provide a measure of the variation in emphasis upon a given goal at the 68 universities studied. For example, the top goal, Protect Academic Freedom, and the bottom one, Cultivate Students' Taste, have standard deviations in the low 80s, meaning that at a few universities the mean emphasis on academic freedom dropped to as low as 3.70, and the mean emphasis on cultivating student taste rose to as high as 2.60. Since a similar variation is evident for the goals adjacent to those two, in a small number of universities the average position of these goals would change places (Protect Academic Freedom would drop to second place, and Ensure Confidence of Contributors would rise to first, for example). For this reason, the ranking in the table must be considered rough, and attention should be given only to comparing goals at widely differing positions in the table (e.g., a top goal with one in the middle).[2]

---

report on such variation would be a report on the observers, not on the planet. But the replies to the second question deal with the planet. Variations would refer to opportunity to observe (perhaps clouds obscure the view in one place), state of repair of the telescope, errors in sighting, and so forth. We would assume that such variation should be small if we have a large number of observers. A few will make mistakes; a few will look at the wrong planet; but most will be looking at the same thing. Again, the planet may really look different from varying points, but we would hope the observer would take this into account, or that such variation would be true of only some and not most observers. If there remained *substantial* disagreement, we would have to conclude that the observers had misunderstood the instructions, or perhaps that the planet was changing its characteristics, or that it was no planet at all.

So too with goals. We felt that large standard deviations meant that errors in observation were so large that we could not conclude that such a goal existed or at least that we could not measure its importance. The standard deviations in Table 3 do not provide this information. Because of space limitations as well as our desire to spare the reader the tediousness of searching through tables, we decided not to publish tables providing, for all 68 universities, the goal means at each university and the standard deviation at the university for each of the 47 goals. On the average, the standard deviations were around .7. With an average response rate at each university of 68, the standard error of a given mean on a campus would come to less than 0.2. Hence, for a mean of say 3.50, successive sampling would result in 95 percent of the samples falling between 3.48 and 3.52. Such variation would affect the ranking on a given campus, but we minimized the effect further by breaking distributions into thirds. Hence, the variance rarely affected the ordinal position of the goal (that is, rarely shifted a goal which fell in the bottom third to the middle third, for example).

[2] The goals with the highest standard deviation, Educate to Utmost High School Graduates and Accept Good Students Only are strongly influenced by the fact that the former is important in public and the latter in private universities. We examine these variations in detail below.

TABLE 3 *The goals of American universities, 1971*

Goal number[a]	Goal	Category[b]	Rank	Mean[c]	Standard deviation
4	Protect academic freedom	MO	1	3.90	.82
40	Ensure confidence of contributors	A	2	3.62	.75
47	Maintain top quality in important programs	P	3	3.62	.74
45	Increase or maintain prestige	P	4	3.62	.74
17	Train students for scholarship/research	SI	5	3.46	.75
31	Ensure favor of validating bodies	A	6	3.41	.78
15	Keep up to date	P	7	3.39	.78
25	Carry on pure research	R	8	3.37	.83
43	Involve faculty in university government	MA	9	3.37	.85
37	Prepare students for useful careers	SI	10	3.34	.72
22	Maintain top quality in all programs	P	11	3.33	.84
10	Disseminate new ideas	S	12	3.32	.82
46	Protect students' right of inquiry	MO	13	3.31	.84
7	Cultivate students' intellect	SE	14	3.29	.79
39	Carry on applied research	R	15	3.27	.76
38	Provide community cultural leadership	S	16	3.25	.72
21	Ensure efficient goal attainment	MA	17	3.24	.85
26	Keep costs down	A	18	3.22	.79
13	Give faculty maximum opportunity to pursue careers	MO	19	3.21	.77
1	Hold staff in face of inducements	A	20	3.20	.75
18	Preserve cultural heritage	S	21	3.17	.81
41	Reward for contribution to profession	MA	22	3.16	.76
44	Provide student activities	MO	23	3.16	.76
36	Develop students' objectivity	SE	24	3.15	.81
34	Prepare student for citizenship	SI	25	3.13	.78
3	Encourage graduate work	MA	26	3.12	.70
33	Run university democratically	MA	27	3.12	.89
29	Produce well-rounded student	SE	28	3.11	.80
24	Prepare students for status/leadership	SI	29	3.09	.78
20	Involve students in university government	MA	30	3.07	.80
19	Satisfy area needs	A	31	3.05	.84
16	Affect student with great ideas	SE	32	3.03	.78
2	Let will of faculty prevail	MA	33	3.01	.84
32	Maintain balanced quality in all programs	P	34	3.00	.80
27	Reward for contribution to institution	MA	35	2.98	.75

Goal number[a]	Goal	Category[b]	Rank	Mean[c]	Standard deviation
30	*Assist citizens through extension programs*	S	36	2.96	.86
14	*Develop pride in university*	MO	37	2.93	.77
28	*Protect students' right of action*	MO	38	2.91	.85
5	*Provide special adult training*	S	39	2.80	.89
11	*Educate to utmost high school graduates*	A	40	2.80	1.01
8	*Develop students' character*	SE	41	2.79	.87
12	*Keep harmony*	MA	42	2.79	.80
35	*Accept good students only*	A	43	2.77	.92
42	*Emphasize undergraduate instruction*	MA	44	2.76	.84
6	*Develop faculty loyalty in institution*	MO	45	2.74	.82
23	*Preserve institutional character*	P	46	2.70	.96
9	*Cultivate students' taste*	SI	47	2.41	.83

[a] These numbers are provided to enable the reader to check the exact wording of the goal in the questionnaire (Appendix C) if he wishes to do so.

[b] These are abbreviations which classify the goals into our main categories, as follows: SE, student-expressive; SI, student-instrumental; R, research; S, direct service; A, adaptation; MA, management; MO, motivation; P, position.

[c] Ties did not occur. Apparent ties are due to rounding to two decimals.

If we take, as a rough measure of importance, those goals that fall beyond one standard deviation from the mean of the goals of the table itself, we find that five goals emerge as the top goals of American universities in 1971. They are:

1 Protect Academic Freedom

2 Ensure Confidence of Contributors

3 Maintain Top Quality in Important Programs

4 Increase or Maintain Prestige

5 Train Students for Scholarship/Research

Three important and unexpected findings emerge from this list. First is the preeminent place given to protecting academic freedom. An examination of the literature on higher education dealing with university goals would not have led one to the prediction that this one would be top-rated; in fact, it is usually discussed as a "problem" or in terms of famous historical cases, such as E. A. Ross, Thorstein Veblen, or George Santayana. That our respondents rated it first as a goal means not that they value it highly (although they do) but that, as they perceive it, their university shows signs—

in words and actions—that protecting academic freedom is a very important goal. Its high rank is then a sign that, whether this is considered a precarious value or not,[3] the university is moving in the direction of protecting it. Protecting academic freedom is, moreover, one of the goals which is always ranked high in each university.

Protecting academic freedom appears, then, to be basic to universities. We did not define what we meant by the term *academic freedom,* and consequently, there might be different interpretations placed upon this finding. To some of our respondents the term was used in the classical sense relating to freedom to teach. To others the issue may be considerably broader, involving such questions as whether the campus should be a sanctuary from external forces. In still other cases the term may mean freedom from tight legislative or state control. We had used the term *protection* of the faculty's right to academic freedom in the interest of narrowing the definition. To judge from a number of the comments made, wide differences in interpretation remain. Nevertheless, with a preponderance of our respondents indicating that this goal, however defined, is of great importance, it becomes obvious that the various nuances are not creating significant differences.

The goal Protect Academic Freedom is a support goal. This leads us to the second unexpected finding about these top five goals: four out of the five are support goals. At the very least, this finding casts doubt on the claim that university administrators and faculty are not aware of bureaucratic realities. Ensure Confidence of Contributors and Increase or Maintain Prestige are measures for increasing institutional security. The goal of maintaining quality in important programs to the institution may very well be tied to the increasing of university prestige. Thus it is that a university public relations official may point out, for example, that three of its programs have Nobel prize winners on the faculty, or he might state that a given school of the university ranked in the top five on some kind of survey that had been made.

That these goals rank considerably higher than such output goals as Cultivate Students' Intellect, Produce Well-Rounded Student, or Provide Special Adult Training suggests that American universities show signs of having become institutionalized. More

---

[3] It could become a goal in a university in which academic freedom was at a low point and strong efforts were made to improve it, as well as in a situation where it is well protected.

concern is displayed for goals that support the institution, and the output goals are taken for granted. While the public often grouses about the inability of college graduates to read or write, it is usually unable to do anything about it, and there are no commonly agreed upon objectives tests to check on the quality of university products. (The university itself, if pressed, may claim that it is the public schools' "job" to teach literacy.) The public at large, and even representative bodies such as legislatures, are seldom in a position to prescribe to the university, with the result that the university has not been called upon to define its own priorities to any great extent.

The third striking finding is that students show up in only one of the top goals: Train Students for Scholarship/Research. Although one cannot attach significance to the frequency with which any particular set of goals shows up in an analysis (since the number of goals is arbitrary), the students are nevertheless the subjects of 18 of the 47 goals. Hence, this showing of one of the 18 in the top six could even be a chance occurrence. Nor is the particular goal one that has been featured in student protests in recent years; instead, it is one dear to the hearts of the faculty and that small group of students intending to become faculty at distinguished universities.

If we turn next to the goals ranked at the bottom (beyond one standard deviation below the mean), we find they are as follows with the lowest ranking listed first:

1 Cultivate Students' Taste

2 Preserve Institutional Character

3 Develop Faculty Loyalty to Institution

4 Emphasize Undergraduate Instruction

5 Accept Good Students Only

6 Keep Harmony

7 Develop Students' Character

8 Educate to Utmost High School Graduates

9 Provide Special Adult Training

The actual statement of the bottom goal was: "Make a good consumer of the student—a person who is elevated culturally, has good taste and can make good consumer choices." This goal may have been assigned such a low position since consumption is related to commercialism and as such is distasteful to many members of the academic community. Yet the recent interest in the consumer movement and the tendency of faculty and administrators to consider themselves as possessing elevated taste might have led one to expect a considerably higher ranking for this goal. Develop Students' Character has similar content and is assigned a similarly low place.

The second-lowest goal, Preserve Institutional Character, seems to be in direct conflict with some of the goals closer to the top. While our respondents are indicating that they regard resistance to change to be of very minor importance among the goals of the university, they are placing great emphasis upon ensuring the confidence of supporters. Oftentimes the way to ensure this confidence is to resist change. It is evident from the next-lowest goal that our respondents do not believe that much is done to try to build faculty loyalty to the university instead of the faculty's own professional fields. This is entirely consistent with the low ranking given to the goal of emphasizing undergraduate instruction, even at the expense of graduate work. Graduate work tends to be associated with the various disciplines which, in turn, attract faculty loyalty. Undergraduate instruction tends to focus more attention on the concept of a "college" and is apt to develop a core of faculty loyal to the college rather than to their own particular specialty.

The low position assigned to Provide Special Adult Training suggests little interest in catering to the nonregular daytime student (note that Assist Citizens Through Extension Programs is not much higher on the list). The two goals dealing with selection policy on student admissions are also found in the bottom group (the goals being Accept Good Students Only and Educate to Utmost High School Graduates), but this placement may be partly because this table includes both private and state universities which assign different priorities to those goals. That they are not ranked high suggests that universities are able to control their admissions and feel no need to divert resources to doing so. Finally, the low position of Keep Harmony is not surprising, since the actual statement of the goal referred to keeping harmony between departments. Its lack of importance is indicative of the relatively loose structure we described in Chapter 1.

It must be kept in mind that all these goals fall between the score of little importance and the score of medium importance. No single goal is considered absolutely unimportant, although there are, of course, individual respondents who have indicated as much. Nevertheless, the scores on the lowest group show a substantial difference from the scores of the top group.

In sum, if we take seriously the perceptions of approximately 70 well-placed and influential observers on 68 campuses, the major universities of the United States emphasize support goals over output goals, especially the protection of academic freedom and other goals related to the pursuit of personal faculty careers. There is little emphasis upon teaching undergraduate and nonregular students, and little concern for loyalty to the university itself as a place of employment or with the admissions policy of the institution.

GOAL PREFERENCES– 1971 Our respondents were asked to indicate not only how important a particular goal may be at the university but also how important it should be. Presumably, if there were substantial differences, the organization would have to be considered unstable. There would be many frustrated people who would function only in a nominal manner and, obviously, as many as possible would leave the institution at the earliest opportunity.

By asking people to indicate what the goals should be, we are asking also for an expression of educational and organizational philosophy. Oftentimes the differences between what is and what should be might be very substantial, but the goal itself may be of relatively little importance. Under these conditions the individual may be expressing a particular preference as a matter of principle and not as a matter for immediate action. The results for the 1971 survey are shown in Table 4.

The following goals (ranked from top to bottom) are the preferred goals (beyond one standard deviation above mean) in American universities:

1 Protect Academic Freedom

2 Cultivate Students' Intellect

3 Train Students for Scholarship/Research

4 Keep up to Date

5 Maintain Top Quality in All Programs

6 Maintain Top Quality in Important Programs

7 Disseminate New Ideas

8 Develop Students' Objectivity

9 Ensure Efficient Goal Attainment

TABLE 4 *Goal preferences in American universities, 1971*

Goal number[a]	Goal	Category[b]	Rank	Mean[c]	Standard deviation
4	Protect academic freedom	MO	1	4.27	.73
7	Cultivate student's intellect	SE	2	4.11	.76
17	Train students for scholarship/research	SI	3	4.07	.63
15	Keep up to date	P	4	4.04	.71
22	Maintain top quality in all programs	P	5	4.03	.80
47	Maintain top quality in important programs	P	6	4.01	.68
10	Disseminate new ideas	S	7	4.00	.80
36	Develop student's objectivity	SE	8	3.98	.69
21	Ensure efficient goal attainment	MA	9	3.92	.79
46	Protect students' right of inquiry	MO	10	3.81	.81
27	Reward for contribution to institution	MA	11	3.80	.71
43	Involve faculty in university government	MA	12	3.71	.79
29	Produce well-rounded student	SE	13	3.70	.86
45	Increase or maintain prestige	P	14	3.68	.76
34	Prepare student for citizenship	SI	15	3.66	.80
8	Develop students' character	SE	16	3.63	.96
16	Affect student with great ideas	SE	17	3.60	.84
40	Ensure confidence of contributors	A	18	3.57	.80
14	Develop pride in university	MO	19	3.55	.83
26	Keep costs down	A	20	3.53	.78
1	Hold staff in face of inducements	A	21	3.51	.77
25	Carry on pure research	R	22	3.51	.81
18	Preserve cultural heritage	S	23	3.50	.88
33	Run university democratically	MA	24	3.50	.91
41	Reward for contribution to profession	MA	25	3.48	.77
6	Develop faculty loyalty in institution	MO	26	3.46	.86
39	Carry on applied research	R	27	3.46	.79
38	Provide community cultural leadership	S	28	3.44	.74
13	Give faculty maximum opportunity to pursue careers	MO	29	3.39	.85
37	Prepare students for useful careers	SI	30	3.39	.79
2	Let will of faculty prevail	MA	31	3.37	.87
30	Assist citizens through extension programs	S	32	3.32	.88
5	Provide special adult training	S	33	3.30	.84
31	Ensure favor of validating bodies	A	34	3.25	.87

Goal number[a]	Goal	Category[b]	Rank	Mean[c]	Standard deviation
32	*Maintain balanced quality in all programs*	P	35	3.25	.97
19	*Satisfy area needs*	A	36	3.18	.89
24	*Prepare students for status/leadership*	SI	37	3.12	.96
11	*Educate to utmost high school graduates*	A	38	3.11	1.21
20	*Involve students in university government*	MA	39	3.08	.88
44	*Provide student activities*	MO	40	3.07	.84
42	*Emphasize undergraduate instruction*	MA	41	3.02	.96
3	*Encourage graduate work*	MA	42	3.01	.70
12	*Keep harmony*	MA	43	2.97	.89
35	*Accept good students only*	A	44	2.94	.97
28	*Protect students' right of action*	MO	45	2.93	.96
9	*Cultivate students' taste*	SI	46	2.75	1.03
23	*Preserve institutional character*	P	47	2.22	.96

[a] These numbers are provided to enable the reader to check the exact wording of the goal in the questionnaire (Appendix C) if he wishes to do so.

[b] These are abbreviations which classify the goals into our main categories, as follows: SE, student-expressive; SI, student-instrumental; R, research; S, direct service; A, adaptation; MA, management; MO, motivation; P, position.

[c] Ties do not occur. Apparent ties are due to rounding to two decimals.

Protecting academic freedom once again scores very high, which indicates that our respondents believe it is properly the number one goal. For the rest, both students and output goal preferences score higher than they did as goals, suggesting a possible "guilty conscience factor." For example, while our respondents see Develop Students' Objectivity as appearing in 22d place (see Table 3), they believe it should be in 8th place.

The lowest-ranked preferred goals (counting up from the bottom) are:

1 Preserve Institutional Character

2 Cultivate Students' Taste

3 Protect Students' Right of Action

4 Accept Good Students Only

5 Keep Harmony

6 Encourage Graduate Work

7 Emphasize Undergraduate Instruction

These tended to be consistent with the rankings of goals in Table 3. It is worth noting, however, that the standard deviations of these bottom goals are relatively high, suggesting that they reflect variation in ranking among universities. In a considerable number of universities they would rank higher. We should note that Emphasize Undergraduate Instruction does somewhat better as a preference than it did as a goal, but again, the standard deviation is relatively high, which means that in quite a number of universities it may retain its position in the bottom group.

Sins of Goal Omission and Commission— 1971

The comparison of rankings in Tables 3 and 4 is carried out more systematically in Table 5. Playfully we use the term *sin of goal omission* to refer to a situation in which our respondents think a goal is not emphasized as strongly as it should be (the preference ranking is higher than the goal ranking), and the term *sin of goal commission* for the opposite situation in which it is believed that the goal is receiving more emphasis than it deserves. Bearing in mind our earlier caution about paying attention only to large differences, we have included in Table 5 only those shifts in rank that of 12 or more. It must be noted that these are only changes in rank and are not changes in mean score. It is distinctly possible for a goal to have a higher mean score as a preference than as a goal and still lose position in rank relative to the other goals. In general, the mean scores of the preferred goal table are higher and the range from the top mean to the bottom mean represents a greater spread. In 1971, for example, there are nine preferred goals which have a higher mean score than the highest in the goal list. This is not surprising, and in many ways it reflects the vitality of universities as organizations. There is a general belief that we must do more and that, in one manner or another, we should advance on most fronts.

The greatest sins of omission or, in other words, the points upon which it is felt the university must do much better fall into several different categories. Six of the goals involve students: the development of student character, affecting the students permanently with the great ideas of history, turning out a well-rounded student, developing students' objectivity, developing student intellect, and making the student into a good citizen, are among the top nine goals with this criteria. The other three have to do with the institution, and they fit into a pattern. Our respondents are saying that

TABLE 5 *Sins of goal omission and commission, 1971*		

Goal number	Goal	*Size of rank difference between goal and preference*[a]
Goals underemphasized		
8	*Develop students' character*	26
27	*Reward for contribution to institution*	24
6	*Develop faculty loyalty in institution*	19
14	*Develop pride in university*	19
16	*Affect student with great ideas*	15
29	*Produce well-rounded student*	15
36	*Develop students' objectivity*	14
7	*Cultivate students' intellect*	12
34	*Prepare student for citizenship*	12
Goals overemphasized		
31	*Ensure favor of validating bodies*	26
37	*Prepare students for useful careers*	19
3	*Encourage graduate work*	17
40	*Ensure confidence of contributors*	16
44	*Provide student activities*	16
25	*Carry on pure research*	13
39	*Carry on applied research*	12
38	*Provide community cultural leadership*	12
13	*Give faculty maximum opportunity to pursue careers*	12

[a] Figures are the difference in ranking Tables 3 and 4. For example, Develop Students' Character was in 42d position as a goal but in 16th as a preference, the difference being 26, as shown above.

institutions are being short-changed by faculty members, that the reward system should be based on the contributions of individuals to the institution rather than to the professional field, and that faculty loyalty and pride in the university should somehow be developed to a much greater extent than is presently the case. Another way of looking at this situation is to consider these three as the goals of localism as opposed to cosmopolitanism. It must be kept in mind, however, that none of these are among the high-ranking goals and have only moved up in a position relative to others.

The nine goals that our respondents believe are overemphasized are more diverse. Heading the list is the goal of ensuring favorable appraisal of validating and accrediting bodies. Few academics are enthusiastic about the process of evaluation of this kind. The decline in rank may indicate criticism of the amount of time and effort spent on making a good impression as well as the leverage which sometimes is exercised by the various validating bodies as a form of outside control. The entire process of appraisal and validation is at best considered to be a necessary evil. It must be kept in mind that this goal ranks as one of the very top goals and, thereby, represents one of the major conflict situations. The growing discussion of the role of accreditation in American higher education is an indication of the conflict that seems to be developing.

The second largest sin of goal commission is that of preparing students for useful careers. Once again, this is a fairly high-ranking goal which evidently should be ranked quite a bit lower. There is general recognition, we believe, that American higher education has placed a great emphasis upon career preparation. As long as the percentage of the population going to college remains high, we can expect that this emphasis is not going to change. On the campus, however, there has always been a feeling that students should concentrate their time and effort upon obtaining the best education possible rather than worrying about what they are going to do when they get out of school.

The third sin of commission, the encouraging of graduate study, is a recognition that universities have placed too much emphasis at the undergraduate level on the identifying and recruiting of graduate students. Through the mechanism of graduate teaching assistantships they have further abetted the encouraging of graduate work, possibly at the expense of the undergraduate program. Our respondents indicate that such emphasis should be discouraged. Other goals, including those involving research, in which sins have been committed seem to fall into a similar pattern. It is interesting to note, for example, that the ensuring of confidence on the part of supporters is now apparently a goal which should be played down. This goal ranked second on the list of goals, but it ranks eighteenth on the preferred list. Much like the goal of ensuring favorable appraisal of validating bodies, it is quite evident that administrators and faculty wish that this function could be deemphasized. People within the organization would probably like to have the confidence implied in the goal statement but would prefer not to have to work at it in a special way.

We are fortunate to have comparable data from two periods of time enabling us to make an evaluation of change. By comparing the goal rankings of our 1971 study with the earlier study made in 1964, we can note the shifts that indicate actual change. To expect major changes in fundamental goals and objectives within the short span of seven years, however, is not very realistic. Change is not likely to be very swift in an organization which is characterized by the tongue-in-cheek observation that it is easier to move a cemetery than to change a curriculum.

Yet the seven-year interval between the two studies was filled by extraordinary events, and it could be asserted that these events were sufficiently important so as to bring about a major shift in the goals hierarchy of American universities. In 1964, for example, the magnitude of campus unrest was very small compared to the next several years. Federal government largesse graced the university in such abundance that members of the academic community had assumed that it was to be a permanent way of life. Furthermore, the demand for graduates at all degree levels—bachelor's, master's, and doctoral—seemed to be insatiable.

By 1971 many of these conditions had reversed. Student unrest, after peaking, had subsided except for occasional outbursts. Federal largesse had certainly diminished, and graduates were having a tough time locating jobs. Along with a decline in federal money great "belt tightening" took place among state and local governments. The public at large and young people in particular began to question the worth of the college degree in human as well as economic terms; enrollments reached a plateau and started to decline. It is not possible to describe the dynamic path by which we moved through this period, but it is certainly worthwhile to compare the goal rankings of 1964 with 1971.

While many changes have taken place, our findings seem to indicate that from the perspective of perceived and preferred university goals, there does not appear to have been as much change as many people have suggested. This is true of the output goals as well as the support goals. Table 6 sets forth a comparison of the rank order of the 47 goals and goal preferences.

Only two marked changes occurred in goal rankings from 1964 to 1971: the goals of involving faculty and students in the government of the university have moved up in rank substantially. The goal of involving the faculty in the government of the university

TABLE 6 *Goals and goal preferences, 1964–1971*

Goal number	Goal	Goal rank 1971	Goal rank 1964	Preference rank 1971	Preference rank 1964
4	Protect academic freedom	1	1	1	1
40	Ensure confidence of contributors	2	4	18	26
47	Maintain top quality in important programs	3	3	6	7
45	Increase or maintain prestige	4	2	14	11
17	Train students for scholarship/research	5	6	3	2
31	Ensure favor of validating bodies	6	9	34	34
15	Keep up to date	7	5	4	6
25	Carry on pure research	8	7	21	16
43	Involve faculty in university government	9	25	12	19
37	Prepare students for useful careers	10	13	29	32
10	Disseminate new ideas	11	11	7	5
22	Maintain top quality in all programs	12	8	5	4
46	Protect students' right of inquiry	13	17	10	10
7	Cultivate students' intellect	14	14	2	3
39	Carry on applied research	15	12	27	30
38	Provide community cultural leadership	16	16	28	28
21	Ensure efficient goal attainment	17	10	9	9
13	Give faculty maximum opportunity to pursue careers	18	22	30	25
1	Hold staff in face of inducements	19	15	20	18
26	Keep costs down	20	24	22	35
18	Preserve cultural heritage	21	19	23	20
36	Develop students' objectivity	22	23	8	8
41	Reward for contribution to profession	23	26	25	21
44	Provide student activities	24	27	40	43
3	Encourage graduate work	25	18	42	27
33	Run university democratically	26	29	24	22
34	Prepare student for citizenship	27	20	15	14
29	Produce well-rounded student	28	21	13	17
24	Prepare students for status/leadership	29	28	38	33
20	Involve students in university government	30	45	39	46
19	Satisfy area needs	31	34	36	42
16	Affect student with great ideas	32	30	17	15
2	Let will of faculty prevail	33	36	31	24

Goal number	Goal	Goal rank 1971	Goal rank 1964	Preference rank 1971	Preference rank 1964
32	Maintain balanced quality in all programs	34	35	35	31
27	Reward for contribution to institution	35	32	11	13
30	Assist citizens through extension programs	36	31	32	36
28	Protect students' right of action	37	41	45	40
14	Develop pride in university	38	33	19	23
5	Provide special adult training	39	37	33	38
11	Educate to utmost high school graduates	40	39	37	37
12	Keep harmony	41	43	43	41
8	Develop students' character	42	38	16	12
35	Accept good students only	43	40	44	39
42	Emphasize undergraduate instruction	44	44	41	44
6	Develop faculty loyalty in institution	45	42	26	29
23	Preserve institutional character	46	46	47	47
9	Cultivate students' taste	47	47	46	45

stood in the middle of the total distribution of goals in 1964, whereas in 1971 it had moved to ninth place. The higher ranking of this particular goal manifests itself on campuses in a variety of ways. One of the universities in our study did not have a faculty senate in 1964, but it had a very active one in 1971. Other consultative devices have been set up to involve faculty to a much higher degree. The nature of the problems on campus often has been such that administrators have welcomed faculty participation and a measure of faculty responsibility. It also has been convenient for administrators to cite an amorphous organization of faculty as authority for some contemplated action or postponement. Regardless of the reason, involving faculty in university government is now a high-ranking goal.

Involving students in university government has also moved up in goal ranking, but it really had no other direction to go. In 1964, involving students in university government was seen to be one of the least important goals in universities. Although it has not moved to the top, its 1971 position in thirtieth place makes it an almost middle-ranking goal. Much has been made of student involvement as a part of the educational process, and, something therefore to be applauded. It also has been very popular to suggest that students should have a hand in running the university because, after all, it is their education. That the goal in 1971 has still only a lower-middle ranking at best indicates that administrators and faculty do not believe it has the same priority as involving the faculty in decision making.[4] Whether the goal of student involvement will become of greater importance in the years to come is difficult to say. The years between 1964 and 1971 were generally explosive ones. Oftentimes student involvement in policy decisions was granted as a concession to prevent worse things from happening. In more normal periods, the rapid turnover of students and their likely preoccupation with other matters may prompt faculty and administrators to return to the 1964 opinion that student involvement is not very important. While students may have coerced administrators into making more opportunities for involvement, there is no indication that they will have the same impact upon external power centers such as trustees, legislators, and the public at large.

Looking now at the right-hand columns of Table 6, we see that the goal preference rankings have not shifted appreciably either. As with goals, only two preferences have shifted appreciably. Keep Costs Down has risen in rank from 35th to 22d position and Encourage Graduate Work has dropped from 27th to 42d place. Neither finding is surprising or suggestive of any important shift in the values of professors and faculty over the seven-year period of the study.

By comparing the first and third or second and fourth columns with each other, it is possible to compare the sins of goal omission and commission in the two years. We have already presented the 1971 picture in Table 5. It is not necessary to present a new table here. Instead we can merely note that the following goals in Table 5

---

[4] Hefferlin (1969, pp. 148–149), in a book on program changes between 1962 and 1967, comments: "Many Americans mistakenly believe that students have recently had great power over curricular matters, and a majority of them apparently think that students already possess too much power. (In a Gallup poll of December, 1968, for example, more than half of the persons over thirty years old who were interviewed stated that they did not think college students should have a 'greater say concerning the academic side of colleges.') The fact is, however, that students have possessed little power at all during the past decade. They have not controlled the resources that would effect change, and they have not had the opportunity of a buyer's market to exercise their options." Our own data on perception of student power (see pp. 122–135) would support Hefferlin's claim. There is a distinct gap between perceptions of change in that power and the evaluation of its amount in comparison to other power holders.

were new for 1971, not being present either as sins of omission or commission in 1964. The following goals were thought to be under-emphasized in 1964: Develop Pride in University, Produce Well-Rounded Student, Cultivate Student Intellect, and Prepare Student for Citizenship. The following goals were believed to be overem-phasized: Encourage Graduate Work, Do Pure Research, and Give Faculty Maximum Opportunity to Pursue Careers. Only one goal thought to be underemphasized in 1964 dropped out in 1971, namely Let Will of Faculty Prevail. These findings suggest con-cern that the university is not doing enough for students, while paying too much attention to the needs of faculty and to research goals. Yet these changes represent no more than feelings or con-cerns. The lack of any appreciable shift in the goal rankings and preference rankings of Table 6 remains compelling.

Given the volume of comment and the actual attention paid to student dissent, these findings are surprising. Assuming that they are valid, there are several possible explanations. First, it may be that there has in fact been little change in the goals or values of faculty and administration at the major universities in the United States. Perhaps these persons simply were unable to change; per-haps the universities themselves were unable to change. Perhaps the faculty and administration believed, even under attack, that their values and goals were worth defending and preserving. A second possibility is that universities did change, but in ways not reflected in goals or goal preferences. We can hardly deny that possibility, but it does not bear on the question considered here — the lack of change in goals and goal preferences. It is possible that universities changed in internal organization, in admission policies, and in makeup but in such a way that those changes resulted in the pursuit of the same goals. Such is not likely, but cannot be ruled out immediately.

A third possibility is that the changes which have so much dominated public perception have resulted in the generation of new institutions — community colleges, experimental colleges, new state colleges, and even new universities. Since we studied the same institutions in 1971 as in 1964 we would not detect the ferment going on elsewhere.[5]

---

[5] Hefferlin (1969) was unable to find strong differences in program reform in different types of institutions, though he did note that religious colleges were more prominent among "dynamic" institutions.

There is one change in goal emphasis since 1964 which provides some support for this third interpretation. If we compare the means and standard deviations of all goals and goal preferences (the mean of means, and standard deviation of that mean) in 1964 and 1971, we obtain the following results:

	1964		1971	
	Mean	*Standard deviation*	*Mean*	*Standard deviation*
Goals	3.20	.30	3.14	.28
Goal preference	3.52	.44	3.47	.44

The standard deviations are about the same in the two years, but the means have dropped. It is, of course, hazardous to attribute significance to a shift in scores, but since it occurred with both goals and goal preferences, it is worth speculating on its possible meaning. A shift downward in scoring means literally that our respondents in 1971 were more likely to check "of medium importance" than "of top importance," more likely to check "of no importance" than "of little importance." Such a shift may signify that our respondents are becoming more conservative in their estimates of what is possible and of what they believe should be possible. A top rating to a goal reflects a belief that the university is definitely moving in that direction. A lower rating seven years later reflects either doubt that it is possible to move that far or a recognition that perhaps one ought to settle for more modest targets. If a sense of diminished possibility has grown up between 1964 and 1971, then those goals which are now felt to be less achievable may be those which other institutions are beginning to take over. This may be particularly likely for the service goals, such as providing evening classes, which were ranked low in any case. We will pursue these speculations further in our final chapter.

GOAL CONGRUENCE AND INCONGRUENCE The degree of agreement between goal emphasis and goal preference may be termed goal congruence; the lack of agreement may be termed goal incongruence. Its significance is worth noting. If there is general agreement on a campus that a particular goal is important and is receiving the emphasis it should have, we can infer an absence of basic conflict over that goal. If, however, a situation should exist in which a given goal is reported to be of great importance, although the preference of the respondents at that university is that the goal should receive less emphasis, then we have a situation where potential conflict exists. The same would hold for a goal in which the ranking was quite low, but there were strong feelings that the goal should be ranked very high. Some of these conflicts are more important than others because the goals are more significant. Although it is unwise to generalize too much about the degree of goal congruence and the mobility of individuals, conflict in goals will likely lead to personnel turnover, to considerable internal debate and possible friction, and to general instability.

Because our respondents come from a wide variety of backgrounds and, with few exceptions, have had exposure to more than one university either as a student, a faculty member, or an administrator, most of them have had ample opportunity to compare universities. Although we suspect that many of them are attracted to a university which has developed a goals hierarchy which they find compatible with their own values, we know that others have not. As one professor in our sample put it:

We used to try and place our top Ph.D. candidates at schools where they would have comparable scholarship values because we believed that both would be happier under those conditions. Now we find that some of our best Ph.D. candidates are more concerned with the university environment, the community as a place to live and geographic location than they are with scholarship values. Either we are breeding incipient areas of conflicts on many campuses, or else our students are much more willing to compromise and adjust than they have in past years.

This professor believes, obviously, that the goals profile at a given university is established and that people who are educated at universities with similar patterns would automatically want to stay within their own "family." Thus it is that the major Middle Western state universities, for example, have tended in the past to trade Ph.D.'s as they become new faculty members. In the 1960s when colleges and universities were expanding and the demand for faculty was high, one of the common complaints of new schools was their inability to attract top faculty candidates from major Ph.D. programs. This situation has eased somewhat since 1970, but it is still present in many places. Congruence, therefore, may tend to be the product of an incestuous relationship which has existed among the leading Ph.D. degree granting schools.

While we may speculate further about whether the organization shapes the man or the man shapes the organization, we know that the presence of a great many goals in which there is a high degree of congruence would seem to indicate that people at universities are reasonably satisfied with the goal hierarchy and believe it to be about right.

Measuring Goal Congruence

The notion of sins of omission and commission provides us with a picture restricted only to very large differences in ranking. In addition, it is an aggregate measure based on goal averages from all universities. Here we turn to a more sensitive measure which can assess the strength of the relationship between the actual emphasis given to the goal and the emphasis respondents believe the goal should receive.

In measuring the degree of emphasis on a goal or goal preference, two perspectives are possible. For illustration, take the goal Assist Citizens Through Extension Programs, for the cases of the University of Minnesota and the University of Washington. It is possible to examine the emphasis given to that goal at the University of Minnesota in comparison to other goals at that university and find that it occupies a position in the middle. This goal also occupies a middle position at the University of Washington. But when we compare the two universities with each other, the emphasis on this goal at the University of Minnesota is higher than it is at the University of Washington. This is what we would expect from the traditional land-grant emphasis at Minnesota, in contrast to the University of Washington, which is not a land-grant institution.

We call the former comparison *Within* analysis and the latter, *Across*. We shall be employing both types of analyses throughout the book. Hence it is worth emphasizing that the two kinds of analyses give different information although they are correlated, albeit weakly. The Across analysis reveals stratification of universities, whereas the Within analysis stratifies goals. For the Across analysis we range all universities from high to low on the goal and split the distribution into thirds. Hence a university occupies a high, medium, or low position relative to other universities. In Figure 1 the upper portion presents the data for the goal Assist Citizens Through Extension Programs cross-classified for goal and goal preference. The marginals in Figure 1 illustrate our procedure of dividing up the distribution into thirds. For this goal, 21 universities were placed in the bottom, 23 in the middle, and 24 at the top. The corresponding figures for goal preference are 26, 21, and 21. Inspection of the table reveals that there is clearly a strong relationship, which is measured by the size of Goodman and Kruskal's

FIGURE 1 *Sample illustrating contrast between Goals-Across and Goals-Within for Assist Citizens Through Extension Programs, 1971*

ACROSS UNIVERSITY ANALYSIS

		Goal preference			
		Low	*Medium*	*High*	*Sum*
Goal: Assist Citizens	*Low*	18	3	0	21
	Medium	7	12	4	23
	High	1	6	17	24
	Sum	26	21	21	68

Gamma = .893

WITHIN UNIVERSITY ANALYSIS

Goal: Assist Citizens	*Low*	25	13	0	38
	Medium	1	12	1	14
	High	1	11	4	16
	Sum	27	36	5	68

Gamma = .889

gamma, namely, .893 (see Appendix B for explanation). In sum, the table leads us to conclude that if a university falls in the upper third of the distribution in emphasis on that goal, it also falls in the upper third in emphasis on the goal preference, and so forth. In a sense, we could say that it falls "in the company" of universities emphasizing that goal and that goal preference. This is what we mean by saying that the Across analysis stratifies universities.

If we look at the bottom part of Figure 1, we see the Within analysis illustrated. Here we take each of our 68 universities and divide the goals *within each university* into thirds. Then we classify the university in terms of whether it ranks a given goal in the upper, middle, or lower third. Note that it is possible for all 68 universities to classify a given goal in the top third (such is the case for Protect Academic Freedom, for example) of the goals at each university. Hence the marginals may present a skewed distribution. In the sample case, although 16 universities put this goal in the top third, only 5 put it there as a goal preference. But the gamma is .889, suggesting a strong relationship here also. That is, if a university ranks the goal in the bottom third, it tends also to rank it in the bottom third of its goal preferences. This is true of 25 of the 68 universities. Similarly, universities giving the goal a middle ranking also classify it in the middle of their preferences. Those are the major facts accounting for the high gamma, however, for there is little tendency for those universities who rank it high on their goals also to rank it high on their preferences. One reason is simply that there is little room to "move around" because of the skewed marginals: there are only five universities which classify it in the top third as a preference. Nevertheless, the relationship is there.

Goal Congruence: Across Measure

Table 7a lists the findings on goal congruence for Across analysis, a *finding* being defined as a relationship exceeding the 5 percent level of significance. This table also enables us to compare the 1971 findings with those obtained in 1964. In Table 7b we list the goals that do not reach significance in 1971, with the gammas listed for those that did in 1964.

An examination of Table 7a reveals that there are nine goals which attained significance in 1971 which did not do so in 1964, whereas two which were significant in 1964 dropped out in 1971. Hence, there was a net gain of seven, for a total of 32 goals which are congruent in 1971 compared to 25 in 1964.

The 5 percent level of significance would lead us to expect that of 47 goals, some two or three might show up by chance alone. That 25 showed up in 1964 enabled us to rule out any likelihood that chances were operating in generating findings. The situation is even more remarkable in 1971. Such a finding suggests that the tendency toward stratification reflected by such findings in the Across analysis in 1964 has become even more pronounced. In sum, if a university falls in the company of one set of universities on one goal, it tends to fall in the same set on the goal preferences. The nature of this stratification will occupy our attention in the next chapter. We can anticipate that discussion by saying that the evidence suggests that the tendency of universities to be either elitist or egalitarian — already evident in 1964 — is more strongly pronounced in 1971. One can speculate on the reasons for this development. One plausible explanation is that the curtailment of federal funds has deprived many schools of the ability to compete on an equal footing. Now that those funds are diminished, there is more recognition of the need for a "differentiated product" based upon resources available and upon perceived needs to be met.

Table 7b accounts for the remaining 15 goals in which the low degree of congruence fell below our cutoff point of a 5 percent significance level. Presumably these 15 goals represent areas of possible or incipient controversy. Of these, 4 are output goals, and 11 support goals. Three of the four output goals relate to students, and six of the eleven support goals are classified as manage-

		Degree of
	Goal	*congruence*[a]

TABLE 7a
Congruence
between
perceived and
preferred goals:
Across

Output goals

Student-expressive

8	Develop students' character	.652[b]
29	Produce well-rounded student	.623[b]
36	Develop students' objectivity	.479

Student-instrumental

37	Prepare students for useful careers	.860
34	Prepare student for citizenship	.595[b]
9	Cultivate students' taste	.861
24	Prepare students for status/leadership	.685[b]

Research

25	Carry on pure research	.868
39	Carry on applied research	.874

Direct service

5	Provide special adult training	.973
30	Assist citizens through extension programs	.893
18	Preserve cultural heritage	.647
38	Provide community cultural leadership	.502[b]

Support goals

Adaptation

31	Ensure favor of validating bodies	.726
11	Educate to utmost high school graduates	.874
19	Satisfy area needs	.963
26	Keep costs down	.540
1	Hold staff in face of inducements	.511[b]
35	Accept good students only	.960[b]

Management

12	Keep harmony	.468
43	Involve faculty in university government	.626
20	Involve students in university government	.761
42	Emphasize undergraduate instruction	.668

Motivation

13	Give faculty maximum opportunity to pursue careers	.467
4	Protect academic freedom	.861
44	Provide student activities	.800
46	Protect students' right of inquiry	.590
28	Protect students' right of action	.607

TABLE 7a (continued)	Goal	Degree of congruence[a]
	Support goals (continued)	
	Position	
	47 Maintain top quality in important programs	.512 [b]
	22 Maintain top quality in all programs	.537
	23 Preserve institutional character	.850
	45 Increase or maintain prestige	.544 [b]

[a]Goodman and Kruskal's gamma. See Appendix B for explanation.
[b] New finding in 1971. Not present in 1964.

ment goals. The low congruence of the management goals is most noteworthy. Several deal with the reward system (Reward for Contribution to Institution and Reward for Contribution to Profession) indicating that the basis for rewards, at least as far as these two measures are concerned, is far from certain. Two of the management goals deal with methods of operation, Ensure Efficient Goal Attainment and Run University Democratically. The basis for selection of administrators and their behavior, whether democratic or autocractic, are also issues of considerable debate in the university community. The two remaining management goals (Let The Will of Full-Time Faculty Prevail and Encourage Graduate Work) are more directly concerned with the faculty role, which is a hotly debated question today. A large number of comments (see Appendix A) made by our respondents were concerned with this question. Questions about the reward system are also directly related to faculty concerns. The low congruence may be a possible explanation of the growing debate about faculty collective bargaining.

The adaptation goal of ensuring confidence on the part of those who support the university was congruent to a very high degree in 1964, but not in 1971. When it is noted that this goal moved up in rank among all university goals from fourth to second place and at the same time the preference score moved from 26th to 18th, it becomes obvious that this disparity in general ranking makes a finding of high congruence almost impossible.

Goals Congruence: Within Measure

Table 8a presents the findings using our Within measures. There is an astounding number of 38 goals out of the 47 with high degrees of congruence; by contrast, only 20 goals so ranked in 1964. There are 22 new goals on the list, and only 3 that were congruent in 1964 have dropped off.

TABLE 7b *Lack of congruence between perceived and preferred goals: Across*

Goal	Degree of congruence[a]
Output	
Student-expressive	
7 *Cultivate students' intellect*	
16 *Affect student with great ideas*	
Student-instrumental	
17 *Train students for scholarship/research*	
Direct service	
10 *Disseminate new ideas*	(congruence 1964 = .569)
Support	
Adaption	
40 *Ensure confidence of contributors*	(congruence 1964 = .562)
Management	
2 *Let will of faculty prevail*	
3 *Encourage graduate work*	
21 *Ensure efficient goal attainment*	
27 *Reward for contribution to institution*	
33 *Run university democratically*	
41 *Reward for contribution to profession*	
Motivation	
6 *Develop faculty loyalty in institution*	
14 *Develop pride in university*	
Position	
15 *Keep up to date*	
32 *Maintain balanced quality in all programs*	

[a]Goodman and Kruskal's gamma. See Appendix B for explanation.

Only one output goal shows a low degree of congruence, leaving eight support goals in that category.

The Within measure is subject to possible bias because of a "halo effect" whereby the respondent checks the same importance for "is" and "should be" in answering all questions. An inspection of the questionnaires themselves, the many comments made by the respondents, and the absence of such an effect in 1964 indicate that the possible bias present is quite minimal. We must conclude therefore that there is substantial agreement on most campuses as to the relative priorities of most of the goals. Indeed, in the case of 10 of them whose scores are 1.000 the congruence is perfect in that

	Goal	Degree of congruence [a]
	Output goals	
	Student-expressive	
7	Cultivate students' intellect	1.000 [b]
29	Produce well-rounded student	.854
36	Develop students' objectivity	1.000 [b]
8	Develop students' character	.540 [b]
	Student-instrumental	
37	Prepare students for useful careers	.605
24	Prepare students for status/leadership	.798
17	Train students for scholarship/research	1.000 [b]
9	Cultivate students' taste	1.000 [b]
34	Prepare student for citizenship	.680
	Research	
25	Carry on pure research	.812
39	Carry on applied research	.877 [b]
	Direct service	
5	Provide special adult training	.845
30	Assist citizens through extension programs	.889
38	Provide community cultural leadership	.820
10	Disseminate new ideas	1.000
18	Preserve cultural heritage	.750
	Support goals	
	Adaptation	
40	Ensure confidence of contributors	.468 [b]
31	Ensure favor of validating bodies	.565 [b]
11	Educate to utmost high school graduates	.759
35	Accept good students only	.981 [b]
19	Satisfy area needs	.929 [b]
1	Hold staff in face of inducements	.870
	Management	
43	Involve faculty in university government	.703
20	Involve students in university government	.824 [b]
33	Run university democratically	.758 [b]
12	Keep harmony	1.000 [b]
42	Emphasize undergraduate instruction	.778 [b]
3	Encourage graduate work	.932
21	Ensure efficient goal attainment	.545 [b]

TABLE 8a
Congruence between perceived and preferred goals: Within

Goal	Degree of congruence[a]
Support goals (continued)	
Motivation	
4 Protect academic freedom	1.000[b]
13 Give faculty maximum opportunity to pursue careers	.841
46 Protect students' right of inquiry	.790
Position	
22 Maintain top quality in all programs	.750[b]
47 Maintain top quality in important programs	1.000[b]
15 Keep up to date	1.000[b]
45 Increase or maintain prestige	1.000[b]
23 Preserve institutional character	.967[b]
32 Maintain balanced quality in all programs	.536[b]

[a]Goodman and Kruskal's gamma. See Appendix B for explanation.
[b] New finding in 1971. Not present in 1964.

all universities rank both the goal and the goal preference in either the upper, middle, or lower third.

The inescapable conclusion drawn from the many findings using the Within measure—almost double the number found in 1964—is that beneath the surface conflicts a more general meeting of the minds is gradually taking shape upon the definition of university goals. The job of the many planning committees and the hours and hours spent by administrators and faculty in drafting documents of purpose have apparently borne fruit. It seems that the adversity faced by universities since 1964 has promoted a degree of unity one would not have expected from surface observations of conflict and dissension.

Before we are carried away by the large amount of apparent conflict resolution which these findings indicate, we must note that a number of goals (9) still have low degrees of congruence (see Table 8b). There is only one output goal (Affect Students with Great Ideas of History) in which there is low congruence, and this represents a change from 1964 when congruence prevailed. In those schools in which the goal itself ranked high, the goal preference ranked low, and vice versa. Why this should take place is obviously a matter of speculation. One plausible explanation is that the liberal arts ideal which this goal typifies is no longer held with any degree

TABLE 8b *Lack of congruence between perceived and preferred goals: Within*

Goal	Degree of congruence[a]
Output	
Student-expressive	
16 *Affect student with great ideas*	(congruence 1964 = .668)
Support	
Adaptation	
26 *Keep costs down*	
Management	
41 *Reward for contribution to profession*	
27 *Reward for contribution to institution*	
2 *Let will of faculty prevail*	(congruence 1964 = 1.000)
Motivation	
44 *Provide student activities*	
28 *Protect students' right of action*	(congruence 1964 = .857)
14 *Develop pride in university*	
6 *Develop faculty loyalty in institution*	−.728

[a] Goodman and Kruskal's gamma. See Appendix B for explanation.

of certainty. In some cases, however, it might mean that the pressures of professionalism have run their course and that a desire to return to a more general curriculm is reasserting itself. A large number of comments (see Appendix A) indicated the hope of regaining that former state in which the goal Affect Students with the Great Ideas of History was of much greater importance. This would seem to indicate a goal preference that may be out of line with the actual goal itself.

The support goals indicate once again the problem of the reward system. There is little agreement that the reward system should be based either upon contribution to the institution or the contribution that the faculty member makes to his own profession. Both concepts are with us but in widely varying degrees. As indicated earlier in connection with the Across measure, it is likely that the low congruence on these goals may be a prelude to the coming of more collective bargaining.

The goal of letting the will of the full-time faculty prevail is an indication of a possible power struggle. In 1964 this goal was in the bottom third as a goal and preference at all universities. Since that time the growth of faculty power has raised the goal score into the middle third and even the upper third, whereas the preference score has tended to remain somewhat lower although not entirely in the lower third.

The motivation goals with low congruence are rather unique. There is no apparent general agreement about providing student activities or protecting the students' rights to advocate direct action. This latter had a high degree of congruence in 1964, but events of the last eight years have made this a controversial issue.

Finally, the two goals of developing pride in the university and developing loyalty to it are goals in which there is no general agreement on most campuses. Developing loyalty on the part of the faculty to the university rather than only to their own jobs or professions has almost perfect noncongruence. Almost all schools rank this goal in the lower third as a goal and in the middle and upper third as a preference. This finding represents very strong evidence of cosmopolitanism in American universities. Whether the abundance of goals in congruence will eventually work to develop a degree of localism in higher education remains to be seen.

SUMMARY Our examination of the goal structure of American universities in 1971 led us to the finding that the top goals involve the protection of academic freedom and the achievement of a variety of support goals related to the careers of faculty and administrators. The emphasis leads us to believe that American universities are showing strong signs of maturity—of taking output goals for granted while they concentrate on the institutionalization of the organization. Undergraduate teaching and loyalty to the institution itself are ranked far down, which does not mean that they do not occur but only that other matters occupy the attention of key persons in universities.

When we turned to feelings about the way things should be, there was some variation, suggesting a guilty conscience about the private concerns revealed by the goal emphasis. Six student goals are felt to be underemphasized, but our respondents resist appraisal on these and other sins of omission and commission.

However one might feel about those findings for 1971, a comparison with 1964 reveals that seven years of turmoil have resulted in practically no change in goals or goal preferences. Involving the faculty in university government has moved up, and so has involving students in university government. But they are the only goals that have changed position appreciably, and the student goal has moved only from a position almost at the bottom to one somewhat higher up, but still in the lower part of the distribution.

Finally, the examination of data on goal congruence and incongruence leads to evidence that universities are becoming differentiated from one another, or becoming stratified, rather than continuing to try to compete with one another in all programs and goals. Along with this trend (evident in 1964 but more strongly observable in 1971) is a distinct and striking trend toward congruence within universities between goals and goal preferences—that is, an increasing tendency for persons to feel that the goals at the university are receiving the emphasis they should be receiving. Is this merely the smug complacency of an establishment? The troubles of the last seven years would hardly be expected to produce complacency. Tentatively, we think these findings represent evidence that the seven years have not so much shaken up American universities as they have shaken them down. Conflicts have been successfully resolved; compromises have been made; and universities show strong signs of stability.

3. Patterns of Differentiation

Our analysis thus far has treated all 68 universities as if they were an undifferentiated whole. Yet most academics, as well as laymen, assume that there are differences among universities and that those differences are important. Some universities are assumed to be "better" than others, as shown by the keen competition of students to enroll in them. In recent years much criticism has been leveled at all universities—and especially at large ones—for their supposed emphasis upon research rather than teaching. Some universities, however, are much more heavily committed to research than others (as measured, for example, by the volume of contract research), and some universities have large graduate programs and award many Ph.D.'s, whereas others do not. Because we have ignored these differences thus far, our analysis in the previous chapter may be misleading. A goal which received a medium score from all 68 universities may well have received a high score in public universities and a low score in private universities. One receiving a low score on the average may still have received a high score in those universities emphasizing graduate work.

We explored such differences in both 1964 and 1971 and shall report on those findings in this chapter. The particular measures chosen included the usual comparisons made by students of universities, with special emphasis on those for which reliable data could be secured for all universities. The measures used in both 1964 and 1971 were as follows:

1 Type of control (public or private)

2 Research and scholarly productivity ("productivity" for short) as measured by:

a Volume of contract research[1]
b Percentage of graduate students in the student body
c Number of doctorates awarded

3 University prestige

4 Amount of student unrest

These measures, which we came to refer to as *global*,[2] were found to relate to the goal structure of universities in important ways. But there were two obvious global measures which we do not report on here—location and size. Both these measures were fully examined in 1964. Location was measured in two ways—geographical region and urban versus rural location; size was measured by the number of full-time staff and the size of student body, including full-time-equivalent students. Results were sketchy in both cases (see Gross & Grambsch, 1968, pp. 43–45). For example, it was found that increasing size of staff was positively related to the goals of doing pure research, disseminating new ideas, and keeping up to date. The size of the student body was found to be positively related to the goals of providing cultural leadership to the community, carrying on applied research, and encouraging graduate work. Although one might be tempted to begin theoretical speculations to account for such findings, such a small number of correlations is well within the number expected by chance alone, given the

[1] Calculated for the year for which information was available closest to the survey year.
[2] Following the usage proposed by Lazarsfeld and Menzel (1969) for describing properties of "collectives." They suggest the following classification: (1) *analytical*, for properties "obtained by performing some mathematical operation upon some property of each member" (e.g., average income of inhabitants of census tracts, average age of university presidents); (2) *structural*, for "properties obtained by performing some operation on data about the relations of each member to some or all of the others" (e.g., asking students at each university to describe how "close" or "distant" they feel from members of the faculty and then measuring the extent to which such closeness varies in the social sciences as compared to the physical sciences); and (3) *global*, in which the "properties do not require information about the properties of individuals" (e.g., classifying societies by whether they use money or not, classifying cities as run by a city manager or a council). Such measures have also been called "emergent" and "syntalic." Lazarsfeld and Menzel remind us (1969, fn. 15, p. 506) that the claim that global properties "are not based on information about the properties of individual members" does not mean that they bear no relationship at all to the behavior of individual members. Indeed, the point is often to examine just such a relationship.

number of goals examined. As we noted earlier, such a finding will come as a surprise to some[3] and cannot be easily attributed to a lack of size variation in the sample; about half of the universities had student bodies of 15,000 or over, and the smallest had about 3,000. We ought to consider the effect, however, of a critical mass. A place does not usually become a full university, in our sense of the term, until it reaches a population of 5,000 to 10,000 and our universities are usually well over that figure. A sample which includes denominational colleges (which may not exceed 1,000 in student body, and less than 100 in faculty) or liberal arts colleges, as well as universities, would certainly show relationships to size. Perhaps size does not correlate with university goals because it is not a variable, or at least varies within limits too narrow in comparison to the variation among universities in goals.

Similar observations apply to the study of university location. In 1964 we found that a university's geographical location was almost totally unrelated to its goals or goal preference structures. The rural-urban distinction yielded more findings, such as an association of goal preferences with a practical service orientation in rural universities, and a somewhat elitist set of preferences for

---

[3] For example, Meyer (1972, p. 440), after a study of city, county, and state departments of finance, concludes: ". . . one cannot underestimate the impact of size on other characteristics of organizations." See also the discussion of size in Hodgkinson (1971) as well as the findings in Blau (1973).

On preparation of our manuscript for publication, we had second thoughts about the plausibility of the argument we have offered for *not* examining the effects of size on goals. After all, one can settle the matter by performing the calculations. This we have done and can report an average Pearsonian correlation of .370 between goals and enrollment. Although this is not zero, it is far from impressive—size accounting for about 1.4 percent of the variance. It is worth noting that we get higher correlations for other size measures. For example, for graduate enrollment the average correlation is .470, for number of doctorates it is .472, and for federal obligations (grants, etc.) it is .492. These results suggest to us that when size is measured by some output measure it is more strongly related to organization goals than when measured by number of students, which is a kind of client measure. Finally, in the interests of heading off a controversy on this matter, we should note that studies are unfortunately not always comparable because of differences in definitions. For example, Scott and El-Assal (1969) report a correlation of .58 between enrollment and number of student demonstrations. We find a correlation of .018. But the institutions are different, and Scott and El-Assal appear to find the major differences between schools with 10,000 or more students and those smaller. Fully 57 of our 68 universities have 10,000 or more students; only 3 have under 8,000.

those in urban areas. But even these findings seem to result from a confounding of rural-urban with other global variables such as private-public and prestige.

The lack of significant findings in 1964 led us to eliminate, given a reduced budget, the variables of location and size from our 1971 study. We felt that the continued movement of population and the tendency for the decline of regional traditions made it even more unlikely that location would yield significant findings. We have already reported that the universities in our population had a high proportion with 15,000 or more enrolled students. When we turned to 1971 data, we found this tendency to be even more pronounced; some universities had about held their own, but there was a strong tendency for universities to have increased in size.[4] At the same time, the effect appeared to shift the modal peak to a somewhat higher level, rather than push the numbers of many past the 40,000 mark. If anything, then, the range of variation in size was even less than in 1964. We felt that since size had yielded so few findings in 1964, it was likely to yield even fewer in 1971.

Our method of analysis is similar to that used in measuring goal congruence (see Chapter 2). We have arrayed the universities from top to bottom and have trichotomized the range (Across and Within) so as to determine the upper, middle, and lower thirds for both the goals and the goal preferences. Using Goodman and Kruskal's gamma we are able to identify those particular goals which are associated, either positively or negatively, with a given criterion. We are also following the same approach of using the Across and Within measures that are described in Chapter 2.

TYPE OF CONTROL: PUBLIC VERSUS PRIVATE A distinction has always existed between private and public universities in the United States. Private universities, for the most part, are older institutions. They have prided themselves on more selective admissions policies, and it is generally assumed that they have had freedom to pursue goals of excellence, unfettered by the "deadening hand" of legislatures and governmental controls. The faculty were presumed to have enjoyed higher pay, smaller classes, and the more traditional cloistered life. The private universities were best

---

[4] It was such an increase that forced us to sample in the lower administrative levels, and to use a smaller sampling ratio for faculty than we did in 1971. We had not anticipated the enormous growth in quite a number of universities and found ourselves with insufficient funds to cover the mailing costs.

typified by the "ivy league," and to this day the use of that term has been largely associated with "private education."

More recently, in the period since World War II, the impact of federal programs such as the World War II GI Bill, the National Defense Education Act (NDEA), and National Science Foundation (NSF) Fellowship Programs, plus the federal research programs has tended to blur the distinction between private and public universities. Some public universities have been as successful as private universities in raising outside funds. They have mounted fund drives among alumni and other "friends" to raise money in the same manner as private universities. Private universities have undertaken special education programs in their respective communities, often in direct competition with public universities. As a result many people, in academic circles and beyond, regard the differences between the two groups as minimal ones which may disappear altogether over time.

In our 1964 study many significant goal relationships indicated considerable differences between private and public universities. If it is correct to hypothesize that the type of control now creates differences, then we should have fewer distinguishing marks in the 1971 study. Conversely, if there are more significant findings than in 1964, it would seem to indicate that the goals hierarchy as well as the goals preferences at public and private universities are tending to diverge.

Type of Control: Across Measure Table 9 identifies the goals on which private universities place relatively higher emphasis than do state universities. There is a total of 17 goals that fall into this category. Six are new in 1971 in that they were not statistically significant in 1964. On the other hand, three goals in which the relationship was significant in 1964 have dropped off the list, making a net increase of three. With respect to goal preferences, there are 10 significant relationships, 4 of which are new, with only 1 dropping out, leaving a net increase of 3. The net increase in both goals and goal preferences relationships indicates that private universities and public universities are diverging in their goals' pattern.

The goal that seems to typify private universities by exhibiting the highest gamma score and, therefore, the strongest relationship is Accept Good Students Only. It appears that persons at private universities look on this goal as their most distinguishing characteristic, and they not only believe it is an important goal but also

TABLE 9
*The relationship
between type of
control and
university goals
(private
universities):
Across*

	Goals	Goals preference
Output		
Student-expressive		
7 Cultivate students' intellect	.830	
16 Affect student with great ideas	.754	
36 Develop students' objectivity	.795	.547
Student-instrumental		
17 Train students for scholarship/research	.716	
Research		
25 Carry on pure research	.523^a	.538^a
Direct service		
18 Preserve cultural heritage	.433^a	.507^a
Support		
Adaptation		
35 Accept good students only	.881	.902
40 Ensure confidence of contributors	.472	
Management		
41 Reward for contribution to profession	.511^a	
3 Encourage graduate work	.713	
21 Ensure efficient goal attainment	.722^a	
Motivation		
4 Protect academic freedom	.807	.731
13 Give faculty maximum opportunity to pursue careers	.554	.607
46 Protect students' right of inquiry	.680	
Position		
22 Maintain top quality in all programs	.670^a	.857
47 Maintain top quality in important programs	.712^a	.632^a
45 Increase or maintain prestige	.652	.495^a
23 Preserve institutional character		.534
Relationships in 1964 not significant in 1972		
Student-instrumental		
17 Train students for scholarship/ research		.525
Direct service		
10 Disseminate new ideas	.531	
Position		
15 Keep up to date	.552	
23 Preserve institutional character	.573	

^{a}New finding in 1971. Not present in 1964.
NOTE: Figures are gammas. See Appendix B.

want to emphasize it further. We also found this emphasis in 1964, and it is worthy of special mention because it identifies the "eliteness" of private universities (Shils, 1973). The second strongest relationship is the goal Cultivate Students' Intellect. There are actually three student-expressive goals with strong private university emphasis. The other two are Affect Students with Great Ideas of History and Develop Students' Objectivity. All three stamp the private university as "intellectual." Furthermore, the student-instrumental goal of Training Students for Scholarship/Research reinforces this view. Notice, however, that only one of these four student goals has a corresponding goal preference (Develop Students' Objectivity). Public universities have equally high goal preferences for these goals. Therefore, they are not distinguished as private school emphases, with the one exception.

Two findings dramatize changes which are taking place. First, the goal Train Students in Scholarship/Research in 1964 was emphasized by private universities as a goal preference, but not as a goal. In 1971 the preference has become a reality, and the goal, but not the goal preference, was emphasized. Evidently, private universities set out to differentiate themselves in this manner and have made major strides in doing so. Second, consider the opposite pattern for the goal Preserve Institutional Character. In 1964 this goal was emphasized in private universities, but it was not a goal preference; whereas, in 1971 it is no longer emphasized, but has now become a goal preference. Most likely the ravages of seven years of student unrest, protest, and change, plus economic adversity, have induced a state of greater anxiety on private university campuses than on those of public universities — hence, a preference to hold what they have.

The interesting newcomers to the 1971 list are Carry on Pure Research and Preserve Cultural Heritage. These were not heavily emphasized goals in 1964 but have become so in 1971; especially noteworthy is our respondents' belief that they should be goal preferences as well. Both these goals are indicative of the national character which private universities are assuming. Pure research and the cultural heritage are not related to state boundaries, regions of the country, or to any particular community.

Table 10 sets forth the essential democratic and public service nature of public universities. There are only eight goals with distinguishing relationships. Five goals that were significant in 1964 are no longer significant; there are only three newcomers to the list, and thus there is a net loss of two.

	Goals	Goals preference
Output		
Student-expressive		
29 Produce well-rounded student		.450
Student-instrumental		
9 Cultivate students' taste	.508[a]	.767
34 Prepare student for citizenship		.569
Research		
39 Carry on applied research	.569	.781
Direct service		
5 Provide special adult training	.530[a]	.704
30 Assist citizens through extension programs	.910	.850
38 Provide community cultural leadership	.805[a]	.570
Support		
Adaptation		
31 Ensure favor of validating bodies		.581
11 Educate to utmost high school graduates	.983	.861
19 Satisfy area needs	.694	.691
Management		
41 Reward for contribution to profession		.573
20 Involve students in university government		.454
33 Run university democratically		.453[a]
Motivation		
44 Provide student activities	.546	
Position		
15 Keep up to date		.730[a]
Relationships in 1964 not significant in 1972		
Student-instrumental		
37 Prepare students for useful careers	.603	.675
Adaptation		
26 Keep costs down	.626	
1 Hold staff in face of inducements		.697
Management		
20 Involve students in university government	.801	
12 Keep harmony	.688	
42 Emphasize undergraduate instruction	.599	

TABLE 10
The relationship between type of control and university goals, (public universities): Across

[a]New finding in 1971. Not present in 1964.
NOTE: Figures are gammas. See Appendix B.

There are fourteen distinguishing relationships among goal preferences, with only two of them being new. Since two goal preferences are no longer emphasized, the net change is zero.

The goals which public universities emphasize tend to run in a direction opposite that of private universities. Two student-instrumental goals are present, although it should be pointed out that neither is a high-ranking goal. The goal of Carry on Applied Research directly contrasts with the private university emphasis upon doing pure research. The service goals are emphasized very highly, as both goals and goal preferences.

The most outstanding public university emphasis is the goal Educate to Utmost All High School Graduates (gamma $= .983$). The very strong relationship this goal exhibits with state universities reflects a felt need and obligation. The goal preference emphasis on this goal is also very strong.

Some of the goals which public universities formerly emphasized in contrast to private universities are worthy of mention. In 1964, for example, public universities could be distinguished from private universities by their relative emphasis upon the goal Involve Students in University Government. In 1971 this distinction cannot be made. Public and private universities give equal weight to this goal. As a matter of goal preference, however, public universities emphasize this goal in both 1964 and 1971.

Similarly, a distinguishing mark of state universities in 1964 was their emphasis on the goal Emphasize Undergraduate Instruction. In 1971 this distinction also disappears, for institutions with each type of control give equal emphasis to this goal. It must be pointed out, however, that the goal of emphasizing undergraduate instruction even at the expense of graduate education ranked very low in the total hierarchy of goals of American universities (see Tables 3 and 6).

To summarize, by using the Across measure there are 25 goals in which significant relationships identify a goal emphasis in either public or private universities. When this number is subtracted from the total of 47 goals, 22 goals remain which exhibit no significant difference of emphasis between public or private universities. In this latter group of 22, however, only 3 goals come from the 10 highest-ranking goals of American universities (see Table 3). They are the goals of ensuring favor of validating bodies, involving faculty in university government, and preparing students for useful careers. Seven of the ten top-ranking goals (including the five highest) were emphasized by either public or private schools. This is a clear indication that differences between these two are over goals that our respondents believe to be important, while the similarities tend to be clustered around unimportant or lower-ranking goals. It must be concluded that differences between public and private universities remain and have undoubtedly widened since 1964, contrary to the opinion of many people.

Type of Control: Within Measure Analyzing the rankings of the 47 goals Within each university by type of control has produced a surprisingly large number of significant relationships which did not exist in 1964, indicating that private universities now emphasize many more goals than they did formerly. Table 11 shows a total of 27 significant relationships; whereas in 1964 a similar table showed only 13. Moreover, 11 of the new relationships are goals, and only 5 are goal preferences. Two significant relationships of 1964 are no longer present, so there is a net increase of 14. The sheer number of new findings reveals many more ways in which private universities have differentiated themselves from public universities than formerly. The number of new goals which private universities emphasize is especially striking. Eight of the new goals are support goals, and only three are output goals. These three—namely, Develop Students' Character, Train Students for Scholarship/Research, and Carry on Pure Research—also receive high-ranking emphasis using the Across measure. We can say with some confidence, therefore, that the output goals which private universities emphasize are those which stress the intellectual and the scholarly development of students and the conduct of pure research.

Private universities now appear to emphasize many more support goals than formerly. Of the eight new findings, four are matters of particular interest to faculty, two are of special interest to students, and the remaining two are of direct concern to the institution as a whole. The presence of so many new findings is still further evidence of the developing distinction between private and public universities. The support goals tend to reveal more of the character of the institution. It is not surprising to note that the goal Ensure Confidence of Contributors is now a goal emphasized by private universities, and our respondents believe, moreover, that it is the right emphasis and should be a goal. Furthermore, private universities also believe that the goal Develop Faculty Loyalty in Institution is a goal that should continue to be emphasized. Eco-

		Goals	Goals preference
Output			
Student-expressive			
7	Cultivate students' intellect	.786	
16	Affect student with great ideas	.769	.557
36	Develop students' objectivity	.872	
8	Develop students' character	.552[a]	
Student-instrumental			
17	Train students for scholarship/research	1.000[a]	
Research			
25	Carry on pure research	.470[a]	.650[a]
Direct service			
10	Disseminate new ideas	.451	
18	Preserve cultural heritage		.720
Support			
Adaptation			
35	Accept good students only	.946	.890
26	Keep costs down		.889[a]
40	Ensure confidence of contributors	.474[a]	.461[a]
Management			
41	Reward for contribution to profession	.601[a]	
3	Encourage graduate work	.490[a]	1.000
21	Ensure efficient goal attainment	.553[a]	
2	Let will of faculty prevail	.454[a]	
Motivation			
13	Give faculty maximum opportunity to pursue careers	.534	.910
44	Provide student activities		.884[a]
46	Protect students' right of inquiry	.756[a]	
28	Protect students' right of action	.516[a]	
6	Develop faculty loyalty in institution	.607[a]	.714[a]
Relationships in 1964 not significant in 1972			
Student-instrumental			
24	Prepare students for status/leadership	.563	
Motivation			
28	Protect students' right of action		.714

TABLE 11
The relationship between type of control and university goals, (private universities): Within

[a]New finding in 1971. Not present in 1964.

NOTE: Figures are gammas. See Appendix B.

nomic adversity seems to bring goals such as these to the fore because they are necessary to the survival of the institution.

One of the major topics of conversation on almost all campuses today is student action on political and social issues. Students of the 1950s were often called apathetic and interested only in their own pursuits toward the college or graduate degree (see Lipset, 1972, Ch. 5). It is now part of history, of course, that in the decade of the 1960s students became active on issues relating to the war in Vietnam, environmental protection, governmental structure, and various social injustices. In 1964 the goal Protect Students' Right of Action ranked very low (see Table 6), with no distinctive recognition relative to either private or public universities. Private universities, however, indicated in 1964 that this goal *should* have been emphasized in their universities. With the passage of seven years the responses of these same private universities indicate that this goal *is* now emphasized at their institutions. But now, however, there is a clear indication that our private university respondents believe that this goal *should not* be emphasized to the degree that it is in public universities. It must be noted, however, that this is a low-ranking goal (forty-fifth) for all schools, both public and private, and this finding is not as significant as it would be for a higher-ranking goal.

Table 12 shows the significant relationships indicating goals of greater emphasis on the part of public universities. It should be noted that among the goals there are only two findings not present in 1964. There are three new goal preferences. Although there is only one new finding that appears in both the goal and the goal preference table, it is a rather striking one. It is generally assumed that the goal Provide Special Adult Training must be important in public universities, particularly in those with land-grant origins. In 1964 this goal, surprisingly enough, did not exhibit a significant relationship associating it with public universities. It must be kept in mind that at that time regular college and graduate enrollments were growing substantially, and extension programs and adult education tended to be taken for granted. In 1971, however, both the goal and the goal preference indicate a strong relationship with the public university, thereby confirming a generally held view of the mission of schools under public control.

It is worthwhile noting that none of the position goals can be especially identified with either private or public universities. All universities are apparently quite interested in maintaining their

	Goals	Goals preference
Output		
Student-expressive		
29 *Produce well-rounded student*		.683
Student-instrumental		
34 *Prepare student for citizenship*		.832
Research		
39 *Carry on applied research*	.792	.827
Direct service		
5 *Provide special adult training*	.509[a]	.760[a]
30 *Assist citizens through extension programs*	.960	.932
38 *Provide community cultural leadership*	.818	.808[a]
Support		
Adaptation		
31 *Ensure favor of validating bodies*	.757	
11 *Educate to utmost high school graduates*	1.000	.832
19 *Satisfy area needs*	.747	.669[a]
Management		
27 *Reward for contribution to institution*	.859[a]	
Motivation		
44 *Provide student activities*	.680	
Relationships in 1964 not significant in 1972		
Student-instrumental		
37 *Prepare students for useful careers*	.673	.613
Adaptation		
26 *Keep costs down*	.562	
1 *Hold staff in face of inducements*	.593	.599

TABLE 12
The relationship between type of control and university goals (public universities): Within

[a] New finding in 1971. Not present in 1964.
NOTE: Figures are gammas. See Appendix B.

position because these goals generally rank quite high, both as goals and as goal preferences.

In summary, it would seem that our analysis has demonstrated that the type of control in American universities means more than the question of who holds the title to the buildings or the amount of the tuition. There are many goal emphases that distinguish private and public universities from each other. To judge from our bench mark of 1964, the number is growing rather than diminishing.

PRODUCTIVITY One of the most publicized issues in American education has been that of teaching versus research. The doctrine of "publish or perish" typifies the controversy. Critics of the system insist that the doctrine does exist as policy in fact and assert that it represents a misplaced set of values. Defenders of the system will argue that the effects of this policy are greatly exaggerated, but that it is a justifiable policy because the university has an obligation to push forward the frontiers of knowledge and the faculty needs the additional spur in order to do so. The term *productivity,* therefore, has generally been interpreted as research output, and not as a balance of teaching, research, and service. We are using the term *productivity* to mean *research output* with full recognition that this index offers only a limited perspective on the larger question of how productivity should be fully interpreted.

It is difficult to measure productivity, even using our narrower definition, when taken as a whole. Therefore, we have decided to use several measures which might shed some light on the relationship of university goals to productivity. The question is: What goals are emphasized at universities that exhibit higher rather than lower productivity?

The measures we have chosen are: (1) volume of contract research, (2) percentage of graduate students in the student body, and (3) number of doctorates awarded. All three of these measures exhibit considerable variation in the range from top to bottom, and strong relationships (high gamma scores) thus will be of considerable significance.[5]

Contract or sponsored research is a well-publicized university activity which has grown to tremendous proportions in the period since World War II. Contract research dollars are so vital to some university departments that if they were withdrawn completely the department would be a mere skeleton of its former self. While all universities have taken steps to minimize this situation, there has been concern about the way in which the federal government, state and local governments to a certain extent, and private founda-

---

[5] There are other measures which might have been used, such as a list of major articles and books published by each faculty during a given year, but such particulars begin to overlap too greatly with a measure of "quality" (or prestige), which we consider below.

tions have influenced the university's total program (see Orlans, 1962). Indeed, in the late 1960s many universities had instituted seminars for faculty in how to apply for research grants. If there is a problem with the doctrine of "publish or perish," it is quite evident that part of the problem stems from the impact of contract research.

Because contract research usually involves faculty members, it is reasonable to assume it is a measure of productivity. Although only a portion of the university faculty are involved directly in contract research, it is very likely that even those faculty members who do not work directly on contract research are affected and possibly benefited from its importance in the university. Universities have exacted an overhead charge on most contract research, which returns a portion of the grant to the total budget in ways that provide direct assistance to faculty who are working on nonsponsored research. Its impact thus is spread widely beyond the people directly affected.[6]

Our other measures of productivity are tied to the graduate emphasis of the university. If there is a large graduate emphasis, then it might be assumed that there is a corresponding emphasis upon scholarship and productivity on the part of the faculty. The growth in graduate programs during the past ten years makes this assumption slightly more questionable, but we believe it is still valid. The number of programs has been growing, but the number of students in the newer programs remains small, and the graduates even fewer. As has already been indicated, we are using two different approaches to graduate emphasis. The percentage of graduate students in the total student body is a good indication of relative emphasis. Universities in our study range from a high of 65 percent to a low of 10 percent. Because we are using only percentages and not actual population, it must be kept in mind that some of the largest graduate populations are in universities where they constitute only a small proportion of the entire student body.

The other approach indicating graduate emphasis is the number of doctorates produced in a given year. This measure represents sheer size. Nevertheless, it is often said that faculty turn out doctorates in their own image, and therefore the numbers in them-

---

[6] Our data on contract research support are drawn from *Federal Support to Universities* . . . (1970).

selves are important because of the impact they make on universities as a whole. We believe that it is valid to assume there is a direct correlation between the number of doctorates produced and the productivity of the faculty. Our source of data for the 1971 survey was Hooper (1970).[7]

Rather than discuss these measures independently, we believe it is more justifiable to pay attention only to those findings which are present in at least two of the three measures. Consequently, Tables 13 to 16 represent the summary tables of goals and goal preferences, first using the Across followed by the Within measures.

Productivity: Across Measure

Table 13 shows that there are four goals in which there is a significant relationship on each of the three measures. Furthermore, they are all positive relationships indicating goals which are emphasized at universities where faculty productivity is high. Sixteen goals exhibit a significant relationship on two out of three measures. In no cases in any of the above comparisons are the signs among indicators different. In other words, if the goal was strongly empha-

[7] On the 1964 Survey, see Gross and Grambsch (1968).

TABLE 13 *Relationship between faculty productivity and university goals: Across*

Goals	Volume of contract research	Percent of graduate students in student body	Number of doctorates awarded	Total relationships
Output				
Student-expressive				
7 *Cultivate students' intellect*	.483	.686		2
8 *Develop students' character*			—.457[a]	
16 *Affect student with great ideas*		.534		
36 *Develop students' objectivity*	.631	.697		2
Student-instrumental				
9 *Cultivate students' taste*	—.499	—.499		2
17 *Train students for scholarship/research*	.566	.618		2
34 *Prepare student for citizenship*	.469			
Research				
25 *Carry on pure research*	.794	.514	.616	3

TABLE 13 *(continued)*

Goals	Volume of contract research	Percent of graduate students in student body	Number of doctorates awarded	Total relationships
Direct service				
5 Provide special adult training		−.503ᵃ		
10 Disseminate new ideas	.747		.552	2
18 Preserve cultural heritage	.523ᵃ	.443		2
30 Assist citizens through extension programs		−.782ᵃ		
38 Provide community cultural leadership		−.470ᵃ		
Support				
Adaptation				
1 Hold staff in face of inducements	.707ᵃ		.604ᵃ	2
11 Educate to utmost high school graduates		−.725		
19 Satisfy area needs	−.445	−.711		2
31 Ensure favor of validating bodies	−.560ᵃ		−.512	2
35 Accept good students only	.484	.820		2
Management				
2 Let will of faculty prevail	.460ᵃ			
3 Encourage graduate work	.737	.630	.567	3
41 Reward for contribution of profession	.662		.633	2
42 Emphasize undergraduate instruction	−.567	−.548		2
Motivation				
4 Protect academic freedom	.475	.654		2
13 Give faculty maximum opportunity to pursue careers	.695	.601	.469	3
44 Provide student activities		−.648ᵃ		
46 Protect students' right of inquiry	.553	.531		2
Position				
15 Keep up to date	.588		.601	2
22 Maintain top quality in all programs	.582	.644	.456	3
45 Increase or maintain prestige	.595		.528	2
47 Maintain top quality in important programs	.467	.561		2

ᵃ New finding in 1971. Not present in 1964.

NOTE: Negative (−) values indicate emphasis at universities with lower productivity. Figures are gammas. See Appendix B.

sized in any one, e.g., contract research, then it was also strongly emphasized (in the same direction) on the other one or two as the case may be.

The four goals which are significantly related on all three measures are as follows:

25 Carry on Pure Research

3 Encourage Graduate Work

13 Give Faculty Maximum Opportunity to Pursue Careers

22 Maintain Top Quality in All Programs

Each of these four represents a remarkably consistent point of view. Universities in which the goal of carrying on pure research is emphasized are undoubtedly places where one would expect the larger volume of contract research. One would also expect that the percentage of graduate students in the student body would be quite high and that the number of doctorates awarded would be numerous. Encourage Graduate Work seems to follow Carry on Pure Research. Those universities which encourage graduate work tend to turn out doctorates and also to have an abundant supply of graduate students for much of the "slave labor" on contract research projects.

The other two goals which appeared on all three measures are also quite consistent. Give Faculty Maximum Opportunity to Pursue Careers shows that schools that emphasize this goal are intimately tied up with a good graduate program and evidently encourage contract and grant research. Finally, the goal Maintain Top Quality in All Programs has a dual importance. Those schools that emphasize this goal are in the best position to attract good graduate students and, of course, to turn out large numbers of doctorates. The association with contract research is somewhat more tenuous, but nevertheless, it is still present. Schools which have many millions of dollars in contract research, for example, are those in which excellence in all their programs is more likely to be found.

The goals (two out of three) in which a significant relationship is associated with measures of faculty productivity include such goals as Protect Academic Freedom, Hold Our Staff, Train Students in Methods of Scholarship, plus various student-expressive goals such as Develop Students' Objectivity and Cultivate Students' Intellect. These findings are to be expected.

On the other hand, goals such as Ensure Favorable Appraisal of Validating Bodies, Satisfy Area Needs, and Emphasize Undergraduate Instruction are all associated with universities of lower productivity. By implication, therefore, universities which emphasize these goals are those in which graduate and research values are less important.

Turning now to the goal preferences, we find that there are many fewer significant relationships. Admittedly, there are four goals that appear on all three of the measures (one positive and three negative); however, only six appear on two out of the three (two positive and four negative). There is then only a total of 10 that appear on two or more of the measures. Evidently the unanimity of goal emphasis gives way to some disagreement as to the goals which should be emphasized. The four goal preferences which appear to be significantly related on each of the three measures are as follows:

25   Carry on Pure Research (positive)

29   Produce Well-Rounded Student (negative)

31   Ensure Favorable Appraisal by Validating Bodies (negative)

19   Satisfy Area Needs (negative)

It appears that Carry on Pure Research is the only finding which is significantly related to all three of the productivity measures as both a goal preference and a goal. It is an indication that universities with high productivity think this is about right. However, the others are all negative and are preferences that tend to be emphasized when productivity is low. Produce a Well-Rounded Student, for example, is certainly a different kind of student-expressive goal than are the goals Develop Students' Objectivity or Cultivate Students' Intellect. More significant, however, is the fact that satisfying area needs appears to be associated with a lower faculty productivity. Obviously, satisfying area needs is not accomplished by turning out large numbers of doctorates nor by engaging in large amounts of contract research. We may conclude that the Across measure generates a significant number of findings which seem to be entirely consistent and also to support one another.

TABLE 14 *Relationship of faculty productivity to university goals preferences: Across*

Goals preferences	Volume of contract research	Percent of graduate students in student body	Number of doctorates awarded	Total relation-ships
Output				
Student-expressive				
7 Cultivate students' intellect	—.563[a]			
8 Develop students' character	—.563		—.540	2
29 Produce well-rounded student	—.541	—.635	—.490	3
Student-instrumental				
9 Cultivate students' taste	—.456	—.720		2
34 Prepare student for citizenship		—.602		
37 Prepare students for useful careers		—.534		
Research				
25 Carry on pure research	.766	.541	.643	3
39 Carry on applied research		—.776		
Direct service				
5 Provide special adult training		—.593		
30 Assist citizens through extension programs		—.905		
38 Provide community cultural leadership		—.459		
Support				
Adaptation				
11 Educate to utmost high school graduates		—.613		
19 Satisfy area needs	—.471	—.720	—.459	3
31 Ensure favor of validating bodies	—.669	—.567	—.593	3
35 Accept good students only	.578	.655		2
Management				
20 Involve students in university government	—.451[a]	—.484		2
21 Ensure efficient goal attainment			—.465	
27 Reward for contribution to institution	—.460[a]	—.680		2
33 Run university democratically		—.576		
42 Emphasize undergraduate instruction	—.538	—.606		2
Motivation				
4 Protect academic freedom	.541	.612		2
44 Provide student activities	—.494[a]	—.459		2

Goals Preferences	Volume of contract research	Percent of graduate students in student body	Number of doctorates awarded	Total relation- ships
Position				
15 *Keep up to date*		$-.687$		
22 *Maintain top quality in all programs*	.450[a]	.580		2

[a] New finding in 1971. Not present in 1964.

NOTE: Negative ($-$) values indicate emphasis at universities with lower productivity. Figures are gammas. See Appendix B.

Productivity: Within Measure   When productivity is related to the degree of goal emphasis within each university, we obtain the results shown in Table 15. The general picture is similar to that for the Across analysis, with a somewhat smaller number of goals related to two or more of the productivity measures. Some of this effect appears to be due to the occasional tendency of gamma, as a measure, to generate a "1.000" in cases of highly skewed distributions. For example, gammas of 1.000 showed up for all three productivity measures for the goal Increase or Maintain Prestige, but those results were due to the goal being ranked high in practically all universities. Hence the gamma is "produced" by the one university where this is not the case, with a resultant zero in one cell.

The goals which are found to be related to all three productivity measures are:

17   Train Students for Scholarship/Research (positive)

25   Carry on Pure Research (positive)

34   Prepare Student for Citizenship (negative)

37   Prepare Students for Useful Careers (negative)

31   Ensure Favor of Validating Bodies (negative)

19   Satisfy Area Needs (negative)

In general, we secure further support for the differentiation by productivity, which showed up in the Across measure, with the new goal (Prepare Students for Useful Careers) being consistent with the other negatively related goals.

When we turn to the findings for goal preferences (Within mea-

TABLE 15 *Relationship between faculty productivity and university goals: Within*

Goals	Volume of contract research	Percent of graduate students in student body	Number of doctorates awarded	Total relation- ships
Output				
Student-expressive				
7 Cultivate students' intellect		.670[a]		
16 Affect student with great ideas		.526		
29 Produce well-rounded student	—.571[a]		—.651[a]	2
36 Develop students' objectivity		.635		
Student-instrumental				
17 Train students for scholarship/research	.733	.932	.710	3
34 Prepare student for citizenship	—.641	—.687[a]	—.566	3
37 Prepare students for useful careers	—.672	—.463	—.460	3
Research				
25 Carry on pure research	.689	.452[a]	.676	3
39 Carry on applied research		—.700		
Direct service				
5 Provide special adult training		—.460		
10 Disseminate new ideas	.753		.531	
30 Assist citizens through extension program		—.766		
38 Provide community cultural leadership		—.576		
Support				
Adaptation				
1 Hold staff in face of inducements	.508[a]		.630[a]	2
11 Educate to utmost high school graduates		—.552		
19 Satisfy area needs	—.514	—.682	—.455	3
26 Keep costs down	—.514			
31 Ensure favor of validating bodies	—.796	—.681	—.605	3
35 Accept good students only	.669	.925		2
40 Ensure confidence of contributors	—.783[a]		—.654[a]	2
Management				
3 Encourage graduate work	.621			
12 Keep harmony		.450[a]		
41 Reward for contribution to profession	.496		.440	2
42 Emphasize undergraduate instruction	—.564[a]			

Goals	Volume of contract research	Percent of graduate students in student body	Number of doctorates awarded	Total relation- ships
Motivation				
13 *Give faculty maximum opportunity to pursue careers*	.578	.594		2
44 *Provide student activities*	.473	−.767		2
46 *Protect students' right of inquiry*	.468[a]	.627		2
Position				
15 *Keep up to date*		.513[a]	.474[a]	2
22 *Maintain top quality in all programs*		.679[a]		
32 *Maintain balanced quality in all programs*		.516[a]		
47 *Maintain top quality in important programs*		.489[a]		

[a] New finding in 1971. Not present in 1964.

NOTE: Negative (−) values indicate emphasis at universities with lower productivity. Figures are gammas. See Appendix B.

sure, Table 16), we discover more relationships than was the case for the Across analysis and the corresponding goals analysis. There are 6 goal preferences showing significant relationships to all three productivity measures and 15 which are related to two of the measures. The goal preferences showing relationships to all three productivity measures are:

29 Produce Well-Rounded Student (negative)

25 Carry on Pure Research

18 Preserve Cultural Heritage (positive)

35 Accept Good Students Only (positive)

 3 Encourage Graduate Work (positive)

 6 Develop Faculty Loyalty in Institution (positive)

Here we have the opinions of our respondents on how things should be. Where productivity in a university is high, there is a strong feeling that the university should not be trying to produce a well-rounded student, but should concentrate instead on scholarly activity and research production. Carrying on pure research is not

TABLE 16 *Relationship between faculty productivity and university goals preferences: Within*

Goals preferences	Volume of contract research	Percent of graduate students in student body	Number of doctorates awarded	Total relation-ships
Output				
Student-expressive				
8 *Develop students' character*	—.526		—.668	
29 *Produce well-rounded student*	—.607	—.708	—.587[a]	3
Student-instrumental				
34 *Prepare student for citizenship*		—.649[a]		
Research				
25 *Carry on pure research*	.871	.752[a]	.735	3
39 *Carry on applied research*		—.618[a]	.476[a]	2
Direct service				
5 *Provide special adult training*	—.489	—.621		
18 *Preserve cultural heritage*	.754[a]	.924	.664	3
30 *Assist citizens through extension programs*	—.480[a]	—.918		2
38 *Provide community cultural leadership*	—.450[a]			
Support				
Support-adaptation				
1 *Hold staff in face of inducements*	.458		.473[a]	2
11 *Educate to utmost high school graduates*		—.456[a]		
19 *Satisfy area needs*		—.674[a]	—.568	
30 *Assist citizens through extension programs*		—.918		
31 *Ensure favor of validating bodies*	.467[a]			
35 *Accept good students only*	.920	.882	.668	
40 *Ensure confidence of contributors*	.831[a]		.496[a]	2
Management				
3 *Encourage graduate work*	1.000[a]	1.000[a]	.795[a]	3
20 *Involve students in university government*	—.504[a]	—.537[a]		2
21 *Ensure efficient goal attainment*	—.761[a]		—.634[a]	2

Goals preferences	Volume of contract research	Percent of graduate students in student body	Number of doctorates awarded	Total relationships
27 *Reward for contribution to institution*	−.592	−.893		
33 *Run university democratically*		−.474[a]		
42 *Emphasize undergraduate instruction*	−.806[a]	−.820[a]		2
43 *Involve faculty in university government*		.509	.507	2
Motivation				
6 *Develop faculty loyalty in institution*	.551[a]	.580[a]	.506[a]	3
13 *Give faculty maximum opportunity to pursue careers*	.534[a]	.625		2
28 *Protect students' right of action*		.543		
44 *Provide student activities*	.640[a]		.654[a]	2
46 *Protect students' right of inquiry*	.571[a]	.602[a]		2
Position				
32 *Maintain balanced quality in all programs*		.519[a]		

[a] New finding in 1971. Not present in 1964.

NOTE: Negative (−) values indicate emphasis at universities with lower productivity. Figures are gammas. See Appendix B.

only a goal (see Table 15) which is emphasized more than other goals at the university. Encouraging graduate work should also be stressed, an aim which is, of course, predictable, given an emphasis on research. The goal Accept Good Students Only appears to come in here because of the association between research productivity and "quality" (or prestige), which we will discuss below. Finally, discovering the goal Develop Faculty Loyalty in Institution is a surprise, and standing alone it takes on a rather poignant quality. A defensible inference is that in the face of the high costs of productivity (that is, the goals that have to be sacrificed to attain it), there is some uneasiness that faculty have forgotten the institution that employs them—that, in plain language, they are ingrates who take the institution too much for granted.

All things considered, the costs associated with following the path of specialization in research and scholarly production are great. There are definite and predictable sets of goals which characterize universities of high and low productivity. High productivity means focusing on research and graduate study and placing less emphasis upon traditional goals such as producing well-rounded students, loyalty to the local institution, or satisfying the needs of persons in the local areas. The high costs have led some universities to question whether this pursuit is worthwhile. As we saw in the case of private and public universities, there is evidence that the gap between high- and low-productivity institutions remains as strong as it was in 1964 and may be widening. This fact, then, provides one more indication that the universities are beginning to diverge in type and become more differentiated.

PRESTIGE   Prestige is a vague quality which accrues to organizations in a wide variety of ways. It conveys ideas of leadership, of power, and, above all, of excellence. The high ranking assigned by our respondents to the goal of Increase or Maintain University Prestige is an indication of the value placed upon it. It is eagerly sought after by those who do not have it, and those universities that have achieved prestige do everything they can to uphold it. Prestige in universities is possibly of more significance than it is in other organizations. Attracting faculty and students, as well as foundation and other research grants, becomes considerably easier if the university is perceived to be a place of prestige (see Caplow, 1964, Ch. 6; Blau, 1973, pp. 275–278).

The measurement of organizational prestige is a controversial matter (see, for example, Lewis, 1968; Knudsen & Vaughn, 1969; and Shamblin, 1970), perhaps because persons become upset at where the measure may place their own organization. Such seems to be the case especially with universities, leading to what Caplow (1964) has called the "aggrandizement effect"—the tendency to rate one's own organization higher or even near or at the top in comparison to others of a similar kind. Part of the controversy has to do with the question of the relationship of prestige to "quality." Prestige is essentially a reputational measure—what one's colleagues think of one's institution or department—and of course, a department of high "quality" may not be rated very highly, possibly because it is not well known, or because its quality is restricted to a small number of highly esoteric areas. Yet this did not prevent

Cartter (1966) from entitling the most famous recent study of departmental reputation *An Assessment of Quality in Graduate Education*. Whatever the problems in measuring (or even defining) prestige (see Ben-David, 1971, Appendix B), they are far fewer than in measuring "quality" since it is an even touchier subject than prestige, and one more affected by subjective judgment. Measures such as citations in the research literature, number of Nobel Prize winners on the faculty, and recipients of other awards and honors in the departments (Astin, 1965), have been tried by various researchers (see Cole & Cole, 1967; Crane, 1965, 1970; Zuckerman, 1967). But apart from being difficult to measure on a comparative basis, many of these measures (such as citations or proportion of awards won by a department) are very severely skewed in distribution, with most departments in any given area not securing any at all. Further, however measured, quality turns out to be correlated with prestige, partly because quality is, of course, one of the factors persons take into account in rating a colleague or department. It may well be that prestige in a more dynamic measure, in the sense that faculty members and administrators are more likely to be galvanized into action by a low prestige rating (or pleased by a high one) since it is a statement of what one's colleagues think of one's department. Few academics do not highly respect the opinions of their colleagues. Hence, prestige (rather than quality, however measured) is probably the variable that would exhibit enough variation to show correlations with goals.

For our 1964 ranking of prestige, we made use of a modification of Cartter (1966) as described in Appendix B. For 1971 we made use of the updated report (Roose & Andersen, 1970) with similar modification. Part of the dispute over reputation concerns the very small differences generated by one measure as compared to another. We have sought to avoid this problem by dividing our universities into four main levels of prestige. These we found to be defensible, because while argument exists over whether University A should be above University B, there is practically no dispute on the broad assignment of universities into major strata.

Prestige Measure: Across
The goals which are related to prestige (see Table 17) are indeed many in number. There are 17 goals which are emphasized by those schools with high prestige, while there are 8 goals which are emphasized by those schools with lower prestige (those having negative scores in Table 17). The remaining 22 goals are not distinguishable

TABLE 17
*The relationship
between
prestige and
university goals:
Across*

	Goals	Goals preference
Output		
Student-expressive		
7 *Cultivate students' intellect*	.622	
29 *Produce well-rounded student*		—.716
16 *Affect students with great ideas*	.560	
36 *Develop students' objectivity*	.722	
8 *Develop students' character*		—.568
Student-instrumental		
17 *Train students for scholarship/research*	.756	
9 *Cultivate students' taste*	—.560	—.719
34 *Prepare student for citizenship*		—.523
Research		
25 *Carry on pure research*	.928	.787
Direct service		
5 *Provide special adult training*	—.516[a]	—.514
30 *Assist citizens through extension programs*	—.544	—.530
10 *Disseminate new ideas*	.800	
18 *Preserve cultural heritage*	.699	
38 *Provide community cultural leadership*		—.465
Support		
Adaptation		
31 *Ensure favor of validating bodies*	—.627	—.774
11 *Educate to utmost high school graduates*	—.451[a]	—.589
35 *Accept good students only*	.679	.656
19 *Satisfy area needs*	—.702	—.685
26 *Keep costs down*	—.538	
1 *Hold staff in face of inducements*	.757[a]	
Management		
41 *Reward for contribution to profession*	.752	—.648[a]
20 *Involve students in university government*		—.634[a]
43 *Involve faculty in university government*	.470	
27 *Reward for contribution to institution*		—.606
12 *Keep harmony*		—.477
42 *Emphasize undergraduate instruction*	—.547	—.571
3 *Encourage graduate work*	.783	

	Goals	Goals preference
21 *Ensure efficient goal attainment*	.492[a]	−.532
2 *Let will of faculty prevail*	.519[a]	
Motivation		
4 *Protect academic freedom*	.630	.626
13 *Give faculty maximum opportunity to pursue careers*	.860	
46 *Protect students' right of inquiry*	.681	
14 *Develop pride in university*		−.639
Position		
22 *Maintain top quality in all programs*	.731	
47 *Maintain top quality in important programs*	.682	
32 *Maintain balanced quality in all programs*	.522[a]	
15 *Keep up to date*	.749	
45 *Increase or maintain prestige*	.747	
Relationships in 1964 not significant in 1972		
Student-instrumental		
37 *Prepare students for useful careers*	−.504	−.598
Direct service		
10 *Disseminate new ideas*		.455
Adaptation		
26 *Keep costs down*		−.531
Motivation		
13 *Give faculty maximum opportunity to pursue careers*		.521

[a]New finding in 1971. Not present in 1964.

NOTE: Negative (−) values indicate goal is emphasized at universities with lower prestige. Figures are gammas. See Appendix B.

between high or low prestige to any significant extent. The 15 goals associated with high prestige give us a picture of the prestigious university of today. The output goals listed in order of the strength of the emphasis are as follows:

25 Carry on Pure Research

10 Disseminate New Ideas

17 Train Students for Scholarship/Research

36 Develop Students' Objectivity

18 Preserve Cultural Heritage

7 Cultivate Students' Intellect

16 Affect Students with Great Ideas of History

The output goals which are emphasized by those schools with lower prestige are relatively few, and the relationship is not nearly as strong; nevertheless, they are goals that our respondents tell us are emphasized, relatively, at universities of lower prestige. They are as follows:

9 Cultivate Students' Taste

30 Assist Citizens Through Extension Programs

5 Provide Special Adult Training

Of the seven output goals on which universities of high prestige place relatively important emphasis, four are in the upper third of all goal rankings and six of the seven are in the upper half. In contrast, the three goals which are emphasized relatively by lower prestige schools are all in the bottom third of goal rankings (see Chapter 2). This would appear to indicate that on those goals that all schools deem to be important the higher prestige schools lead. Conversely, the lower-ranking schools emphasize goals that all schools tend to rank quite low.

The support goals differentiate universities possibly even more than output goals do. There is a total of 15 support goals in which universities of high rank place relative emphasis. Five of the goals which have the strongest relationship indicating the greatest emphasis by high-prestige schools are as follows:

13 Give Faculty Maximum Opportunity to Pursue Careers

3 Encourage Graduate Work

1 Hold Staff in Face of Inducements from Other Schools

41 Reward for Contribution to Profession

15 Keep up to Date

It should be noticed that three out of these five are directly related to the needs of the faculty; in addition, the other two have a strong but indirect relationship. This would seem to indicate that universities of high prestige pay especially close attention to the "care and feeding of faculty," more so than do their colleagues in schools further down the prestige ladder.

At the opposite end of the scale, the five support goals which are emphasized at those schools with lesser prestige are as follows:

19 Satisfy Area Needs

31 Ensure Favorable Appraisal of Validating Bodies

42 Emphasize Undergraduate Instruction

26 Keep Costs Down

11 Educate to Utmost All High School Graduates

None of these goals is directly related to faculty, but seem to concentrate instead on special institutional needs and services. With one exception (Ensure Favorable Appraisal of Validating Bodies), the goals stressed by lesser-prestige schools are in the lower half of goal rankings; all five support goals emphasized by universities of high prestige are in the upper half.

There are seven new findings in 1971, and only one of the 1964 findings has dropped out. This net increase of six new findings strengthens the conclusion that differences in prestige are of major proportions in American universities. Possibly some of the explanation lies in the rapid expansion of higher education. With so many new institutions coming into being, the major institutions are having to work much harder at maintaining their prestigious positions. Salary differentials have narrowed in many instances; faculty and students alike have become more impressed with the amenities of life which go with climate, recreational location, etc., rather than with scholarly achievement and large libraries. Whether a shift will ultimately take place so that prestige levels will narrow rather than widen depends partly upon levels and types of funding, and the pressures exerted by state and federal governments toward equality in research funds and the admission of students qualified or otherwise, plus a host of unknown factors.

The goals preferences which are found in Table 17 exhibit the same general direction as that of the goals themselves, but there is a smaller number of findings. Among the output goal preferences, for example, there is only one (Carry on Pure Research) which is emphasized by universities of high prestige. The others are emphasized by schools of lesser prestige. This list is worthy of special mention because it indicates the decided preference for "nonscholarship" goals. The list is as follows:

9   Cultivate Students' Taste

29 Produce Well-Rounded Student

8   Develop Students' Character

30 Assist Citizens Through Extension Programs

34 Prepare Student for Citizenship

5   Provide Special Adult Training

38 Provide Community Cultural Leadership

A plausible explanation is that universities with lesser prestige are growing more attuned, through proximity and otherwise, to the felt needs of students and the community, and our respondents are expressing the view that their universities need to stress these goals more than they do. Possibly some of the universities of lesser prestige have given up thoughts of stressing those factors that the high-prestige universities deem to be important and are settling for a different type of university with a goal emphasis more in keeping with what they believe to be their obligations.

The support goal preferences exhibit much the same general phenomena as that of the output goals. Only two relationships indicating emphasis by higher-prestige universities are present (Accept Good· Students Only and Protect Academic Freedom). The other ten are all relationships indicating a preference emphasis by those universities of lesser prestige. One ordinarily assumes that goal preferences are general intentions or, in some cases, even dreams of what should be. It is most surprising to find that universities of lesser prestige are not expressing desires to imitate the higher prestige universities but rather are stressing a preference for an entirely different set of values. In only two out of the ten cases do the lesser prestige schools express a preference for a goal that the higher prestige schools say, in fact, is emphasized now among them. On the other eight the preferences are either congruent with their goals or exist where there is no goal indication of emphasis on either side. This state of affairs seems to suggest that although there are great differences in the goal emphasis of the universities differentiated by levels of prestige, it does not follow necessarily that our respondents, especially from the lower-level schools, believe that the differential should be narrowed. They do not express a distinct preference for those goals that seem to be the hallmark of the high-prestige universities. Instead, they appear to be delineating a set of relationships of their own.

Prestige Measure: Within
The Within measure is possibly a clearer indication of the relative values held by universities of different prestige levels. Table 18 presents the findings using the Within measure. Among the output goals there are no significant findings associated with high prestige that are not also findings already reported in the earlier section concerning the Across measure. The goals associated with lower-prestige universities are, likewise, almost the same, but there are several additions from the list presented earlier. Most noteworthy are the two goals Prepare Students for Useful Careers and Prepare Student for Citizenship. These two goals evidently rank sufficiently high in the goal hierarchy of schools of lesser prestige that a strong relationship exists. The support goals are also quite similar to the support findings for the Across measure, although the strengths of the relationships may have changed either up or down.

Most surprising is that there is a total of 12 new findings over 1964; only one goal relationship has dropped out. Seven of the new findings are positive relationships indicating that they are goals that are emphasized at universities of higher prestige, and five are goals which tend to be emphasized at schools of lesser prestige. Every sign points to a widened differential based on prestige. Furthermore, the Within measure tends to be based upon more conscious acts than the Across measure. For a university to rank a goal in the upper third of its rankings is a good indication of a meeting of the minds on that particular campus.

The goal preferences which are listed in Table 18 reveal somewhat fewer findings, especially among the output goals. While there are 11 new findings in 1971 that did not exist in 1964, 6 findings have dropped off the list. Of these six, four have been translated into reality in that they are now significant goal findings, whereas in 1964 they were significant goal preference findings. On the other hand, two goal preferences were apparently not translated into reality. Of these two, the goal Protect Students' Right of Action is most interesting. In 1964 there was a very strong relationship indicating that high-prestige universities believed that this goal should be emphasized. In 1971 this is no longer the case,

		Goals	Goals preference
Output			
Student-expressive			
7	*Cultivate student's intellect*	.477[a]	
29	*Produce well-rounded student*	—.542[a]	—.759
36	*Develop students' objectivity*	.581[a]	
8	*Develop students' character*		—.452
Student-instrumental			
37	*Prepare students for useful careers*	—.806	
17	*Train students for scholarship/research*	1.000	
34	*Prepare student for citizenship*	—.820	
Research			
25	*Carry on pure research*	.887	.910
Direct service			
5	*Provide special adult training*	—.549[a]	—.478[a]
30	*Assist citizens through extension programs*	—.539	—.594
10	*Disseminate new ideas*	.842	
18	*Preserve cultural heritage*		.886
Support			
Adaptation			
40	*Ensure confidence of contributors*	—.752[a]	.552[a]
31	*Ensure favor of validating bodies*	—.909	—.445
11	*Educate to utmost high school graduates*	—.567	—.560
35	*Accept good students only*	.729	—.560
19	*Satisfy area needs*	—.733	—.724
26	*Keep costs down*	—.616	
1	*Hold staff in face of inducements*	.615[a]	
Management			
41	*Reward for contribution to profession*	.579	
43	*Involve faculty in university government*	.454[a]	
20	*Involve students in university government*		.495[a]
27	*Reward for contribution to institution*		—.735
42	*Emphasize undergraduate instruction*	—.640[a]	—.524[a]
3	*Encourage graduate work*	.487[a]	.903[a]
21	*Ensure efficient goal attainment*		—.667[a]
2	*Let will of faculty prevail*	.462	

	Goals	Goals preference
Motivation		
13 Give faculty maximum opportunity to pursue careers	.803	.572
44 Provide student activities	−541[a]	.692[a]
46 Protect students' right of inquiry	.682[a]	
6 Develop faculty loyalty in institution		.682[a]
Position		
22 Maintain top quality in all programs	.682	−.667[a]
15 Keep up to date	.569[a]	−.667[a]
23 Preserve institutional character		.667[a]
Relationships in 1964 not significant in 1972		
Student-instrumental		
37 Prepare students for useful careers		−.619
Direct service		
18 Preserve cultural heritage	.541	
Management		
43 Involve faculty in university government		.751
2 Let will of faculty prevail		.769
Motivation		
46 Protect students' right of inquiry		.895
28 Protect students' right of action		.951
14 Develop pride in university		−.825

[a] New finding in 1971. Not present in 1964.

NOTE: Negative (−) values indicate goal is emphasized at universities with lower prestige. Figures are gammas. See Appendix B.

and there are no significant findings for it either as a goal or as a goal preference. The trials and tribulations over the seven-year period have exacted their toll.

It must be concluded that on both the Across and Within measures prestige is a strongly differentiating factor and, from all indications, it will continue to be of importance. It is possible that in the future it might be more difficult to develop even a rough prestige measure because of the indication that universities of lower prestige are apparently not quite as interested in competing with top universities. Whether these goal preferences will be translated into reality in the future is, of course, problematical, but the prospect is not something to be dismissed lightly.

STUDENT
UNREST

One of the most widely discussed topics in recent years is that of student unrest. Ever since the period when "free speech" became a cause célèbre on the Berkeley Campus of the University of California, the issue of student protest has exploded beyond campus boundaries and has been duly noted in the press the world over. In the maze of antiwar protest groups and various kinds of student movements, it is sometimes difficult to remember that the student unrest issue came to the fore almost overnight. The legitimacy or illegitimacy of the students' goals is a subject of controversy on almost every campus and, indeed, in almost every household. Every institution of higher learning is touched in one way or another, sometimes violently, but in all cases quite effectively by some form of student organized movement. To cite only a few examples: (1) The doctrine of *in loco parentis* has almost completely disappeared as a policy and in many cases student discipline has shifted from the dean of students to the district court; (2) students are now serving on university committees and are involved, at least nominally, in the government of the university itself; and (3) almost every university has a committee or commission charged with defining its goals, restructuring the organization, and questioning almost every phase of the establishment with the view toward ordering change and all that it portends.

At the time of our 1971 study, we were confronted with a special problem in causal attribution. Although it is possible to identify the sites of active student protest (as publicized) in a small number of universities in the period 1964–1967, beyond that date student protest became quite general. For example, although the Berkeley campus of the University of California provided the first open expression of widespread student protest, later protest was as likely to take place at San Francisco State College and other colleges and universities in the Bay Area. Indeed, protest became worldwide (Lipset & Altbach, 1969), threatening the stability of governments in such countries as France and Japan. Hence it becomes very difficult to identify protest with particular universities or colleges in the manner we have tried to do with our global variables.

In addition, student protest has clearly had as its target major problems and dissatisfactions in the larger society. In fact, protesters in the early 1960s made it clear that they were not alienated from the university and were generally quite satisfied with the university itself (see Semas, 1971). When we set out to try to discover whether student protest is associated with type of university (as measured by goals), we can hardly expect many findings. In addition, as Veysey (1965, Ch. 4) notes, student complaints about the university are very old, dating from the founding of the first universities and continuing without cessation up to the present day. While such complaint and protest are cyclical, usually the periods of relative quiescence need more explaining than those of protest. As Lipset (1972, Ch. 1) notes, students as a group are particularly likely to respond to criticism of society, being young, idealistic, and having both the leisure and lack of immediate responsibility that enable them to join a protest for considerable periods of time. Added to those factors is the general tendency, even in rigidly controlled police states, for the police and agents of government to hesitate (sometimes for only short periods to be sure) before taking action on a campus.

In spite of these caveats, we thought it worthwhile to see whether university goal structure—which proved so differentiating with reference to other global variables—might shed some light on student unrest as well. We handled the measurement problem by making use of the U.S. Senate report on campus disorders (United States Senate, 1969), which attempted systematically to "rate" universities.[8] We adopted our usual self-protective procedure of eschewing individual scores and grouping the universities into three groups—Low, Medium, and High.

Student Unrest: Across

The first important factor to note in Table 19 is that the size of the relationships (gammas) is of relatively low magnitude compared to those of the other measures we have been examining. Furthermore, of the total of 15 goal relationships, there are only 2 which are significant with respect to lower amounts of student

[8] A similar procedure was used by Wynn (1970). This classification was found to correlate fairly closely with that of Collins (1970), based on reports in the *New York Times* on reactions to the Cambodia incursion as well as to the Kent State killings. Such a correlation is rather striking since, as we have said, by that time protest was likely to be very widespread and difficult to measure as to extent in different universities.

	Goals	Goals preference
Output		
Student-expressive		
29 Produce well-rounded student		—.658
8 Develop students' character		—.638
36 Develop students' objectivity	.446	
Student-instrumental		
24 Prepare students for status/leadership		—.570
34 Prepare student for citizenship		—.552
9 Cultivate students' taste	—.479	
Research		
25 Carry on pure research	.537	.502
Direct service		
10 Disseminate new ideas	.659	
Support		
Adaptation		
19 Satisfy area needs	—.611	—.543
1 Hold staff in face of inducements	.531	
26 Keep costs down		—.461
31 Ensure favor of validating bodies		—.472
Management		
43 Involve faculty in university government	.484	
41 Reward for contribution to profession	.504	
12 Keep harmony		—.526
21 Ensure efficient goal attainment		—.597
2 Let will of faculty prevail	.492	
3 Encourage graduate work	.444	
Motivation		
13 Give faculty maximum opportunity to pursue careers	.509	
46 Protect students' right of inquiry	.544	
4 Protect academic freedom		.470
14 Develop pride in university		—.472
Position		
22 Maintain top quality in all programs	.561	
15 Keep up to date	.518	
45 Increase or maintain prestige	.489	

NOTE: Negative (—) values indicate an emphasis at universities with lower student unrest. See Appendix B.

unrest. The other 13 are all related positively to student unrest, indicating that the universities which stress these goals are plagued with a higher order of student unrest.

The top five goals which seem to receive significant emphasis at those universities experiencing a high degree of student unrest are as follows:

10	Disseminate New Ideas
22	Maintain Top Quality in All Programs
46	Protect Students' Right of Inquiry
25	Carry on Pure Research
1	Hold Staff in Face of Inducements

Most noteworthy is the conspicuous absence of any student-expressive or -instrumental goal on this list. Only one goal appears which relates to students (Protect Students' Rights of Inquiry), but it is an institutional goal, and we are sure that many members of the academic community would deny that an emphasis upon it was in any way a causal factor of student unrest. On the other hand, citizens at large will likely interpret this finding as a confirmation of their belief that universities are entirely too permissive. The other four goals in which the relationship was the strongest are generally associated with faculty, thereby supporting the contention of many student activists that the overwhelming concern of administrators and faculty is over those matters that are directly related to faculty rather than to students. One fact bears repeating: the findings on student unrest are not as differentiating as most of the other measures we have used. When findings exist, they are not very strong. Student movements tend to blanket the country, and while differences in intensity exist, all campuses appear to be affected.

The findings with respect to goal preferences present a strange contrast to those for goals. Only two goals are found both as goals and goal preferences: Carry on Pure Research (found at universities with high student unrest) and Satisfy Area Needs (found at universities with low student unrest). Almost all the rest are found in universities where protest is low. In sum, there seems to be a set of goals found in places of high student unrest. These are goals associated with pure research, high quality and originality, and protecting students' right of inquiry. Where those goals are deemphasized, student unrest is low. On the other hand, a set of quite unrelated goal preferences characterizes places of both low and high unrest. In the main, these are the service-oriented, practical goal preferences that we have also associated with universities of lower prestige and those with low productivity.

To put this finding another way, student unrest tends to be found on campuses whose goals relate to pure research, high quality and originality, and protecting students' rights of inquiry. We cannot say whether these goals "cause" the unrest but the view of the Carnegie Commission (*Reform on Campus,* 1972) is plausible: that certain kinds of institutions—those carrying on experiments and hence oriented to change and innovation—probably attract the radical, both as student and professor. These tend also to be the more prestigious institutions and faculties (see Lipset, 1972, p. 201). The combination of an experimental attitude and higher quality faculty (more likely to be activist in all areas, including participation in community affairs—conservative as well as radical) makes it easy for radical students, who are generally critical of societal institutions, to get a more receptive hearing. Given also the readiness of most students to respond to leadership, as noted earlier, such institutions may well be the initiators of discontent.

But we also find a set of goal preferences associated with student discontent, and these consist largely of deemphasis of the land-grant, service, student-oriented kinds of goals. That is, where unrest is high, one finds not merely a high-quality, innovative faculty, but also a feeling that the university should *not* be concerned about providing a practical course of training for students or serving the local area. This seems to add up to a kind of arrogance which hardly implies an end to student unrest or to hostility from citizens, regents, and sources of funds and other resources.

Student Unrest: Within   The results using the Within measure are found in Table 20. There are somewhat more findings than in using the Across measure, but in general, they are pointed in the same direction. While there is some changing of the order, actually four out of the top five goals listed using the Across measure are also present as positive relationships using the Within measure. This tends to confirm the findings. The top five relationships indicating goals that are emphasized by universities with higher amounts of student unrest are as follows:

10 Disseminate New Ideas

25 Carry on Pure Research

22 Maintain Top Quality in All Programs

2 Let Will of Faculty Prevail

36 Develop Students' Objectivity

Here again only one student goal is distinguished using the Within measure. The other four goals are more closely concerned with faculty and faculty relationships.

The goals that seem to be associated with universities experiencing lower amounts of student unrest are, in the case of the Within measure, much more numerous than we had discovered earlier using the Across measure. For example, the goal of emphasizing undergraduate instruction is quite strongly associated with universities that have had lower student unrest. Preparing students for useful careers and for leadership and citizenship are also apparently important in the same type of schools.

The goal preferences found in Table 20 are correspondingly not far different from the Across measure. That is, our analysis of the relationship between student unrest and universities has tended to support the general thesis advanced by Lipset (1972) that the university itself, though increasingly a target of student revolutionaries, is not itself an important "cause" of such unrest. Uni-

		Goals	Goals preference
TABLE 20 *The relationship between student unrest and university goals: Within*	**Output**		
	Student-expressive		
	29 *Produce well-rounded student*		—.554
	8 *Develop students' character*	—.521	—.605
	36 *Develop students' objectivity*	.466	
	Student-instrumental		
	37 *Prepare students for useful careers*	—.650	
	24 *Prepare students for status/leadership*	—.618	
	34 *Prepare student for citizenship*	—.541	
	Research		
	25 *Carry on pure research*	.544	.697
	Direct service		
	10 *Disseminate new ideas*	.561	
	18 *Preserve cultural heritage*		.670

	Goals	Goals preference
Support		
Adaptation		
31 Ensure favor of validating bodies	−.716	
35 Accept good students only		.632
19 Satisfy area needs	−.541	−.538
1 Hold staff in face of inducements	.456	
40 Ensure confidence of contributors	−.452	
Management		
43 Involve faculty in university government	.461	.535
27 Reward for contribution to institution		−.626
42 Emphasize undergraduate instruction	−.758	
3 Encourage graduate work		.735
2 Let will of faculty prevail	.504	
Motivation		
13 Give faculty maximum opportunity to pursue careers	.495	
44 Provide student activities		.911
46 Protect students' right of inquiry	.460	
Position		
22 Maintain top quality in all programs	.522	
15 Keep up to date	.502	
45 Increase or maintain prestige	.488	.444
47 Maintain top quality in important programs	.488	

TABLE 20 (continued)

NOTE: Negative (−) values indicate an emphasis at universities with lower student unrest. See Appendix B.

versities, being the kinds of places they are, provide opportunities for critics of society to congregate. These critics may be students or faculty. Further, there is a close association between the liberal political positions of such faculty and prominence in research, as well as in participation in government-sponsored programs of research and inquiry (including those condemned by student radicals). Hence, one finds on the campuses of the most eminent researchers and scholars a mix which provides a favorable atmosphere for student unrest touched off by injustices in the larger society. In the end, as students are frustrated by the difficulty they experience in attempting to change the larger society, and when they discover that the faculty as a whole is both with them and against them (in the sense of hesitating to take sides because of their commitment to scholarly values of objectivity), the students turn against the university itself. As time goes on, the students at one university follow the example of those at the leading universities, making it difficult to distinguish campuses characterized by high discontent from others. The phenomenon becomes widespread and endemic, as it always has been in universities.

THE DIFFEREN-TIATION OF UNIVERSITIES This chapter was designed to examine the validity of regarding American universities as a single system, an undifferentiated whole composed of institutions that were becoming more alike. The view has been expressed that as universities become more alike, they are ever more sharply to be contrasted with state colleges, small liberal arts colleges, and community colleges. Whatever the contrast may be (and we believe it is a large one, as we shall discuss in Chapter 6), our findings make it very difficult to claim that universities are growing more alike. Rather, public and private universities show an increasingly diverse set of goals. Universities differ strongly from the more productive to the less productive, with some evidence that the less productive are giving up on the competitive struggle and becoming oriented to their own goals. There are very large goal and goal-preference differences between the most- and the least-prestigious universities. Even student unrest, though apparently endemic to the campus, can be distinguished in extent by the sort of goals universities exhibit. The goals of universities seem then not only to be ways of describing the activities of universities but also to be highly sensitive to variations from campus to campus. There are—and this is our most important finding—distinct signs that universities are more sharply differentiated than they were in 1964, so that it seems increasingly inappropriate to think of "university" as a uniform category of analysis. Although some of our colleagues were critical of our limiting ourselves to a "mere" 68 universities, even these 68 appear to fall into several distinct types. Even the word "type" is misplaced, for it implies that they all fit on the same scale, but our evidence is that universities are dividing into noncompeting clusters, each cluster beginning to define its own area in its own way.

4. Power Structures

Given our commitment to look upon universities as organizations, the concern with the identification and ordering of goals that has occupied our attention in Chapters 2 and 3 is understandable. Yet, merely to present a description of those goals and the changes in them would be to leave us with a view of universities from the outside. We would be able to discern the general direction of the organization, but little of its internal dynamics. We would not be in a position to make predictions for the future nor even to understand the shape of goal structures themselves.

It seemed essential that we should turn our attention to those persons who define the goals and move the organization toward attaining them. Theoretically, one could imagine a situation of power equalization (Strauss, 1963)[1] in which *all* concerned participants would influence goals equally, through a town meeting arrangement or through some set of organized message transmission in the manner of sealed bids on a municipal contract. Even the least hierarchical of organizations seems to be far from such a model, though some, of course, wish to move in that direction. Nevertheless, we thought we would begin by identifying those who would likely play at least a small role in goal definition and attainment. Then we would ask our respondents whether some were more important than others, and to what extent: As might have been expected, we found a definite power structure in existence, with some persons and groups perceived as having far more influence than others.

Identification of such a power structure seemed not merely of interest in itself. Rather, we were interested in it for the light it might shed on goals. We assumed that power holders would have

---

[1] Strauss attributes the term to Harold Leavitt.

a causal impact, in the sense that they would affect or even determine goals and the manner of their attainment. Such is not an obvious assumption, for it is quite possible that the causal direction is just the reverse. For example, it is possible that universities with a certain type of goal structure (perhaps as a consequence of historical factors) attract certain kinds of persons into positions of high influence, or the goal structure facilitates the accretion of power to those persons. If so, instead of assuming that "power holders cause goals," we could say that goals "cause" certain kinds of power structures to emerge.

Whatever the direction of causation might be, it seemed to us that the identification of important power holders would relate not merely to the scientific problem of increasing knowledge about universities, but to the applied problem of changing them. Although our concern in this volume is with chronicling the significant changes between 1964 and 1971, we wish to note not only the kinds of changes that represent mere drift but also those that might have been or could be directed. In distinguishing "pure" from applied social sciences, Gouldner (1957) points out that the applied scientist goes beyond interest in prediction to interest in control, even when predictive relationships may represent the greater scientific achievement. He writes:

> . . . no matter how high an inverse correlation is found between the rate of urbanization and the birth rate, the applied demographer can do little to reduce the birth rate by manipulating the degree of urbanization. Demographers can, however, focus on an item, namely, contraceptive materials and information, which they can control, at least in greater measure. Even if urbanization and industrialization are much more highly correlated with the birth rate than is the degree of available contraceptive material and information, the latter assumes strategic significance because of its controllability (Gouldner, 1957, pp. 96–97).

So too, agents of change in society focus upon housing or street design, which may bear only a modest relationship to social problems, but which are manipulable.

In the case of universities, goals are similarly difficult to modify directly. They characterize general directions for the university which, over time, become traditional and even sanctified. A service orientation, for example, is often justified (if questioned at all) by its relationship to the traditional American values of egalitarianism and helping one's neighbor. The "ivory tower" goals associated with the intellect or the classical disciplines are not even felt to require justification. A frontal attack on goals is likely, therefore, to be met with powerful resistance. But if there is a causal relationship between goals and power holders, one may be able to proceed indirectly to change goals by changing power holders. Note that this approach might bear fruit whatever the direction of causation. If power holders "cause" goals, then a change in power holders would presumably result in changes in goals. On the other hand, if certain goals attract a particular type of power holder or make it easy for certain kinds of persons to assume power, then changing the power holders might again, in time, cause the goals to languish for lack of persons likely to implement them. Although such an indirect approach will likely produce only small goal changes, those changes may well be larger than would result from a direct attack on goals themselves.

As described in Chapter 1 (pp. 31–34), our procedure was simply to identify persons and categories of persons who might play some role in the definition of goals as well as in their achievement. Our own experience, as well as pretest results, resulted in a decision to ask about the power of the following persons or categories of persons (stated in alphabetical order):

Alumni

Chairmen of academic departments

Citizens of the state, considered as a category

Dean of the graduate school

Dean of liberal arts (or arts and sciences)

Deans of professional schools

Faculty

Federal government

Sources of grants or endowments (called "Grants" in tables)

Legislators

Parents

President

Regents

State government

Students

Vice-presidents (or provosts)[2]

[2] Considered as a group.

These were not, of course, necessarily comparable, e.g., asking a person to compare "federal government" with the president of the university, but we found that our respondents had no difficulty with this question. These persons or categories were all recognized as centers of power which do affect goals.

The form of the question, as described in Chapter 1, asked the respondent "how much say" each of these persons or categories of persons had about university goals. Respondents were reminded that a person might have "a lot of say" in his own department, for example, but little about the goals of the university as a whole. In this way, we hoped to avoid the practice of simply asking for "power holders" without specifying the area or scope of the power. The overall power structure of the 68 universities, for both 1964 and 1971, is presented in Table 21.

The mean scores for each power holder have been ordered from 1 through 16 in both 1964 and 1971. These averages are, of course, affected by variations among universities, but there are not so

TABLE 21
The overall power structure of American universities, 1964–71

Power holder rank order	1971			1964		
	Rank	Mean	Standard deviation	Rank	Mean	Standard deviation
President	1	4.52	.69	1	4.65	.62
Regents or trustees	2	4.36	.81	2	4.37	.82
Vice-presidents	3	4.06	.81	3	4.12	.82
Deans of professional schools	4	3.50	.80	4	3.62	.84
Dean of liberal arts	5	3.41	.83	6	3.56	.89
Dean of graduate school	6	3.35	.89	5	3.59	.89
Faculty	7	3.35	.92	7	3.31	.97
Legislators	8	3.20	1.35	9	2.94	1.37
Chairmen	9	3.10	.88	8	3.19	.93
Federal government	10	2.89	.95	10	2.79	1.06
State government	11	2.80	1.09	11	2.72	1.21
Students	12	2.77	.79	14	2.37	.82
Grants	13	2.68	.93	12	2.69	1.06
Alumni	14	2.58	.79	13	2.61	.90
Citizens	15	2.11	.94	15	2.08	1.02
Parents	16	1.94	.73	16	1.91	.87

many of those variations as might be expected. Inspection of the standard deviations reveals relatively little variation, with the size of the larger ones (legislators, federal government, state government, grants, and citizens) largely attributable to the "public–private" distinction, as we shall note below.

Turning then to the rank order in the table, we note first the striking correspondence between the rank order in 1964 and in 1971. Particularly noteworthy is the fact that students, felt by so many to have increased their power, are perceived as having done no more than move up two positions, remaining in the bottom set of power holders. We will return to this finding presently. For the moment, the correspondence in rank order in the two years makes it easy for us to examine the rank order in the two years without having to jump back and forth in our discussion.

In American universities, then, the person perceived by our respondents as having the most say about university goals was, and still is, the president. To some, this will not seem surprising. After all, he (and it is, overwhelmingly, a "he") is the chief executive, identified in the public mind with the university, and perhaps the single person whose decisions carry most weight. Radicals or those taking a Machiavellian view of power might dismiss this finding as a mere artifact of the perceptual process. After all, we did not measure "power," only persons' perceptions of power. Hence, persons pick out the "front man," who is only an agent of "interests" who are the real power.[3] As we noted in Chapter 1, this controversy rages in studies of power, and we do not claim to have resolved it here. We do think, however, that a stronger case can be made for the validity of this finding than can be made in most studies of community or societal power. When one asks a member of a complex society, such as the United States, or even a modestly sized local community to identify the "key" power holders, it is understandable that he will name the more prominent or those in official positions. What else can he do? He can hardly have access to the meetings of the boards of corporations, the strategy conferences of military commanders, or the executive sessions of city councils. So he will do the best he can with whatever information is provided by the mass media. But we are dealing with the perceptions of 70 respondents in the circumscribed ambience of the university in which they work full-

---

[3] See the discussion of the "leg man" in Presthus (1964, p. 50).

time. Further, our population included *all* persons at dean level and above, from a fourth to all chairmen and directors, plus 3 to 10 percent of faculty. We have strong assurance that some of them do indeed have access to secret meetings and other behind-the-scenes activities. In fact, we would guess that the perceptions of power are based, for this group, far less than usual on public statements or assumptions about official position and more upon actual observations of these persons making decisions, justifying courses of action, or actually seeking to bring influence to bear on others (including the respondents). One may, of course, still ask whether they are being honest in their replies, but we hope that the fears of a few might be offset by the courage of others—this being one of the benefits of using large numbers. All things considered, we feel confident that the president belongs at the top of the list. Note also that the mean score in both years is above 4.5, meaning that on a scale in which the maximum score assignable was 5, a mean of such magnitude could only result if a high proportion of persons assigned him a score of 5.

Our respondents' assignment of regents to second position (and, like the president, with mean scores over 4.00) was not anticipated and runs contrary to the tendency of regents to assign to themselves a relatively low power position.[4] Some part of this tendency may be characteristic of all power holders in organizations. They feel relatively powerless in view of the need to secure the cooperation of others in the attainment of planned personal ends. But, in any case, regents are perceived as second in power only to the president. Objective assessments of the power of regents in the United States (Corson, 1960, pp. 49–53) take note of three areas in which regents make major decisions: selection of the president, overall management of university funds, especially investments, and general approval of major changes in educational policy (e.g., approval of black studies programs, or addition of a new professional school). In the case of presidential selection, the regents often preside over the decision rather than make the actual choice, since a representative committee is influential in producing the "short list." In any case, selection of a president is a rare event (perhaps less so in recent years), and some members

---

[4] This is our impression from personal contacts as well as written comments by regents in our 1964 survey. They were surveyed then, but the very small return rate forced us to abandon any attempt to analyze their replies systematically. That experience led us to exclude them as respondents in 1971.

of the regents at a given university may never experience it during their terms of office. Overall fund management and major changes in educational policy also are relatively rare events: some members of the faculty who move on to another university after a stay of three or four years may also not experience any such change. Yet, it remains true that though these involve relatively infrequent actions, they are of obvious importance when they do occur and are highly publicized.

In American universities the regents or trustees often make up the legal government of the university, but this fact may not itself be of major significance in accounting for the high position they are perceived to have on the list of power holders. Our own observation is that many of our colleagues are unaware of the regents' legal position. It seems, however, to be a case of potential power, and it may be that, precisely for that reason (plus ignorance of the fact that such potential power exists), the occasional exercise of such power comes as a shock and leads to an elevated perception of the power of the regents. The faculty is likely to be peculiarly sensitive to this potential power, for it has been used in recent years to fire members of the faculty, occasionally including even tenured persons. Over the period of our study, particular prominence has been given to the political aspects of such firings. Politically motivated firings by a group of laymen who exercise potential power occasionally provide support for the Machiavellian theories referred to earlier.

The third and last of the power holders with a mean score above 4.00 is the vice-president. There seems little surprise in his position. He shares directly in the power assigned to the president; he is the person that often acts as the "inside president" while the president faces outward (making speeches, representing the university, seeking legitimation and money), and he usually shares an office in the part of the campus or building occupied by "central administration." Perhaps more important is the increasing tendency for universities to functionalize the role, with larger universities having as many as five or six vice-presidents. Some of these officers will have clear responsibility for strictly academic functions (one, for example, may be in charge of health sciences, another of all professional schools, another of research) and hence will usually be persons with impeccable academic credentials. Such persons cannot be brushed aside by faculty as "mere paper shufflers."

That deans come next in the rank order would seem to follow

from their official position in the administrative hierarchy. Although little significance can be attached to small rank differences, it is interesting that deans of professional schools head the list in both years. This finding is less a confirmation of faculty fears of growth of "dean power" than it appears, as we shall note below. For the time being, such a primary position may be more properly attributed to the interactional network of the deans of professional schools in comparison to the two other kinds of academic deans. Deans of professional schools experience fewer of the legitimation problems of the other deans — their schools are obviously engaged in activities of value to the community. Hence, they often mingle freely with local business and industrial leaders, with representatives of professional organizations, and with labor union leaders. On campus, their "power" is suggested by the large size of professional schools, in teaching, research, and service staff, as well as by enrollment of students in both regular day classes and evening or extension classes.

The assignment of parents, citizens of the state, alumni, and grant donors to bottom positions suggests that the fears that these persons maneuver behind the scenes are not shared by faculty and administration. The assignment of the more obviously influential legislators and state government to middle positions appears to be a consequence of averaging public and private institutions, as we shall see presently.

Faculty are found just below the deans but above chairmen (and federal government) in both years. Apart from providing some assurance that our respondents were not merely recording persons according to official position (which would have placed chairmen above faculty), the finding has important implications. Some part of the reason for this position is due to the "working faculty," that is, those who serve as chairmen of campuswide administrative committees with important missions related to university goals, such as introduction of new curricula, shifts in admission standards, examining cases of threatened violations of academic freedom, or proposing mergers of two divisions of the university. Surely also, the ranking of faculty at about the same position as federal government is not accidental but related to the fact that particular faculty have acquired power as heads of research institutes as a consequence of receiving large amounts of federal money.

The data in Table 21 represent averaging over 68 universities.

In both 1964 and 1971 we were next concerned with whether such averaging concealed internal variations by type of university that might affect the overall findings.[5] To that end, in 1964 we performed multivariate analysis on the rank order of power holders, making use of the variables of size, productivity (number of Ph.D.'s produced per year), type of control (public-private), quality (prestige, and number of volumes in library), graduate emphasis, and region of the country. The result (Gross & Grambsch, 1968, pp. 79–81) was that the overall relationships were found to hold up strongly with little change for all variables with the main excep-

[5] This is the process of elaboration described by Lazarsfeld (1955) as "interpretation" or "explanation" (wherein a relationship between two variables disappears when a third variable is introduced) or "specification" (wherein the relationship is enhanced). As Blalock (1964, p. 85) points out, such efforts do not destroy the original relationship but constitute "putting frosting on the cake."

TABLE 22a   *A comparison of the power structure of private and of public universities, 1964*

Private			Public		
Power holder rank order	Mean score	Standard deviation	Power holder rank order	Mean score	Standard deviation
President	4.70	.58	President	4.62	.63
Regents or trustees	4.24	.88	Regents or trustees	4.41	.78
Vice-presidents	4.10	.82	Vice-presidents	4.07	.83
Deans of professional schools	3.64	.80	Deans of professional schools	3.53	.79
Dean of liberal arts	3.57	.83	Dean of graduate school	3.53	.85
Dean of graduate school	3.54	.87	Legislators	3.45	1.07
Faculty	3.29	.96	Dean of liberal arts	3.43	.83
Chairmen	3.16	.90	Faculty	3.27	.93
Grants	2.84	1.03	Chairmen	3.13	.87
Alumni	2.53	.84	State government	2.91	1.02
Federal government	2.53	.99	Federal government	2.79	.94
Students	2.25	.69	Alumni	2.57	.80
State government	1.86	.90	Grants	2.49	.89
Parents	1.70	.68	Students	2.34	.73
Legislators	1.63	.92	Citizens	2.28	.88
Citizens	1.43	.63	Parents	1.90	.72

TABLE 22b *A comparison of the power structure of private and of public universities, 1971*

Private			Public		
Power holder rank order	*Mean score*	*Standard deviation*	*Power holder rank order*	*Mean score*	*Standard deviation*
President	4.60	.66	President	4.48	.70
Vice-presidents	4.15	.78	Regents or trustees	4.45	.75
Regents or trustees	4.15	.89	Vice-presidents	4.02	.82
Deans of professional schools	3.69	.84	Legislators	3.80	1.00
Dean of liberal arts	3.63	.82	Deans of professional schools	3.42	.77
Faculty	3.50	.93	Dean of liberal arts	3.31	.82
Dean of graduate school	3.46	.95	Dean of graduate school	3.31	.86
Chairmen	3.30	.88	Faculty	3.28	.91
Grants	2.94	.98	State government	3.13	.99
Students	2.84	.77	Chairmen	3.00	.86
Federal government	2.84	.98	Federal government	2.91	.93
Alumni	2.59	.81	Students	2.74	.80
State government	2.06	.93	Alumni	2.57	.78
Legislators	1.81	.98	Grants	2.56	.88
Parents	1.81	.68	Citizens	2.39	.92
Citizens	1.49	.64	Parents	2.00	.75

tion of type of control. Since the multivariate analysis was so unproductive, we repeated it in 1971 only for the type of control variable and for prestige (which had proved to be an important control variable for other parts of our analysis, especially those on goals). The breakdown by prestige into four levels (as described in Appendix B) was again unproductive.[6] The comparison of power structures in private and public institutions is provided in Tables 22a and 22b.

As can be seen, the main effect of separating universities by type of control in both 1964 and 1971 is that legislators and state government rise in rank in public universities (and fall in private universities), whereas grants rise slightly in private universities. It is interesting to note, however, that though the standard devia-

[6] When we say "unproductive," this does not mean that there were not occasional differences. For example, faculty drops from fourth position in top-prestige universities to eighth in bottom-level universities. But when we ran rank correlations between the four levels, *every* correlation exceeded .990.

tions of these categories drop, they remain relatively high. In other words, even in public universities there is variation in how legislators and state government are perceived and variation in private universities with reference to grants. We would guess that such variation reflects actual differences in the behavior of these power holders. For example, it is only in some states that legislators have taken highly publicized punitive actions toward universities in their states.

Looking back over these first findings on power distribution, one is left with the impression that the power structure in universities is not so different as might have been believed. The most important source of variation appears to be type of control and even that is not a simple distinction, for there remain variations among universities, probably attributable to local conditions. Our data lead us to conclude that the power structure of American universities is remarkably uniform, at least among the 68 under study here.

PERCEIVED CHANGES IN POWER, 1964–1971 The lack of any noticeable change in rank order between 1964 and 1971 was a surprise to the writers. Since we expected some changes, we had included a new question in the 1971 questionnaire. Immediately following the question we have just discussed (that is, the respondent's perception of how much say each power holder has over university goals), we asked the following question:

In reviewing the above list of positions and agencies how has the influence of each on major university policies changed during the past seven or eight years? Has it increased, decreased, or remained about the same?

	Increased markedly	Increased moderately	Remained about the same	Decreased moderately	Decreased markedly
The regents (or trustees)	_____	_____	_____	_____	_____
Legislators	_____	_____	_____	_____	_____
*					
*					
*					
Parents	_____	_____	_____	_____	_____

Our findings on this question are presented in Table 23.

TABLE 23
Changes in
power during
the past eight
years

Power holder by change in power	Mean score	Standard deviation
Students	4.06	.68
Legislators	3.64	.81
Faculty	3.42	.83
Regents or trustees	3.41	.87
State government	3.34	.67
Federal government	3.34	.83
Vice-presidents	3.33	.82
President	3.21	.92
Deans of professional schools	3.12	.63
Citizens	3.09	.54
Grants	3.05	.59
Dean of liberal arts	3.00	.65
Dean of graduate school	2.99	.68
Chairmen	2.97	.61
Alumni	2.96	.54
Parents	2.89	.49

We were quite unprepared for the picture presented in Table 23. It offers a ranking quite out of order with that presented in Table 21. When we break out the data by type of control (Table 24), the picture is again quite different from Tables 22a and 22b, though with the expected elevation of legislators and state government to higher positions in public universities, and grants to a somewhat higher position in private universities.

We may, therefore, confine our attention to Table 23.

Although the power holders in Table 23 have been arranged in order ranging from those who are believed to have increased power the most (students) to those who have actually lost power (parents), this table is one case where assigning ranks to the scores would be misleading. The question itself asked the respondent to score the change in power "over the last seven or eight years" by checking one of: "increased markedly," "increased moderately," "remained about the same," "decreased moderately," and "decreased markedly." A score of 5 was assigned for "increased markedly," a score of 4 for "increased moderately," and so forth. Hence, we can assume that any average score substantially above 3 (for "remained about the same") implies an increase, and a score substantially below 3 implies an actual decrease.

TABLE 24   *Changes in power at public and private universities during the past eight years*

Private			Public		
Power holder by change in power	Mean score	Standard deviation	Power holder by change in power	Mean score	Standard deviation
Students	4.14	.66	Students	4.03	.69
Faculty	3.52	.82	Legislators	3.81	.81
Federal government	3.40	.85	Regents or trustees	3.57	.88
Vice-presidents	3.35	.82	State government	3.41	.70
President	3.33	.93	Faculty	3.37	.83
Legislators	3.19	.59	Vice-presidents	3.32	.82
Deans of professional schools	3.15	.62	Federal government	3.31	.81
State government	3.15	.57	President	3.15	.90
Grants	3.15	.65	Citizens	3.14	.59
Dean of liberal arts	3.08	.65	Deans of professional schools	3.11	.63
Regents or trustees	3.03	.70	Grants	3.00	.55
Chairmen	3.02	.61	Dean of graduate school	2.98	.68
Dean of graduate school	3.01	.66	Alumni	2.97	.53
Citizens	2.97	.38	Dean of liberal arts	2.96	.65
Alumni	2.95	.58	Chairmen	2.95	.61
Parents	2.88	.45	Parents	2.89	.51

The first thing to note about Table 23, then, is that the scores range *above* 3.00, implying a general tendency to believe that the power of *most* of the named power holders has risen. Since our list of power holders is, if anything, too broad, it seems hardly likely that there is a power holder whom we omitted to name whose power has dropped substantially.[7] The phenomenon of an increase in control by all levels is not so strange as it first might seem. It would correspond to what Tannenbaum (1961) speaks of as a "polyarchic model" (in contrast to a laissez-faire or anarchic model), illustrated, for example, in Selznick's discussion of cooptation in the Tennessee Valley Authority (TVA), wherein the coopted groups gain power at the same time as the higher levels in TVA increased their power over the coopted groups (Selznick, 1953).[8]

[7] No persons or categories beyond those named were proposed in pretests, nor was the list criticized by our respondents, who were by no means bashful about volunteering criticism. See the discussion "Comments" in Appendix A.

[8] The example is suggested by Tannenbaum (1968, p. 66).

It suggests a situation in which more resources become available to a wider spectrum of power holders who are now able to influence each other to a greater extent than previously. For our respondents, who are included in the power holders listed, there is apparently a sense that everyone, including themselves, has either held onto his former ability to control others or has increased his control (the chairmen are an exception, to be noted presently).

But even though there seems to be a general rise in ability to control what happens in universities, it is important to note the substantial differences in such control reflected in Table 23. Of those who are believed to have lost power—chairmen, alumni, and parents—the finding for alumni and parents, who were perceived as having very little power in both 1964 and 1971 anyhow, indicates that their position near or at the bottom is becoming ever more secure. For chairmen, who occupied a position in the middle (9th in 1971 and 8th in 1964), the implications are more serious, but before examining them, let us look at the other power holders.

We can separate the rest of the power holders in Table 23 by calling a "considerable" increase in power one in which the average score is over 3.33 (an arbitrary decision, of course, but a reasonable one given the range in the table). If we make such a division of the power holders, then we can say we have two groups, one of which has increased in perceived power more than the other. To avoid awkward language, let us call the first "those whose power is believed to have increased considerably," and the second "those whose power is believed to have remained about the same." Those whose power is believed to have increased considerably, then, include: a set of "outsiders" (legislators, regents, state and federal government) plus students and faculty, whereas those whose power is believed to have remained about the same include administrators of the university, plus citizens and grants. In discussing these groups, we can pass quickly by citizens and grants, since they were both judged to be of low power anyhow (see Table 21), and since the diminution of grant funds from private donors would have led us to expect either that they would do no more than maintain their previous ranking as power holders or even drop in rank.

What we have then is a situation where a group of outsiders (legislators, regents, state and federal government) and students and faculty are believed to have increased their power considerably, whereas administrators in the university are believed either to have retained their power (but not increased it) or, in the case of the lowest level of administrator, the chairmen, have actually lost power. The position of outsiders is not surprising, since their actions are publicized, and it is easy for even small increments to be evaluated as large shifts in power. Such at least seems to be the judgment of our respondents. We must bear in mind that these same respondents indicated that they felt there had been substantially *no* change in the ranking of these power holders, relative to one another, between 1964 and 1971. Thus, while students are perceived to have changed the most, their relative position remains near the bottom, but the little change that is evident (from 14th in 1964 to 12th in 1971) is perceived as a very large change. A somewhat similar argument can be made for state government and legislators, categories which have risen slightly in relative position[9] but are believed to have risen considerably above many others. Particularly impressive is the strong showing of regents, because they also scored so high in relative ranking among all power holders (Table 21). Here then we have a group which shows just the opposite effect we observed for alumni and parents, who, we said, were securing their place at the bottom. Regents or trustees, already very high, are believed to have increased their power considerably. Although they still rank below the president (Table 21), one cannot help wondering whether their strong comparative showing in increased power does not imply some reduction of the power difference between them and the president.

Administrators showed no such increase in power and just held their own or, in the case of chairmen, actually lost power. This finding surely reflects their handling of student and "outsider" criticism and agitation over the past seven years. The sight of students' occupying the president's or dean's office leaves a vivid impression, even though relatively little of enduring quality changes. Even though administrators do not rise in perception of change in power, they do retain their relative rank in middle or higher positions as power holders. In this case, there is no drop in relative rank (see Table 21) between 1964 and 1971, but the decline in absolute amount of power is perceived as large.

In sum, the power structure of universities has not changed,

---

[9] The changes are better viewed by comparing Tables 22a and 22b where type of control is held constant. Among public universities, legislators rose from 6th to 4th rank, and state government from 10th to 9th. Among private universities, legislators rose from 15th to 14th, and state government remained the same (13th) in both years.

if by "structure" we refer to the pattern of relative distribution of power. Presidents still sit firmly at the top; other central administrators are not far behind; and students are near the bottom. But the little gain made by students is felt to be very impressive, especially because no comparable gain is shown by top and central administration. If anything, this conclusion reflects a perception by administrators and faculty that the power of top and central administration is so large that the failure to increase it is something that is impressive (perhaps because no one thought they could not do so if they wished). So too, the power of students to make any change in their relative power was considered so slight that even a tiny increment is felt to be an enormous achievement beyond what was expected. In looking for a metaphor to illuminate this finding, we might think of the powerful political establishment in Rome near the height of its power in ancient days contemplating the slave revolt of Spartacus—marveling that mere slaves could accomplish so much, but never for a moment doubting that its military power could suppress the revolt. It would not be surprising to hear patricians mocking the administration or top army leaders because slaves were giving them so much trouble. We are not implying that administrators are military leaders or that students are slaves, but—well, we will drop the metaphor.

Finally, the perception that the power of the faculty has risen deserves special mention. To some it appears to be a "deviant" finding. Since the attack on universities—from legislators, citizens, and students—is perceived as having reduced the power of administrators, how can it not be perceived as àlso having reduced the power of the faculty? Some of the attack has been clearly against particular members of the faculty, as in the most publicized attempts to fire radical professors. Yet, we must remember that our respondents include the very persons who are presumably the target of such attacks (the professors). How then can they, and their administrators, conclude that faculty power has increased absolutely? Some part of this assessment surely results from the improvement over the last few years in faculty salaries and working conditions, which have, after a long lean period, finally begun to approach decent levels and for some (the entrepreneurial researchers) have become enough at last to provide a thundering answer to a mother-in-law's repeated reminder that her daughter might have married a doctor (a real one, that is). Professors are mostly not yet rich, but they live better than most of them ever have before and better than their peers in the most prestigious of European or British Commonwealth universities. Another factor influencing the evaluation of change in power of the faculty may well be that they have lost comparatively less than members of the administration, who have often suffered public humiliation, as well as being forced to resign. Perhaps a smaller relative loss is perceived as a gain.

But there is another, more subtle aspect to the perceived gain of the faculty. This factor is the effect of the student revolt on the general liberalization of traditional, starched-shirt norms. It is described by Caplow (1971, p. 13), who writes of

> . . . the liberation of faculty members from conventional norms that weighed as heavily upon them as upon undergraduates and for a much longer term of years. The trivial freedoms to wear sweaters and sandals to class, to court nubile undergraduates without public censure, to use obscenities in lectures and correspondence, and to cultivate underworld acquaintances in the community are no less heady than the major freedoms to express dissident political opinions, to espouse radical causes, and, above all, to challenge the judgment of one's seniors about one's professional merits. The competitive grading system to which students object is no more galling than the competitive mechanism within each academic discipline and department—a mechanism which measures scholars for eminence or obscurity. It is no wonder that behind nearly every SDS chapter in its heyday stood a devoted little band of faculty advisors.

Such inferences relate to the position of power holders relative to one another and to changes over time. But the critical question for us goes beyond describing the power structure to the relationship of power to the goals of the university. We turn next to that question.

POWER CLUSTERS   The examination of rank order among power holders provides a useful picture of the power structure. Our next task is to relate the power structure to the goals of universities.

In our report on the 1964 study, our practice was to take up the power holders (legislators, regents, etc.) one at a time and relate the goal emphasis to the power holder being considered (Gross & Grambsch, 1968, pp. 82 ff.). It is more parsimonious, as well as less tedious, if we first examine the relationships among the power holders themselves. For example, in 1964 we found a very similar pattern of goal emphasis in those universities where legislators had power and those where state governments had power (as one would expect). Some part, certainly, of the similar goal distributions is due to the tendency of legislators to be powerful in precisely those states where state governments are powerful.

In order to perform this analysis of relating power holders to one another, we related every power holder to every other power holder, then examined the resultant relationships to seek sets of power holders that show strong relationships to one another. The strong relationships are portrayed in Figure 2a in the form of clusters. Two clusters were found to stand out with particular clarity: (1) legislators—state government—citizens; and (2) dean of liberal arts—dean of professional schools—chairmen. The procedure for measuring relationships was to range the mean value for each power holder at each university on a scale from low to high. Then, the 68 means were divided into thirds, so that a university was classified as "High," "Medium," or "Low," for each power holder. Power holders were then also related to each other. For example, for a given university, legislators might fall in the high third, and state government in the high third. At another, one might fall in the high third and the other in the low third. A high gamma means that they tend to be found together—universities where legislators are perceived as having high power are also those in which state government is so perceived. The gammas show the strength of the relationship for Across analysis[10] and,

[10] The Within analysis sometimes produced gammas of 1 or −1, owing to an anomaly of gamma and similar measures with certain kinds of skewed distributions. The direction of the relationship was, however, as shown in the figures.

FIGURE 2a
Strong power clusters: positive relationships (gammas)

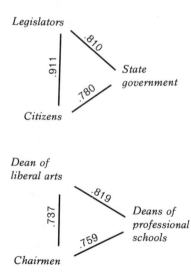

as can be seen, they are very high. To keep the clusters clear, Figure 2a includes only positive gammas. The negative gammas, however, are equally important, and are presented in Figure 2b, together with the positive gammas. Here the positive gammas are placed along the solid lines and the negative gammas are placed on the dotted lines. They may be read as follows: Take the solid line connecting state government and citizens, and the dotted line connecting state government and chairmen. The finding is that those universities falling in groups in which the state government is perceived as having high power relative to other universities, are also universities in which citizens of the state are perceived as having high power (gamma = .780), and in which chairmen of academic departments are perceived as having low power (gamma = −.526). The net impression from Figure 2b is that the legislators—state government—citizens cluster and the

FIGURE 2b *Strong power clusters: all significant relationships (gammas)*

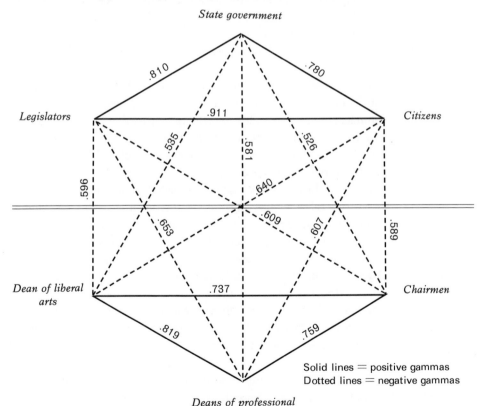

dean of liberal arts—dean of professional schools—chairmen cluster show strong positive relationships within the cluster, and strongly negative relationships between the two clusters. This makes for a good case that the two sets of power holders are worth segregating and may be expected to present similar relationships to goals.

Although the relationship between legislators, state government, and citizens is not surprising, the relationships in the second cluster were unexpected in both 1964 and 1971. A chairman is usually identified by his department members as *primus inter pares,* in many places even serving on a rotating basis (that is, a professor serves a limited term, then returns to his teaching and research duties). That chairmen would be found in the same cluster with two sets of deans is surprising. But even more surprising is the presence of the deans of professional schools. Perhaps this is only surprising to those who identify such deans with outside "interests" or who fear the rapid growth in postwar years of schools of business administration, and the usually large size of the school of education or physical education, and the high salaries and large physical plant associated with schools of medicine and dentistry.

The cluster analysis has been limited only to strong relationships, showing large gammas within the cluster and negative gammas between them. It is worthwhile extending the cluster analysis to all relationships which exceeded the 5 percent level of significance. This has been done for the data of 1971 (though the 1964 picture was substantially the same). The results are presented in Figure 3. Inspection of Figure 3, which, for simplicity, is limited to positive relationships, shows our original clusters, as we would expect, with other power holders related usually to only one or two members of the strong cluster. In the legislators cluster, for example, parents are found related to citizens and regents, whereas federal government is related only to parents. In the deans-chairmen cluster, students come in, but are related only to faculty and chairmen. Donors of private grants are related to deans of professional schools only. Only two power holders manage to bridge the two clusters: namely, the vice-president, whose power is found to be positively related both to the legislators and to deans of professional schools (though the gammas in both cases are relatively low), and alumni, who relate to parents and deans of professional schools. And the president comes in at last, related only indirectly to both

FIGURE 3 *Moderate power clusters*

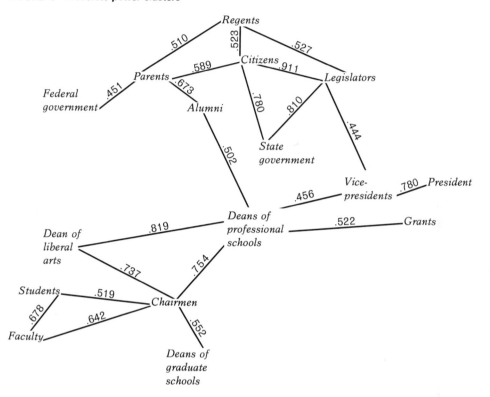

clusters through the vice-president. It is interesting that the vice-presidents do link up with, of all in the cluster at the bottom, the deans of professional schools (who also link with grants and alumni), suggestive of the broad network of influence and interaction that surrounds those deans. Still, the gammas with grants and alumni are not among the highest.

Perhaps the most important conclusion from this cluster analysis is the finding that the power within each cluster is not a zero-sum variable. That is, where state government is powerful, it does not necessarily mean that legislators are not: their power seems to go together. More significantly, where deans of liberal arts are perceived as having high power, so also are faculty and deans of professional schools. It does not follow, then, that an accretion of power to the deans is bought at the expense of the faculty. Quite the reverse—say our data—they go up (or down) together. As we pointed out in our general discussion of power in Chapter 1 (p. 32), one important way in which the faculty may increase its power is through protections offered by sensitive administrators who resist the possible intrusions of regents or legislators. In other words, deans may act on behalf of the faculty, as well as to "control" them.[11]

But the case for assuming that deans or chairmen act on behalf of the faculty requires analysis of the goals associated with each of the clusters. By examining the clusters we will gain insight into what goals these powerholders share and will be able to ask if this agreement provides a basis for common action.

POWER CLUSTERS AND UNIVERSITY GOALS As we pointed out in Chapter 2 (pp. 64–65), the importance of any goal may be looked at from two different perspectives: The goal may be compared with other goals at the same university (Goals Within), or the goal may be compared with the rating given it at other universities (Goals Across). We must now complicate the presentation of findings by pointing out that the same kind of analysis applies to power. Legislators may be compared with, say, deans of professional schools at a given university, where perhaps they may score below the deans, or the legislators at a university may be compared with the perceived power of legislators at another university, where they may score higher. As before, we call comparisons of power within a university *Power Within,* and comparisons across universities *Power Across.* Hence, when relating goal emphasis to various power holders, we can generate four kinds of tables: Power Across related to Goals Across, Power Across related to Goals Within, Power Within related to Goals Across, and Power Within related to Goals Within. These tend to be related, but they give different kinds of information. We have illustrated all four

[11] When examining the members of the "external power cluster" (the upper cluster in Figures 2a, 2b, and 3), one might wonder about the significance of these power holders in private universities. Although we noted (Tables 22a and 22b) that legislators and state government were more important in public than private universities (as one would expect), their influence hardly vanishes in private universities. Such seems particularly to be the case in the years since 1964, when legislatures and state governments have sometimes not hesitated to attack private universities as well as public ones, and also when the severe financial troubles of this period led some of the formerly private universities to "go public." A hostile legislature or state government seems to contribute to an atmosphere which affects private as well as state governments. Whatever the case may be for legislators and state government, however, the external power cluster of Figure 3 shows power holders who obviously are important in private as well as public universities, such as regents, alumni, parents, citizens, and federal government.

FIGURE 4 Samples illustrating relationship of power of legislators to goal 18, Preserve Cultural Heritage

ACROSS UNIVERSITY ANALYSIS

Power across: legislators

Goal: Preserve cultural heritage (18)		*Low*	*Medium*	*High*	*Sum*
	Low	3	7	13	23
	Medium	8	7	6	21
	High	12	8	4	24
	Sum	23	22	23	68

$Gamma = -.496$
$P < .05$

Power within: legislators

Goal: Preserve cultural heritage (18)		*Low*	*Medium*	*High*	*Sum*
	Low	4	9	10	23
	Medium	8	9	4	21
	High	12	8	4	24
	Sum	24	26	18	68

$Gamma = -.417$
$P > .05$

WITHIN UNIVERSITY ANALYSIS

Power across: legislators

Goal: Preserve cultural heritage (18)		*Low*	*Medium*	*High*	*Sum*
	Low	0	3	8	11
	Medium	14	15	12	41
	High	9	4	3	16
	Sum	23	22	23	68

$Gamma = -.575$
$P < .05$

Power within: legislators

Goal: Preserve cultural heritage (18)		*Low*	*Medium*	*High*	*Sum*
	Low	0	7	4	11
	Medium	15	15	11	41
	High	9	4	3	16
	Sum	24	26	18	68

$Gamma = -.427$
$P > .05$

types of analyses in Figure 4 for the example of legislators and the goal Preserve Cultural Heritage.

In each case illustrated in Figure 4, the Across measures are generated by ranging the goal or power holder scores in serial order for all universities, then splitting the distribution into thirds to obtain the high, medium, and low ranks. Our justification, as always, was that the scores (3.22, 3.23, 3.61) carried to two decimal places, represent merely specious precision, even allowing for the dispersions. To say that one power holder ranks one or two steps higher than another represents a truer picture of our data than any claim that 3.23 is "higher" than 3.22. The result of splitting the distribution of Across measures into thirds is to produce around 22 universities in the *sum* columns or rows of the Across measures.

For the Within measures, we range both the goal scores and the power scores within each university from low to high, then split the distribution within the university into thirds. The score is characterized as high, medium, or low according to where it falls in the distribution. Then, to obtain the marginals for high in the Within *sums,* we add up the number of universities in which a given goal or power holder falls in the high part of the distribution. This can be any figure, of course, up to 68, for a goal can be ranked in the top third at each university (Protect Academic Freedom is so ranked), or a power holder can always be ranked in the top third (presidents are so ranked). The result for the *sums* for Within is skewness.

Looking now at the individual tables in Figure 4, consider the table in the upper-left quadrant. This is a Power-Across–Goals-Across measure. Paying attention now to the upper row (3, 7, 13) —that is, to the 23 universities in which the goal Preserve Cultural Heritage is emphasized the least—we find that in 3 of those universities legislators are perceived as having low power in comparisons to other universities; in 7, legislators are perceived as comparatively medium; and in 13 as having comparatively high power. From this row the evidence is that where the goal receives little comparative emphasis, legislators are likely to have high comparative power. The bottom row supports this interpretation. The gamma for the relationship is — .496 (as we would expect), the probability of a gamma so large occurring by chance being less than 5 in 100. As we pointed out in Chapter 1, we consider a piece of information a "finding" only if it does exceed this probability. In sum, the table supports the claim that universities in which legislators have high power (in comparison to other universities) are also universities in which the goal Preserve Cultural Heritage is little emphasized (compared to its emphasis in other universities), and vice versa.

Let us next look at the table in the bottom-right quadrant: the Power-Within–Goals-Within example. This type of analysis corresponds more closely to the individual's perception of both goals and power and hence is easier to interpret. The average person perceives a goal emphasis at his own university and has difficulty comparing it to that at another university. So, too, for the power of legislators. He can more easily compare the legislators he knows to the regents he knows, than he can the legislators in his own state with those in another state. The table shows a zero in the upper-left cell, meaning that there are no universities in which both legislators and this goal are put in the bottom third. There are, similarly, only three in which both goal and power holder are ranked in the top third. Again we have a negative relationship, as suggested by the negative gamma. But in this case, the gamma is too low for significance, hence raising the question that this distribution of scores could be a chance occurrence, or that the relationship is a modest one.

We have here a case in which the Across and the Within analyses do not agree, though the two relationships are found to fall in the same direction (that is, both show a negative relationship between the power of legislators and emphasis on preserving the cultural heritage). We can conclude that when universities are stratified by legislative power and emphasis on preserving the cultural heritage, the same universities fall at the upper or lower part of either distribution. Universities in which legislators have high comparative power are also those that do not emphasize this goal, and vice versa. Within universities, however, it is quite possible for legislators to have more power than other groups but for this goal to be among those most emphasized. From the table in the bottom left, we can conclude that when we stratify universities by the power of legislators, those universities that fall in the upper third tend also to place little emphasis on preserving the cultural heritage in comparison to other goals. One might wish to infer a "causal" connection here—on the assumption that legislators "cause" or interfere with goal emphasis. That is, one might wish to argue that at those universities legislators' power is responsible for the comparative neglect of this goal. But our data do not provide conclusive evidence for such an interpretation, for it could equally be true that the de-emphasis on this goal permits legislators to exercise greater power. This sounds less plausible, but one needs other data than ours to support it in any case.

The information in the table in the upper right offers a possibility of a similar kind of interpretation, but the gamma is here too low for us to claim a finding. Here, the conclusion is that universities are stratified by emphasis on preserving the cultural heritage: Those universities in which it is emphasized highly may also be those in which legislators have high power (compared to regents, deans, etc.) but may also be those in which this is not the case. Again, the direction is negative, but only modestly so.

For simplicity, then, we shall present our tables in the order of the discussion in the previous paragraphs. We shall further abbreviate the presentation by presenting findings for one "representative" of each cluster in Figure 2a, for legislators in the first cluster and for deans of liberal arts in the second cluster. Where appropriate, we shall also present findings for other power holders, since the relationships among them, though often high, are, of course, less than unity.

Power Across and Goals Across   The first set of findings comparing the external power cluster with the internal power cluster is presented in Table 25. The upper part of Table 25 shows the gammas for all findings (that is, where the level of significance exceeds 5 percent), whereas the lower part of the table shows those relationships which were significant in 1964 but not in 1971. The reverse situation (findings which were not significant in 1964 but were in 1971) is indicated in the upper part of the table by an *a* after the gamma value.

Several impressions emerge from the comparisons in Table 25. First, in contrast to the findings in previous chapters, there is an appreciable drop in the number of significant findings below those of 1964. For external power (the legislators), out of 21 findings in 1964, 12 dropped out by 1971; whereas for internal power (deans of liberal arts), 8 dropped out of an original group of 27. If one assumes that "power holders cause goals," then such a drop might suggest a decline in the ability of power holders to influence goals. Or, if one assumes the opposite causal direction (that particular goal patterns provide certain persons or categories of persons with the opportunity to acquire power), then one might conclude that goals no longer offer opportunities for the accumulation of power perhaps because goals are more difficult to achieve

TABLE 25
*Comparison of
relationship of
external power
cluster
(legislators,
state
government,
citizens) and
internal power
cluster (deans of
liberal arts,
deans of
professional
schools,
chairmen) to
university goals:
power Across
and goals
Across*

Goals	External power (legislators)	Internal power (deans of liberal arts)
Output		
Student-expressive		
7 Cultivate students' intellect	—.605	.723
29 Produce well-rounded student	—.549	
16 Affect student with great ideas	—.476	.775
36 Develop students' objectivity		.707
Student-instrumental		
37 Prepare students for useful careers	.548	—.521
24 Prepare students for status/leadership	—.453[a]	
17 Train students for scholarship/research	—.479	.560
Research		
39 Carry on applied research		—.664
Direct service		
30 Assist citizens through extension programs	.637	—.694
38 Provide community cultural leadership	.493[a]	—.463
10 Disseminate new ideas		.596
Support		
Adaptation		
11 Educate to utmost high school graduates	.808	—.531
35 Accept good students only	—.684	.526
19 Satisfy area needs		—.597
Management		
3 Encourage graduate work		.590
21 Ensure efficient goal attainment	—.516[a]	
Motivation		
4 Protect academic freedom	—.591	.752
13 Give faculty maximum opportunity to pursue careers		.655
44 Provide student activities		—.577[a]
46 Protect students' right of inquiry		.695
28 Protect students' right of action		.631
Position		
47 Maintain top quality in important programs		.594
15 Keep up to date		.456

	External power (legislators)	Internal power (deans of liberal arts)
TABLE 25 *(continued)* **Goals**		
Findings in 1964 no longer significant in 1971		
Research		
25 Carry on pure research		.554
Direct service		
5 Provide special adult training		—.459
10 Disseminate new ideas	—.482	
18 Preserve cultural heritage	—.496	.565
Adaptation		
19 Satisfy area needs	.602	
26 Keep costs down	.546	—.521
Management		
41 Reward for contribution to profession		.624
20 Involve students in university government	.567	
12 Keep harmony	.531	
42 Emphasize undergraduate instruction	.605	—.473
Motivation		
13 Give faculty maximum opportunity to pursue careers	—.588	
44 Provide student activities	.501	
46 Protect students' right of inquiry	—.560	
Position		
22 Maintain top quality in all programs		.641
45 Increase or maintain prestige	—.656	.505
23 Preserve institutional character	—.482	

[a] New findings in 1971. Not present in 1964.

NOTE: Negative values (—) indicate an emphasis at those universities where power Across *or* goals Across are low. See Appendix B.

or because power is more difficult to achieve. Both kinds of causation are probably operative, but our data on the perceived change in power (Table 23) showed that external power holders had increased power whereas the internal power holders had lost it. If so, then one would have expected a greater loss of relationships for the latter, when it was the external power holders who showed the greater number of "dropouts" in the findings. If this reasoning is sound, then the second interpretation ("goals attract certain kinds of power holders") would seem more plausible.

This interpretation (that shifts in the structure of universities make it more difficult to "use" goals as a means of accumulating power) receives additional support from an inspection of the actual goals that have dropped out of the rankings of significant relationships. Note particularly those goals that dropped out of both columns (that is, that are no longer related to the power of external or internal power holders): Preserve Cultural Heritage, Keep Costs Down, Emphasize Undergraduate Instruction, and Increase or Maintain Prestige. Two of these goals might be regarded as bread-and-butter items (cost and undergraduate instruction) and two as frills (preserving the cultural heritage and increasing prestige). The dropouts might then be interpreted as showing that the degree of emphasis on frills no longer distinguishes universities in which external power holders are important from those in which internal power holders are important, probably because neither can afford to emphasize frills. On the other hand, bread-and-butter goals no longer distinguish the two kinds of universities precisely because both kinds must pay equal attention to those goals. The conclusion then is that both kinds of power holders are finding goals less easy to achieve, that the goals are, in that sense, manipulating them, rather than the reverse. It is analogous to a situation in which a highly responsive automobile runs so wildly out of control that the driver reacts to it, rather than the reverse. Others of the drop-out goals point in the same direction: Provide Student Activities and Preserve University Character (for external power holders), and Maintain Top Quality in All Programs (for internal power holders) seem to be types of goals that are likely to be regarded as frills in times of trouble (or else are temporarily put to one side). Similarly, the disappearance of the tendency of external power holders to de-emphasize the goal Give Faculty Maximum Opportunity to Pursue Careers and of internal power holders to emphasize the goal Reward for Contribution to Profession (rather than to the university) would point in the direction of turning in of interest to "local" problems (from more cosmopolitan perspectives). Finally, the dropping out of Protect Students' Right of Inquiry, Involve Students in University Government, and especially of Keep Harmony, hardly means that these have become unimportant—quite the reverse. They have disappeared as goals which distinguish universities with different kinds of power structures for the simple reason that those goals have become more important in *all* kinds of universities. Power holders find, in other words, that they have no choice but to implement them as best they can.

In spite of the number of dropouts, the goals that distinguish universities with different kinds of power structures, are sufficient in number to reject the hypothesis of chance generation of findings. At the 5 percent level of significance, we would anticipate only two or three of 47 goals to show up by chance, but the goals in the external power column come to at least four times that number, while those in the internal column come to more than seven times the chance expectation. How then, do the goals in universities with different kinds of power structures differ?

When we compare the goals that fall in the two columns in Table 25 with one another, a striking pattern emerges. In not one case does a goal appear in both columns with the same direction of emphasis, a phenomenon that was also true for all the findings in 1964 (see Gross, 1968, pp. 538 ff.). Either a goal appears in one column and not in the other (e.g., Produce Well-Rounded Student, which is de-emphasized in universities where external power holders are dominant, or Preserve Cultural Heritage, which is emphasized in universities where internal power holders are dominant),[12] or else goals falling in both columns are emphasized in diametrically opposed directions (e.g., Cultivate Students' Intellect, which is emphasized in universities where deans of liberal arts are comparatively dominant, and de-emphasized in universities where legislators are comparatively dominant).

Such a reversal, apart from its intrinsic interest, provides striking confirmation of our earlier finding that the internal and external power clusters show strong relationships with one another within each cluster, and strong negative relationships between the clusters.[13] The conclusion is that universities which are stratified

[12] Our language here is somewhat imprecise because of the complexity of the findings. Strictly speaking, what we should say is: In those universities which are stratified by the power of external power holders (using legislators as representatives of such power holders), then there is a coincidence of stratification by the goal Preserve Cultural Heritage. Such awkward language would come closer to describing the finding. In the interests of readability, we are adopting understandable prose, with a warning to the reader that he should first read the discussion of method in the earlier part of this chapter, as well as in Chapter 1.

[13] This is by no means an obvious conclusion which "follows," by logical implication, from the finding that the power holders are related to one another. Transitivity of findings may be stated as follows: If A implies B, and B implies C, then A implies C. But such transitivity holds only in cases where the relationships between A and B and B and C are near-certainties, or else where one can assume a causal (or asymmetrical) relationship (see Costner & Leik, 1964). Although our gammas are high, they would not justify any inference of being "near-certainties," and we can only speculate on causal direction from our data.

by power holders show patterned differences in goal emphasis. Or, in plain language, it makes a crucial difference for goals what kind of power structure a university exhibits, in comparison to other universities.

What, then, is the substantive nature of this "difference"? By inspection of the goal distribution in the two columns of Table 25 (upper part), we can speak of the goal structure differences as follows: If one stratifies universities by the perceived amount of power of external power holders (legislators, state government, citizens, and, to a less consistent extent, regents, and federal government), and also stratifies them by the perceived amount of power of internal power holders (deans of liberal arts, deans of professional schools, and chairmen, and, to a less consistent extent, faculty, students, and deans of graduate schools), one finds that the two stratified sets of universities are also stratified by goal emphasis in the way shown graphically in Table 26. Here we have organized the findings so that a positive gamma appears as a goal emphasis and a negative gamma as goal de-emphasis. The goal list in the high external power column shows a focus on the practical, traditional, land-grant goal structure—helping citizens and providing an education for all who may profit from it. On the other hand, these universities play down such student-expressive goals as cultivating the intellect, or affecting the student with the great ideas, or producing a well-rounded student. Students are not to be prepared for leadership positions (another elitist kind of goal), nor for careers as scholars and researchers. Most important for faculty, the goal of protecting academic freedom is de-emphasized.[14]

The contrast is evident in looking at the goals in the high internal power column. There we see emphasis on student-expressive goals, along with protecting academic freedom and the elitist goal of Accept Good Students Only. De-emphasized are service and applied functions, as well as relating the university to local needs and

[14] The goal Ensure Efficient Goal Attainment, which, as shown, is de-emphasized in places where legislators have high power, may seem puzzling. In full, the goal statement read: "Make sure the university is run by those selected according to their ability to attain the goals of the university in the most efficient manner possible." Although an immediate impression might be that legislators and state government would be concerned with efficiency, other data that we have suggest that respondents were picking up the concern in this goal with quality. (The goal is more emphasized in private and the more prestigious universities, for example.) Hence, the response appears to reflect a concern with quality, and concomitantly, the power to select administrators who are identified with university goals—that is, a greater ability to be selective in recruitment.

TABLE 26 *Power Across and goals Across: contrasting relationships*

	High external power	High internal power
Goals emphasized	37 Prepare students for useful careers 30 Assist citizens through extension programs 38 Provide community cultural leadership 11 Educate to utmost high school graduates	7 Cultivate students's intellect 16 Affect students with great ideas 8 Develop students' character 17 Train students for scholarship/research 18 Preserve cultural heritage 35 Accept good students only 4 Protect academic freedom 13 Give faculty maximum opportunity to pursue careers 46 Protect students' right of inquiry 47 Maintain top quality in important programs 28 Protect students' right of action 15 Keep up to date
Goals de-emphasized	7 Cultivate students' intellect 12 Produce well-rounded student 16 Affect students with great ideas 24 Prepare students for status/leadership 17 Train students for scholarship/research 35 Accept good students only 4 Protect academic freedom 21 Ensure efficient goal attainment	37 Prepare students for useful careers 39 Carry on applied research 30 Assist citizens through extension programs 38 Provide community cultural leadership 11 Educate to utmost high school graduates 44 Provide student activities 19 Satisfy area needs

serving as an "open door" to all qualified students. The contrast is most vividly drawn by noting goals that are emphasized in universities with one type of power structure *and* which are de-emphasized in those with the other kind of power structure. For example, Prepare Students for Useful Careers is emphasized in universities in which legislators have high comparative power and de-emphasized in universities in which deans of liberal arts have high internal power. If we set such goals down directly opposite one another, we see the following contrast:

High external power	High internal power
Prepare students for useful careers	*Cultivate students' intellect*
Assist citizens through extension programs	*Affect students with great ideas*
Provide community cultural leadership	*Train students for scholarship/ research*
Educate to utmost high school graduates	*Accept good students only*
	Protect academic freedom

The contrast is very impressive, suggesting strongly differing traditions and present atmospheres.[15] It is difficult to believe, then, that universities are becoming "more alike"—a very similar contrast was evident in 1964 (Gross & Grambsch, 1968), and it seems to show no sign of weakening.

Power Within and Goals Within
The examination of Power Across and Goals Across provides evidence in support of a hypothesis that universities are strongly stratified by those dimensions; universities found in the upper part of the distribution in degree of emphasis on a particular goal are also found in a predictable part of the distribution in which power holders are ranked. We turn next to the Power-Within–Goals-Within analysis, in which we examine the extent to which the stratification observed throughout the system is also present within each university. The findings are laid out in Table 27.

The first thing worth noting about Table 27 is that, in contrast to the previous table, there are very few dropouts—three for the external power cluster and four for the internal power cluster. Further, there are 12 new ones in the first group and 7 new ones in the second. Let us recall the distinction between Goals or Power Across and Goals or Power Within. The Across analysis refers to the position of a goal or power holder in the whole system of 68 universities. The Within analysis refers to the position of a goal or power holder within a particular university. In the previous section, we reported a rather large number of dropouts in the Across analysis, a finding we interpreted as meaning that implementing goals is not so dependable an avenue for accumulating power as it once was. We now discover that the Within analysis is not characterized by a large number of dropouts; quite the

---

[15] See the discussion of the "breakdown of consensus" in Trow (1972).

TABLE 27
Comparison of relationship of external power cluster (legislators, state government, citizens) and internal power cluster (deans of liberal arts, deans of professional schools, chairmen) to university goals: power Within and goals Within

Goals	External power (legislators)	Internal power (deans of liberal arts)
Output		
Student-expressive		
7 Cultivate students' intellect	−.799	.581
16 Affect students with great ideas	−.789	.498
36 Develop students' objectivity	−.847	
8 Develop students' character	−.481[a]	
Student-instrumental		
17 Train students for scholarship/ research	−.792	(+)[a b]
Research		
39 Carry on applied research	.743	−.643[a]
Direct service		
5 Provide special adult training	.519[a]	
30 Assist citizens through extension programs	.912	−.608
38 Provide community cultural leader- ship	.690[a]	−.543[a]
Support		
Adaptation		
31 Ensure favor of validating bodies	.771	
11 Educate to utmost high school graduates	.890	
35 Accept good students only	−.933	
19 Satisfy area needs	.700	−.500
Management		
41 Reward for contribution to profession		.653[a]
21 Ensure efficient goal attainment	−.531[a]	
Motivation		
4 Protect academic freedom	(−)[a b]	(+)[b]
13 Give faculty maximum opportunity to pursue careers	−.599	.524[a]
44 Provide student activities	.659	−.513
46 Protect students' right of inquiry	−.696[a]	.500
28 Protect students' right of action		.517[a]
6 Develop faculty loyalty in institution	−.546[a]	
Position		
22 Maintain top quality in all programs		−.701[a]

Goals	External power (legislators)	Internal power (deans of liberal arts)
47 Maintain top quality in important programs	$(-)^{ab}$	
32 Maintain balanced quality in all programs	$-.577^a$	
15 Keep up to date	$-.536^a$	
45 Increase or maintain prestige	$(-)^{ab}$	$(+)^{ab}$
23 Preserve institutional character	$-.541^a$	
Findings in 1964 no longer significant in 1971		
Student-expressive		
36 Develop students' objectivity		.773
Student-instrumental		
37 Prepare students for useful careers	.673	$-.650$
Direct service		
10 Disseminate new ideas	$-.514$	
18 Preserve cultural heritage		.549
Adaptation		
35 Accept good students only		.554
26 Keep costs down	.623	

[a]New finding in 1971. Not present in 1964.

[b]The device of indicating only the direction of a relationship (+ or −) has been adopted for those cases where zero cells in tables produce gammas of unity or minus unity. This is an anomaly of gamma and similar measures (including Q in 2 x 2 tables) which, in our case, follows from the skewness of distributions of certain goals.

NOTE: Negative values (−) indicates an emphasis at those universities where power Within *or* goals Within are low. See Appendix B.

reverse, there is a considerable number of new findings. This means that within universities, a rise of a power holder to influence over other power holders is associated more strongly than ever with a particular goal structure.

An interpretation is as follows. The ability to implement goals of the whole system does not assist a power holder in rising to the top of power within the system. (Or alternatively, being among the top power holders in the system does not mean that one's ability to influence the goal structure is enhanced.) In fact, the opportunity to use goals to increase power has declined since 1964. But what does make a difference is one's position vis-à-vis other power holders in the same university, and one's ability to influence the goal structure within the university. For example, being among the most powerful regents in American universities means less in 1971 than it did in 1964 in terms of the ability of such regents to affect the importance of, say, carrying on applied research than, say, on doing pure research at the University of X. But what has changed is what happens when the regents at the University of X are found to be superior in power to the faculty at the University of X. When that happens in 1971, there is a tendency, stronger than was the case in 1964, for such differential power to be associated with more emphasis on carrying on applied research than, say, on doing pure research at the University of X.

From another point of view, the contrast between the Across and Within findings so far discussed suggests a shifting of the power-goals struggle from the national to the local level. The system as a whole has, perhaps, become too complex to provide avenues for power accumulation through the goals of the system. Or perhaps the system as a whole has become less of a system. The continued cleavage we have reported between private and public universities and between universities at different levels of prestige may suggest a growing fragmentation that makes increasingly questionable the notion of only one status structure among the 68 universities. Hence, being among the most powerful deans of professional schools in the entire system means less than it used to, for the system is less amenable to influence. The picture is analogous to seeking to increase government revenue in a fragmented economy by increasing taxes. If the fragmentation means that persons can evade the tax collector, or get "off" by bribery, then the power of the central government to increase revenue is abridged.

Instead, deans can influence goals at the university where they work, if they are more powerful than the regents, for example. Again, we cannot say in what direction the causation will go— whether obtaining greater power over the regents means greater influence on a particular goal, or whether the emphasis on a particular goal provides the opportunity for the deans to accumulate power. In the previous section, we felt inclined toward the latter interpretation, and it may apply here also, though the reasons are less compelling. Our inference on causal direction was based partly on the greater number of dropouts among the external power holders, whereas here, of course, the difference between power holders is very slight. In any case, the more important point is that power and goals are more strongly related within universities in 1971 than they were in 1964.

We observe again the striking contrast in the direction of relationships between the two sets of power holders. That is, in every case, a goal emphasized in universities where one set of power holders dominates is either not emphasized or actually de-emphasized in the universities dominated by the other set of power holders. The argument for a powerful split within universities between the external and internal power holders gains additional force. It is true not only in the system as a whole but within universities.

The contrast is drawn for us in Table 28. Although there is overlap with the findings from the Across analysis, there are a number of new findings with rather different implications. In the list of goals associated with high external power, we find those associated with practical help to citizens and focusing on applied research. We also find a concern with pleasing client groups (Provide Community Cultural Leadership, Provide Student Activities, and Ensure Favor of Validating Bodies), as well as a distinct de-emphasis on maintenance of quality.[16]

In those where internal power holders dominate, we find the focus on student-expressive goals and a de-emphasis on the service-oriented goals (as we did in the Across analysis) but with a new concern for keeping clients happy. To be sure, there is a different interpretation of what constitutes "happiness": Protect Students'

---

[16] The goal Develop Faculty Loyalty in Institution (full statement: "Develop loyalty on the part of the faculty and staff to the university, rather than only to their own jobs or professional concerns") may seem out of place here; perhaps it is, since the finding is in large part a statistical artifact of a skewed distribution. The table was as follows:

| Develop faculty | Power of legislators | | | |
loyalty in institution	Low	Medium	High	Sum
Low	21	6	38	65
Medium	2	0	1	3
Sum	23	6	39	68

As is obvious, the goal is highly skewed, 65 of 68 universities ranking it in the bottom third of the goals at the university. Hence, the negative relationship is largely an artifact of the "accident" that 39 of the 68 universities rank the power of legislators in the upper third of the distribution at the university, thus producing a preponderance of discordant pairs and hence a negative gamma. For this reason, it might be defensible to regard this finding as misleading and not record it. We decided against this option, but feel that its marginal status justifies a lack of comment on any substantive significance of the "finding."

TABLE 28 *Power Within and goals Within: contrasting relationships*

		High external power		*High internal power*
	39	Carry on applied research	7	Cultivate students' intellect
	30	Assist citizens through extension programs	16	Affect students with great ideas
			17	Train students for scholarship/research
	38	Provide community cultural leadership	4	Protect academic freedom
Goals emphasized	44	Provide student activities	13	Give faculty maximum opportunity to pursue careers
	5	Provide special adult training		
	31	Ensure favor of validating bodies	46	Protect students' right of inquiry
	11	Educate to utmost high school graduates	45	Increase or maintain prestige
			41	Reward for contribution to profession
			28	Protect students' right of action

	7	Cultivate students' intellect	39	Carry on applied research
	16	Affect students with great ideas	30	Assist citizens through extension programs
	17	Train students for scholarship/research		
	4	Protect academic freedom	38	Provide community cultural leadership
	13	Give faculty maximum opportunity to pursue careers	44	Provide student activities
	46	Protect students' right of inquiry	19	Satisfy area needs
	45	Increase or maintain prestige		
	36	Develop students' objectivity		
Goals de-emphasized	8	Develop students' character		
	35	Accept good students only		
	22	Maintain top quality in all programs		
	47	Maintain top quality in important programs		
	32	Maintain balanced quality in all programs		
	21	Ensure efficient goal attainment		
	6	Develop faculty loyalty in institution		
	15	Keep up to date		
	23	Preserve institutional character		

Right of Inquiry and Protect Students' Right of Action are stressed, and Provide Student Activities and Provide Community Cultural Leadership are deemphasized; Give Faculty Maximum Opportunity to Pursue Careers and Reward for Contribution to Profession are also emphasized, as opposed to rewarding the faculty contributions to the institution. We can tabulate the maximal contrast between goals emphasized in settings with one set of dominant power holders *and* deemphasized (rather than simply not appearing as findings) in settings with the other set of power holders as follows:

High external power	*High internal power*
Carry on applied research	*Cultivate students' intellect*
Assist citizens through extension programs	*Affect students with great ideas*
Provide community cultural leadership	*Train students for scholarship/ research*
Provide student activities	*Give faculty maximum opportunity to pursue careers*
	Protect students' right of inquiry
	Increase or maintain prestige
	Protect academic freedom

In sum, where legislators, state government, citizens, regents, and other external power groups have greater power than chairmen, deans, and faculty, one is likely to find goals of a practical character, with a considerable thrust on placating reference or client groups. On the other hand, where the chairmen of academic departments, deans, and faculty have greater power than legislators, state government, etc., one is likely to find an emphasis on goals associated with the classical ideas of a liberal education, along with a concern for ensuring that students have freedom to pursue their own interests. The faculty, moreover, should have the same rights, even when those rights may be opposed to the interests of the university at which they are employed. It is important to bear in mind that these findings emerged from the statements of *both* administrators and faculty. In Chapter 5 we consider the question of whether the results would be different if those two groups were separated out.

The last two comparative tables (Tables 29 and 30) may be discussed together, since their contribution of new information becomes clearer when the tables are related to one another. Both tables exhibit a modest number of dropouts from the 1964 findings which are virtually balanced by the number of new findings. The

TABLE 29 Comparison of external power cluster (legislators, state government, citizens) and internal power cluster (deans of liberal arts, deans of professional schools, chairmen) to university goals: Power across and goals within	Goals	External power (legislators)	Internal power (deans of liberal arts)
	Output		
	Student-expressive		
	7 *Cultivate students' intellect*	—.598	.710[c]
	16 *Affect students with great ideas*	—.479	.617[a]
	36 *Develop students' objectivity*	—.563	.655
	8 *Develop students' character*	—.533[b]	
	Student-instrumental		
	37 *Prepare students for useful careers*		—.521[ac]
	17 *Train students for scholarship/research*		.745[ac]
	Research		
	39 *Carry on applied research*	.604	—.664[c]
	Direct service		
	30 *Assist citizens through extension programs*	.516	—.739
	38 *Provide community cultural leadership*	.488[a]	
	18 *Preserve cultural heritage*		.674[ac]
	Support		
	Adaptation		
	31 *Ensure favors of validating bodies*	.551[b]	—.671[c]
	11 *Educate to utmost high school graduates*	.617	—.582[c]
	35 *Accept good students only*	—.826	.660[c]
	19 *Satisfy area needs*	.487	—.617[c]
	Management		
	42 *Emphasize undergraduate instruction*		—.604[c]
	Motivation		
	4 *Protect academic freedom*		(+)[d]
	13 *Give faculty maximum opportunity to pursue careers*		.624[c]

		External power (legislators)	Internal power (deans of liberal arts)
TABLE 29 *(continued)* Goals			
44	Provide student activities	.449	−.698
46	Protect students' right of inquiry	−.478	.692
6	Develop faculty loyalty in institution	−.704[ab]	
Position			
22	Maintain top quality in all programs	−.507[a]	(+)[dc]
47	Maintain top quality in important programs	−.556[a]	
15	Keep up to date		.484[c]
45	Increase or maintain prestige	−.556[a]	.483[a]
23†	Preserve institutional character	−.551[b]	

Findings in 1964 no longer significant in 1971

Student-instrumental

37	Prepare students for useful careers	.703	

Research

25	Carry on pure research	.511	

Direct service

5	Provide special adult training		−.332
10	Disseminate new ideas	−.495	
18	Preserve cultural heritage	−.575	.498

Adaptation

40	Ensure confidence of contributors	.739	
26	Keep costs down	.542	−.616

Management

41	Reward for contribution to profession		.530
21	Ensure efficient goal attainment	.561	

Motivation

13	Give faculty maximum opportunity to pursue careers	−.525	

Position

22	Maintain top quality in all programs		.618

[a] New findings in 1971. Not present in 1964.

[b] Goal occurring in external power list on this table but not occurring in Table 30.

[c] Goal occurring in internal power list on this table but not occurring in Table 30.

[d] Direction of relationship shown for special cases where zero cells produce gammas of 1.

NOTE: Negative values (−) indicate emphasis at universities where power Across or goals Within are low. See Appendix B.

	Goals	External power (legislators)	Internal power (deans of liberal arts)
	Output		
	Student-expressive		
7	Cultivate students' intellect	—.783	
16	Affect student with great ideas	—.713	.513
36	Develop students' objectivity	—.756[a]	.533
	Student-instrumental		
17	Train students for scholarship/research	—.689[b]	
9	Cultivate student's taste	.489[ab]	
	Research		
25	Carry on pure research	—.465[ab]	
39	Carry on applied research	.532[a]	
	Direct service		
5	Provide special adult training	.541[ab]	
30	Assist citizens through extension programs	.911	—.581
38	Provide community cultural leadership	.632[a]	—.612[c]
18	Preserve cultural heritage	—.482[ab]	
	Support		
	Adaptation		
11	Educate to utmost high school graduates	.950	
35	Accept good students only	—.838	
19	Satisfy area needs	.671	
	Management		
3	Encourage graduate work	—.652[b]	
21	Ensure efficient goal attainment	—.621[ab]	
	Motivation		
4	Protect academic freedom	—.745[b]	.501
13	Give faculty maximum opportunity to pursue careers	—.568[b]	
44	Provide student activities	.540	—.582
46	Protect students' rights of inquiry	—.605	.499
	Position		
22	Maintain top quality in all programs	—.630	
47	Maintain top quality in important programs	—.678	
45	Increase or maintain prestige	—.522	

TABLE 30 Comparison of relationship of external power cluster (legislators, power within state government, citizens) and internal power cluster (deans of liberal arts, deans of professional schools chairmen) to university goals: power Within and goals Across

Goals	External power (legislators)	Internal power (deans of liberal arts)
Findings in 1964 no longer significant in 1971		
Student-expressive		
7 *Cultivate students' intellect*		.758
Student-instrumental		
37 *Prepare students for useful careers*	.469	
Direct service		
10 *Dissemination of new ideas*	−.527	−.533
18 *Preserve cultural heritage*		.613
Adaptation		
31 *Ensure favor of validating bodies*		−.642
11 *Educate to utmost high school graduates*		−.514
35 *Accept good students only*		.550
26 *Keep costs down*	.562	
Management		
20 *Involve students in university government*	.582	
12 *Keep harmony*	.480	
42 *Emphasize undergraduate instruction*	.585	
Position		
22 *Maintain top quality in all programs*		.530
47 *Maintain top quality in important programs*		.547
15 *Keep up to date*	−.469	
23 *Preserve institutional character*	−.487	

[a] New finding in 1971. Not present in 1964.
[b] Goal occurring in external power list on this table but not occurring in Table 29.
[c] Goal occurring in internal power list on this table but not occurring in Table 29.
NOTE: Negative values (−) indicate an emphasis at universities where power Within *or* goals Across are low. See Appendix B.

pattern of reversal of findings for the two sets of power holders comes through again in both tables. This tendency seems to hold whether power and goals are measured internally or externally and whether one is measured externally while the other is measured internally. Given the possibility of measurement error, as well as the crudeness of our variables (allowing only three ranks for power or goals—low, medium and high), we come away impressed with the persistence of the contrast between the relationships of the two sets of power holders and university goals.

When we compare the actual goals (Table 31 and Table 32), there are no surprises, the picture being very similar to Table 28. In settings where external power holders are perceived as having high power, there is the concern with practical help to citizens and applied research, a deemphasis on quality, and a care with keeping client groups satisfied. Internal power holders are found associated with student-expressive goals, protecting students' rights, and concern for the careers of the faculty.

TABLE 31   *Power Across and goals Within: contrasting relationships*

		High external power		*High internal power*
	39	Carry on applied research	7	Cultivate students' intellect
	30	Assist citizens through extension programs	16	Affect students with great ideas
			36	Develop students' objectivity
	31	Ensure favor of validating bodies	35	Accept good students only
	11	Educate to utmost high school graduates	46	Protect students' right to inquiry
Goals emphasized	44	Provide student activities	45	Increase or maintain prestige
	19	Satisfy area needs	23	Preserve institutional character
	38	Provide community cultural leadership	17	Train students for scholarship/research
			10	Disseminate new ideas
			4	Protect academic freedom
			13	Give faculty maximum opportunity to pursue careers
	7	Cultivate students' intellect	39	Carry on applied research
	16	Affect students with great ideas	30	Assist citizens through extension programs
	36	Develop students' objectivity		
	35	Accept good students only	31	Ensure favor of validating bodies
	46	Protect students' right of inquiry	11	Educate to utmost high school graduates
Goals de-emphasized	45	Increase or maintain prestige	44	Provide student activities
	8	Develop students' character	10	Satisfy area needs
	22	Maintain top quality in all programs	37	Prepare students for useful careers
	47	Maintain top quality in important programs	42	Emphasize undergraduate instruction
	6	Develop faculty loyalty in institution		
	23	Preserve institutional character		

TABLE 32 *Power Within and goals Across: contrasting relationships*

		High external power		High internal power
Goals emphasized	30	Assist citizens through extention programs	16	Affect students with great ideas
	38	Provide community cultural leadership	36	Develop students' objectivity
	44	Provide student activities	4	Protect academic freedom
	9	Cultivate students' taste	46	Protect students' right of inquiry
	39	Carry on applied research		
	11	Educate to utmost high school graduates		
	19	Satisfy area needs		
Goals de-emphasized	16	Affect students with great ideas	30	Assist citizens through extension programs
	36	Develop students' objectivity	38	Provide community cultural leadership
	4	Protect academic freedom	44	Provide student activities
	46	Protect students' right of inquiry		
	7	Cultivate students' intellect		
	17	Train students for scholarship/research		
	25	Carry on pure research		
	18	Preserve cultural heritage		
	35	Accept good students only		
	13	Give faculty maximum opportunity to pursue careers		
	22	Maintain top quality in all programs		
	47	Maintain top quality in all important programs		
	3	Encourage graduate work		
	21	Ensure efficient goal attainment		
	45	Increase or maintain prestige		

But a new finding emerges if we go back to Tables 29 and 30 and compare them directly. When we take note of the goals found on one table, but not on the other, an interesting contrast emerges. We have indicated with a *c* the goals associated with external power holders which appear on the one table but not on the other, and have indicated with a *d* those goals correspondingly associated with internal power holders. As can be seen, on Table 29, there are 13 goals marked with a *d* compared with only 1 such goal on

Table 30. That is, when internal power holders (deans, chairmen, faculty) are among the most powerful in the whole university system, we find a strong association with the internal goals of each university. When we look at those goals marked with a ‡ on Table 29, an opposite tendency is exhibited, for there are 4 so marked, compared with 9 on Table 30. Interpreted, this means that when external power holders (state government, legislators, citizens, regents) are in universities in which they have greater power than deans, chairmen, or faculty, there is a strong association with the goals of the university system. The direction of causation can only be speculated upon. Either these external power holders use their power to modify goal emphasis so strongly that the position of the university in comparison to other universities on goal emphasis is affected, or else those universities already stratified by goal emphasis tend to attract external power holders who dominate the internal power holders. In any case, the major point is that external power holders seem to have their impact on the relationship of goals to one another Across universities—and that is a very serious effect indeed. On the other hand, internal power holders seem only to be able to affect goals when they are among the most powerful in the whole system. That is, when the deans, for example, fall in the upper third of the distribution of universities, only then can they affect the goals and, even then, it is the relationship of goals within their own universities that is affected. Being able to affect the relationship of Goals Within is not so impressive as affecting Goals Across, as the external power holders are able to do. To give an example, if the regents at the University of Minnesota are more powerful than the deans of professional schools there (as they are perceived), one finds that encouraging graduate work is depressed below the extent to which it is emphasized at, say, UCLA. In other words, the goal is depressed a great deal. On the other hand, it takes a situation in which the deans of professional schools at the University of Minnesota would be perceived as among the most powerful in all 68 universities for any association with goals to occur, and then the association is with, say, increasing the encouragement of graduate work over emphasis on undergraduate instruction within the University of Minnesota.[17]

Finally, if one inspects the goals themselves, the following clus-

---

[17] This conclusion refers of course only to the comparison of Tables 29 and 30. As Tables 25 and 27 show, there are other relationships with Goals Across.

ters occur. The goals found where external power holders dominate the others within universities involve making the student
into a wise consumer and catering to the educational desires of the
(nonregular, nondaytime) adult, with attendant de-emphasis on research and graduate work, reduced concern for facilitating faculty
professionalism, and reduction in concern for academic freedom.
On the other hand, the goals found where internal power holders
(deans, chairmen, faculty) are among the most powerful of their
kind in the whole university system involve a great concern for
prestige, keeping up to date, disseminating new ideas, cultivating
students' intellect, and assisting pure research, along with a de-
emphasis on preparing students for practical careers. There is
a focus on quality and elitism in admission policy, with little attention to undergraduate instruction, and at the same time an emphasis on assisting the faculty to advance in their careers. Again
the two pictures are strikingly different.

POWER AND GOALS IN AMERICAN UNIVERSITIES In turning to the examination of the power structure of universities, we shift from description to control, from a chronicling of what
has changed to a deeper appreciation of the persons and forces that
make change. Such a shift in perspective provides clues on how
we can manipulate goals so that they are more consonant with
values, or how we can engineer change rather than merely respond
to drift.

We found the rank ordering of power holders in 1971 to be practically identical with that in 1964. At the top were the president,
regents, and vice-president, followed by deans, with parents,
citizens, and students at the bottom. Faculty were in the middle,
but above chairmen, suggesting that the ranking is not a mere
listing of persons by official positions. There was very little difference in rank order by type of university (size, prestige, location,
productivity), except for type of control, with legislators and state
government unsurprisingly ranking higher in public universities
and sources of large private grants ranking a little higher in private
universities. On the whole, the power structure of American universities seemed remarkably uniform from university to university.
Whether this is due to common historical forces, or whether to the
tendency of universities to imitate one another, we cannot say.

Concurrent with this finding ran a strong tendency for persons
to perceive that certain offices or groups had changed in power
absolutely. In particular, students, regents, legislators, and state

government were thought to have increased their power to a greater extent than administrators (president, vice-presidents, deans), while the power of chairmen was thought to have actually declined. Put alongside the actual lack of substantial change in relative position, this finding suggests that tiny changes were so unexpected as to be considered remarkable. For example, students are felt to have changed the most, yet they retain their position near the bottom of the distribution. On the other hand, regents are also felt to have increased power. But they were already next to the top in 1964 and remained there in 1971. Hence, one imagines that respondents felt the regents' power to be so large that even small increments can appear as enormous. Most interesting was the perception that the faculty had increased its power—a finding we attribute to the overall improvement in wages and working conditions that faculty have enjoyed, along with the unrecognized tendency of faculty to support student protest and to profit by the general loosening of campus behavioral norms.

When we examined the relationship of power holders to one another, we found two clusters. One cluster we termed external, for it consists of legislators, state government, citizens, regents, federal government, and parents; a second cluster we called internal, for it embraces chairmen, deans (including deans of professional schools), and faculty. The alignment of deans of professional schools with deans of liberal arts and faculty was striking and suggested a different coalition than many faculty think is the case. In turn, the clustering strongly suggested that power in universities is not a zero-sum variable. That is, because one group has more, it does not follow that another group has less. Powerful deans are not found in universities with weak faculties: quite the reverse. A powerful set of deans is usually found along with a powerful faculty, as a powerful dean of liberal arts is found along with a powerful set of departmental chairmen. One conclusion is that faculties may well maintain their power only when deans and chairmen have the power to provide proper conditions, and that may require that deans and chairmen have a great deal of power indeed. Lest faculty draw too much comfort from this finding, it should be pointed out that power is not a zero-sum for external power holders either: having strong regents or trustees does not necessarily deprive the federal government of power.

The relationship of power to goals produced important findings.

When we examined the relationship of power to goals across all universities, we found there was a considerable drop in the sheer number of relationships since 1964. Goals seem to be more complex and hence more difficult to achieve, or else they provide less opportunity than they used to as an avenue by which potential power seekers may accumulate power. A major reason seems to be a decline in frills and a need for all power holders (external and internal) to give their energies to bread-and-butter goals. But there remains a major variation in goals between the two kinds of power holders. Those universities falling in the top part of the distribution of external power holders are also those found stratified in such a way as to emphasize the practical, land-grant type of goals. In turn, where one examines the stratification by internal power holders, a wholly different set of system goals emerges—those associated with the liberal arts, with protecting academic freedom, and with protecting the quality and prestige of the university.

The examination of power and goals within universities produced a similar set of contrasts, along with goals which emphasize the need to placate citizens and other "outsiders," on the one hand, and the need to placate students (through providing the right to inquire and rights of political action) and faculty (through providing opportunities for them to pursue their professional careers), on the other hand. Since the number of findings did not drop from 1971 (as it did in the Across analysis of the whole system), we suggested that power had shifted from the system level to the local level. Legislators, regents, and citizens were engaged in struggles with deans, chairmen, and faculty which had major effects on the structure of goals within each university. Hence, there was more variability among universities in that impact and possibly the beginnings of a fragmenting of the whole system of universities.

In the end, an examination of further findings led us to the conclusion that a shift in the power of external power holders was likely to have a greater effect on goals than would a corresponding shift in power of internal power holders. For example, if regents were to increase their power over deans, the effect on goals would be considerable. To have a similar effect, deans would have to increase their power not simply over the local regents but increase it to the point where they were among the most powerful deans in the whole system of universities. When we note that the set of goals associated with external power holders is strongly opposed to the set of goals associated with internal power holders, the implications of this finding are serious. The power of deans, chairmen, and faculty are found associated with practically the same set of goals, and those are quite different from those associated with regents, legislators, and state government. Before concluding that these internal power holders are in fact "allies," however, we must examine their goal perceptions and values. This we turn to in Chapter 5.

5. Faculty and Administration: Allies or Opponents?

The examination of university power structures had led to the conclusion that the major cleavage in power to influence university goals is one that pits "outsiders" against "insiders," rather than the celebrated split between faculty and administrators. Arrayed on one side, we found legislators, state government, citizens as a group, regents, federal government, and parents of students. Where the power of any one of these persons or categories was found to be high, there was a tendency (usually strong) for the power of other persons or categories in the same set to be powerful, and similarly for the situation in which the power of any one was low. Arrayed on the other side, we found deans of liberal arts, deans of professional schools, chairmen of academic departments, the faculty, and students. The same tendency for the power of any one to be associated with the power of any other was found.

More important for our purposes was the further finding that quite distinct sets of goals were associated with the power of the two sets of persons or categories. Where outsiders were powerful, goals focused on service and traditional land-grant functions, such as providing adult education and keeping the university an open-door institution for all who might qualify, and manifested a concern with satisfying the needs and earning the approval of sources of funds and validating groups. Where insiders were powerful, traditional liberal arts goals were emphasized, along with a strong feeling that faculty professionalism should be promoted and students should be given rights to inquire into whatever they were interested in and even to engage in political activities.

While one could argue that this split is not inherently surprising, its strength is remarkable, for we were unable to uncover a *single* finding which suggested a goal shared by the two sets of power holders. Because over the last seven years the outsiders, who constitute the major source of funds and other resources, have become increasingly hostile to the insiders, such a strong conflict in goals and the lack of common goals offer little comfort to those who hope for rapprochement or some common ground for peaceful negotiations.

But the obverse of this conclusion is the surprising discovery of so much common ground among faculty and administrators. Where faculty are found to be powerful, so are deans and so are chairmen, a finding which was true in both 1964 and 1971. We call this discovery "surprising" because of the frequent assumption that administration is regarded as being of lesser value than teaching and research. Some part of this antagonism is an expression of the celebrated "local-cosmopolitan" distinction[1] by which the administrators in professionally oriented organizations (Etzioni, 1964, Chap. 8) are regarded as the "servants" of those who carry out the professional functions (professors, doctors, scientists). The downgrading of administration in universities often takes the form of assuming that amateurs can do the work, on a part-time basis, as Riesman (1970, p. 76) observes in the following quotation:

. . . what is wanted (for a university administrator) is a Ph.D. who temporarily gives up his profession to become a part-time amateur manager, and either actually hates such work or appears to despise it.

Indeed the cult of the amateur characterizes American academic life in many of its aspects . . . this is . . . evident in the case of administration. There is a populist element in the American academic's scorn for the specialized understandings and tasks of administration, reminiscent of the attitude toward high civil servants in the Jacksonian era, and part of an old American tradition which makes us assume that a Senator, who has never run anything larger than his own office, can become an instant executive.

Rourke and Brooks (1964, pp. 156–157) put the matter as follows: ". . . the perennial dream of many an academician is that of a university run entirely by professors—a citadel of learning

---

[1] Originally developed in studies of the local community but now frequently applied to the presumed conflict between the orientation of professional employees to their profession on the one hand or their employer on the other. "Administrators" would be held to be by definition oriented to satisfying their employer, whereas faculty members would be oriented to the values of their profession. The concept has been much criticized in recent years (see Grimes & Berger, 1970), but still retains its general validity (see Berger & Grimes, 1973).

undisturbed by the presence of registrars, business managers, or even deans and presidents." This attitude seems not to be a recent one, attributable to the increase in numbers of administrators on most campuses, but rather to have been present from the time when American universities took on their modern form in the 1890s (see Veysey, 1965, pp. 391 ff.).

Although it may not seem noteworthy that faculty adopt such a view of administration, it is worth noting that administrators themselves apparently share this view of their activities. Lunsford (1970, p. 145), for example, cites a 1967 interview study of top campus executives who are reported as seeing themselves ". . . as having drifted into administration half-willingly, often because a higher official had called them to take on institutional responsibility." Of course, such reports refer to public expressions of views which may mask private views, but some part of administrators' diffidence is related to their ambivalence about power. In the United States generally, the naked pursuit of power is frowned upon, so that administrators generally tend to deny ambitiousness, except when it can be justified as seeking to render "service." Such diffidence is particularly likely to be expressed and felt by university administrators, most of whom are, after all, former members of the faculty. Such persons commonly deny any long-term interest in an administrative career, describing themselves as temporarily "helping out," soon to return to their true loves—research and teaching. Whether such declarations can be taken at face value, or whether instead they constitute myths with institutional and self-justifying functions (as Lunsford, 1970, argues)[2] they contribute to the willingness of academics generally to assume that their values and interests reflect a fundamental difference in perspective between the strictly academic on the one hand and the administrative on the other.

Our findings, then, suggest that this split, if it exists, is much less impressive than the cleavage that arrays faculty and administrators against outsiders. At least faculty and administrators appear to have much more in common than is generally assumed. But to show that power and goals are related is not crucial to this issue. For there may remain differences between faculty and administration which are merely dwarfed by the size of the differences

[2] Lunsford's report of an empirical study of 526 university administrators presents a picture of administrators as ambivalent on the subject of power, and employing various kinds of rhetoric in articulating their own positions vis-à-vis "politics" and "pressures" (Lunsford, 1970, p. 131).

both groups have with outsiders. Further, to show that power and goals are so strongly related is still only indirect evidence for a common interest among faculty and administrators. It relies on the following assumptions: If faculty power rises, so does emphasis on liberal arts goals. In turn, if deans' power rises, so does emphasis on liberal arts goals. Hence, since the increase in the power of either results in a similar effect, the original power holders must be similar. But, of course, a similar effect can be produced by very different causes. Hence, we turn here to a direct comparison between administrators and faculty.

The most serious source of possible conflict between role groups in an organization would stem from differences in perception of reality.[3] Given that persons occupy different positions, we should anticipate the possibility that they will see things differently. Such variations cannot be simply dismissed as "bias" in the face of some single "true" picture. An acting assistant professor in a department of English will actually be exposed to very different stimuli than will the dean of the school of home economics. The reports that each makes are both true, assuming each reports accurately what he sees. We shall examine the perceptions of reality of administrators and faculty in the two areas of major concern to our study: goals and power. The questions then will be: Do administrators and faculty see the goals of the university differently? and Do they see the power structure differently? If differences are large, we may anticipate serious difficulties in negotiating to settle such differences, and even in the viability of the whole organization.

Whatever the results on perceptual differences show, we will next wish to know whether faculty and administrators differ in their values. We are not concerned with values in general (aesthetic, political, or personal) but with values relevant to our main concern—the goals of universities. Hence, we will be interested in whether administrators and faculty differ in their goal preferences, in whether they agree on the amount of emphasis that *should be* given to the various university goals. Such differences, if large, would suggest important cleavages.

---

[3] The theme that ideas and values may be reflections of one's social position or interests is, of course, a very old one, going back at least to Plato's metaphor of the cave shadows. Later writers, including Marx, Spencer, and Mannheim, as well as many of the German idealists, developed the theme, and, in recent times, the ethnomethodologists have made important contributions to this aspect of the sociology of knowledge. For representative treatments, see Dreitzel (1970) and Douglas (1970).

We can anticipate our findings at this point: The differences in both perceptions and values are found to be very small. That leads us to a final consideration. Even if the differences are small, do they make a difference? Our approach to that question lies in examining the responses to a series of questions on faculty members' and administrators' morale. We asked such questions as whether they felt they had enough power to get their work done; whether they felt, all things considered, that they would leave their jobs for a different one in another university, or even leave academia altogether. An examination of responses to these questions will help us assess whether existing differences in perceptions and values make a difference for the person's feelings about his work and his commitment to continuing in the university system.

Our role groups will be faculty and administrators, of course. However, it is often worthwhile to split the administrators' category into two subgroups—higher administrators (deans and above) and lower administrators (chairmen of academic departments, directors of research projects, or other units of study).

PERCEPTIONS
OF GOALS

Somewhat different techniques were employed for comparing role groups in 1964 than were employed in 1971. In 1964, gammas were calculated, which however turned out to be very small (none reached the 5 percent level of significance). For that reason, a simpler method to highlight differences among the role groups was employed in 1971—a comparison of goal ranking, as shown in Table 33. In Table 33, the goals are listed in the order in which they were ranked by the higher administrators (deans and above). The other columns in the table show the difference in rank positions between the various role groups, the direction of the difference being shown as "higher rank minus lower rank." For example, the second column shows the rank differences between higher and lower administrators. For the goal Protect Academic Freedom, there is no difference between higher and lower administrators—that is, both ranked it in first place. For the goal next in order, Maintain Top Quality In Important Programs, the rank assigned by the higher administrators minus the rank assigned by the lower administrators is −1. In this case, higher administrators ranked it second, and lower administrators ranked it third. Similarly, in the next column, the figures show the result of the subtraction: rank assigned by lower administrators minus rank assigned by faculty. The last column shows the results: rank assigned by higher administrators minus rank assigned by faculty. Of course, a higher

TABLE 33 *Differences in goal rankings by role groups, 1971*

Goal		Goal as ranked by higher administrators (H)	Rank differences between higher (H) and lower (L) administrators	Rank differences between lower (L) administrators and faculty (F)	Rank differences between higher administrators (H) and faculty (F)
4	Protect academic freedom	1	0	−1	−1
47	Maintain top quality in important programs	2	−1	−1	−2
45	Increase or maintain prestige	3	1	−1	0
43	Involve faculty in university government	4	−3	−9	−12
40	Ensure confidence of contributors	5	1	3	4
17	Train students for scholarship/ research	6	1	−1	0
25	Carry on research	7	−2	−1	−3
15	Keep up to date	8	2	−3	−1
22	Maintain top quality in all programs	9	−1	−3	−4
46	Protect students' right of inquiry	10	−1	−4	−5
7	Cultivate students' intellect	11	−3	−5	−8
10	Disseminate new ideas	12	0	0	0
31	Ensure favor of validating bodies	13	5	3	8
1	Hold staff in face of inducements	14	−5	−9	−14
13	Give faculty maximum opportunity to pursue careers	15	−5	−3	−8
37	Prepare students for useful careers	16	3	6	9
21	Ensure efficient goal attainment	17	1	−1	0
36	Develop students' objectivity	18	−3	−10	−13
38	Provide community cultural leadership	19	2	6	8
39	Carry on applied research	20	5	7	12
33	Run university democratically	21	−3	−9	−12
41	Reward for contribution to profession	22	−1	−3	−4
18	Preserve cultural heritage	23	1	−2	−1
26	Keep costs down	24	6	4	10
34	Prepare students for citizenship	25	−1	−1	−2

Goal	Goal as ranked by higher administrators (H)	Rank differences between higher (H) and lower (L) administrators	Rank differences between lower (L) administrators and faculty (F)	Rank differences between higher administrators (H) and faculty (F)
3 Encourage graduate work	26	−3	9	6
2 Let will of faculty prevail	27	−5	−7	−12
44 Provide student activities	28	3	7	10
29 Produce well-rounded students	29	2	2	4
20 Involve students in university government	30	2	−4	−2
27 Reward for contribution to institution	31	−3	−3	−6
16 Affect students with great ideas	32	1	−3	−2
24 Prepare students for status/ leadership	33	3	8	11
19 Satisfy area needs	34	1	12	13
32 Maintain balanced quality in all programs	35	0	5	5
14 Develop pride in university	36	−1	2	1
28 Protect students' right of action	37	−1	0	−1
30 Assist citizens through extension programs	38	2	7	9
8 Develop students' character	39	0	−6	−6
35 Accept good students only	40	−2	−2	−4
12 Keep harmony	41	−4	3	−1
5 Provide special adult training	42	−2	8	6
6 Develop faculty loyalty in institution	43	0	−3	−3
11 Educate to utmost high school graduates	44	4	1	3
42 Emphasize undergraduate instruction	45	4	−2	2
23 Preserve institutional character	46	0	6	6
9 Cultivate students' taste	47	0	0	0

NOTE: *Rank correlation* $r_{HL} = .981$ H = Deans and higher administrators
                                 $r_{LF} = .928$ L = Directors and chairmen
                                 $r_{HF} = .979$ F = Faculty

number in a column refers to a lower rank (that is, 1 means first and 47 means last).

As stated earlier, in 1964 we related these rankings through gamma, with the result of very low gammas. In 1971, we adopted the simpler device of calculating rank correlations, which are shown at the bottom of Table 33. As can be seen, the three rank correlations (higher compared to lower, lower compared to faculty, and higher compared to faculty) are all extremely high. That is, in both 1964 and 1971, administrators and faculty tended to rank the goals in a highly similar manner. Bearing in mind that we are dealing here with goal perceptions, this result suggests that, in spite of their differing positions on the campus, administrators report that the university is giving about the same emphasis to any given goal as the faculty report. There seems then to be little variation in perceptions of reality, as far as goals are concerned.

Before considering those few goals that do vary substantially, it is worth asking whether the averaging over 68 institutions represented in Table 33 holds up under multivariate analysis. As an easily understood form of such analysis, we present Table 34. Here we present rank correlations for the 68 universities for each of the four prestige levels, and for private and public universities. The rank correlations remain exceedingly high, though there is some slight tendency for the correlations to decline with lower prestige, and for those in public universities to be lower than those in private universities. If this is a reliable finding, then we can say that if there are differences in perception, they are more pronounced among role groups in institutions of lower prestige. (The public-private difference is perhaps an artifact of the correlation—which is low, but positive—between private status and prestige.) Why this should be (if it is the case) can only be answered by further research. Here we might speculate that one of the effects of

	Prestige level				Type of control	
	1 (top)	2	3	4	Private	Public
High administrators related to low administrators	.970	.974	.960	.951	.986	.952
Low administrators related to faculty	.933	.950	.927	.900	.945	.929
High administrators related to faculty	.958	.921	.870	.812	.949	.825

TABLE 34 Rank correlations among role groups in perceptions of university goals, by university prestige, and type of control

prestige is a great uniformity in goals and a greater homogeneity of personnel. The prestige of universities, as we noted in Chapter 3, is measured by asking academics how they rank their colleagues at other universities. Since we are looking at a national sample, such ranking will inevitably tend to reflect universal standards, or at least highly visible ones. Such important interuniversity variables as local reputation, service to local professions, or contributions to local problems must go unrecognized, because they are not widely known. Such a focus on national standards will force evaluators to pay attention only to indicators which have national standing—such as publications, research contributions, leading positions in national scientific societies, and the like. Hence those universities which score high on those variables will, by their very concentration on what it takes to score high, be more homogeneous in makeup. It seems impossible, even for the top universities, to be both of top quality and offer the whole range of services to the local community that other institutions are able to provide.

If we now turn back to Table 33, we may consider those goals ranked differently by the three role groups. The situation in 1971 is not appreciably different from that in 1964. If we adopt as a measure of "substantial" rank difference a difference of nine or more positions, then the following goals were ranked substantially differently by administrators and faculty in 1971. Administrators gave higher ranking than faculty to the following goals:

43 Involve Faculty in University Government

1 Hold Staff in Face of Inducements

36 Develop Students' Objectivity

33 Run University Democratically

On the other hand, faculty gave higher ranking than administrators to the following goals:

39 Carry on Applied Research

3 Encourage Graduate Work

44 Provide Student Activities

24 Prepare Students for Status/Leadership

19 Satisfy Area Needs

30 Assist Citizens Through Extension Programs

Examining these few goals which are seen differently by administrators and faculty, there is little to occasion comment. One would expect that administrators would be more keenly conscious of efforts to Involve Faculty in University Government, for example, since it is the faculty who would complain if such efforts were not forthcoming. On the other hand, faculty might well be less aware of efforts to involve them or tend to deprecate those of which they are aware. A similar argument applies to Hold Staff in Face of Inducements and Run University Democratically. Turning next to those goals ranked higher by faculty, all but one admit to a similar interpretation. For example, one would expect that faculty would perceive the resources allocated to applied research as excessive, in view of the tendency of faculty to emphasize the value of pure research. So too, the usual deprecation of providing a full round of student activities would have the effect of exaggerating their perception of the amount of such activities that do exist. The only unexpected finding is that administrators believe the university is emphasizing Develop Students' Objectivity more than do faculty, and faculty believe the university is emphasizing Encourage Graduate Work more than do administrators. But discovering only one finding on either side is well within the bounds of chance. Hence, given the overall high correlation between the ranks, one comes away impressed with the very great similarity in perception of goals on the part of administrators and faculty.

PERCEPTIONS OF POWER STRUCTURES Our second test of differential perceptions of reality has to do with perceptions of the power structure. Having found that administrators and faculty view the goals of the university in highly similar ways, we next ask whether their differential position in the power structure affects their view of the power structure itself. It is not at all unusual for faculty members to look with suspicion on the many secret meetings of higher administrators — wondering what strange scheme is being concocted in the pipe-smoke-filled rooms. As with goals, one would speculate that any substantial difference in perceptions of the power structure raises questions about the ease with which differences between administrators and faculty may be settled by negotiation. In Table 35, we have separated higher administrators (deans and higher), lower administrators (chairmen and directors), and faculty so that we can observe variations in perceptions of the power structure.

It is clear from Table 35 that the correlation among the percep-

	Rankings		
	Higher administrators	*Lower administrators*	*Faculty*
President	1	1	2
Regents	2	2	1
Vice-presidents	3	3	3
Faculty	4	7	8
Dean-professional	5	4	4
Dean-liberal arts	6	5	7
Dean-graduate	7	6	6
Chairmen	8	9	9
Legislators	9	8	5
Students	10	12	14
Federal government	11	10	10
State government	12	11	11
Alumni	13	14	13
Grants	14	13	12
Citizens	15	15	15
Parents	16	16	16

tions of the three role groups is very high. The only appreciable variation is the tendency of higher administrators to rank faculty and students higher than the others, and a tendency for faculty to rank legislators higher than the others. Even that variation is not large, part of it attributable to the obvious fact that if one rank is out of line, some other rank will have to give way. In any case, we are hardly surprised to find that higher administrators rank students higher than do others, since higher administration has usually been the focus of attack and criticism by students. The last seven years have also seen the creation of new offices in central administration dealing with minority students and women, and other programs representing some of the fruits of "student power." Some part of the higher administrators' perceptions of the power of faculty is relevant to this increase, as we noted in Chapter 4. Faculty have increased in power since 1964, partly because the participation of nonadministrators in university government has generally increased, and partly because the tendency of younger faculty to support a good deal of the student protest has led them indirectly to gain power from subsequent changes.

The tendency of faculty to rate legislators higher than others is surely related to the attack by legislatures on particular faculty members in various universities, usually for holding political beliefs claimed unacceptable or for participating directly in "trashing" of university property or in major demonstrations. Celebrated cases of firings from both state and private universities seem to have made faculty keenly sensitive of the potential power of legislators to affect faculty tenure either directly, or indirectly by stimulating an intolerant atmosphere in the community.

Because we found that the power structure varied by type of control of the university (public versus private) and by prestige level, we thought it worthwhile to see whether these variations in perception held up when type of control and prestige were held constant. This comparison is made in Tables 36 to 41.

In Table 36 the role groups in public universities are compared, whereas in Table 37, the data for private universities are presented. It appears that the situation in public universities is about the same as we have already seen for the general case, whereas in private universities, the tendency for faculty to rate legislators higher is present, but to a much lesser extent. Apparently, this phenomenon is more strongly present in public universities, which is, of course, just what we would expect.

The comparison of universities by prestige levels tends to confirm the overall picture, with some variation. The faculty continues to be ranked higher by top administrators in all four prestige-level universities, as do students, though the picture is a bit confused in second-level universities. Legislators are similarly rated higher by faculty in all four levels. There is a rather odd shift for the deans of professional schools in top-level universities where, as can be seen, they are ranked lowest by the lower administrators (directors and chairmen). This is surprising, but an isolated finding of this kind (in the absence in this case of a statistical test) could well occur by chance. Hence, we essay no speculation on its significance.

The breakdown of role groups by type of control and prestige does not give us much reason to believe that role groups differ in their perceptions of the power structure. The only new point that comes out is the tendency of faculty in public universities to rate legislators especially high, but we would, of course, expect them to. The general finding that higher administrators rank students and faculty higher also hardly reflects different perceptions of reality, but only different experiences whose significance the

	Rankings		
	Higher administrators	Lower administrators	Faculty
President	1	1	2
Regents	2	2	1
Vice-presidents	3	3	4
Faculty	4	8	9
Legislators	5	4	3
Dean-professional	6	5	5
Dean-liberal arts	7	6	8
Dean-graduate	8	7	7
Chairmen	9	10	11
State government	10	9	6
Students	11	12	14
Federal government	12	11	10
Alumni	13	14	13
Citizens	14	15	15
Grants	15	13	12
Parents	16	16	16

TABLE 37
Perceptions of
university power
structure
(private
universities)

	Rankings		
	Higher administrators	Lower administrators	Faculty
President	1	1	1
Vice-presidents	2	2	3
Regents	3	3	2
Dean-professional	4	4	4
Faculty	5	6	8
Dean-liberal arts	6	5	5
Dean-graduate	7	7	6
Chairmen	8	8	7
Students	9	10	11
Federal government	10	11	10
Grants	11	9	9
Alumni	12	12	12
State government	13	13	13
Parents	14	14	15
Legislators	15	15	14
Citizens	16	16	16

TABLE 38
*Perceptions of
university power
structure (top
prestige
universities)*

	Rankings		
	Higher administrators	*Lower administrators*	*Faculty*
President	1	1	1
Regents	2	2	2
Vice-presidents	3	3	3
Faculty	4	4	7
Dean-professional	5	7	4
Dean-liberal arts	6	5	6
Dean-graduate	7	6	5
Chairmen	8	8	8
Students	9	9	13
Legislators	10	10	9
Federal government	11	11	10
State government	12	14	12
Grants	13	12	11
Alumni	14	13	14
Citizens	15	15	15
Parents	16	16	16

TABLE 39
*Perceptions of
university power
structure
(second-level
prestige
universities)*

	Rankings		
	Higher administrators	*Lower administrators*	*Faculty*
President	1	1	1
Regents	2	2	2
Vice-presidents	3	3	3
Faculty	4	4	6
Dean-professional	5	5	4
Dean-liberal arts	6	6	7
Dean-graduate	7	7	5
Chairmen	8	8	8
Federal government	9	10	11
Students	10	9	12
Legislators	11	12	10
Alumni	12	13	13
Grants	13	11	9
State government	14	14	14
Citizens	15	16	16
Parents	16	15	15

TABLE 40 Perceptions of university power structure (third-level prestige universities)	Rankings		
	Higher administrators	Lower administrators	Faculty
President	1	1	1
Regents	2	2	2
Vice-presidents	3	3	3
Faculty	4	7	9
Dean-professional	5	4	4
Dean-liberal arts	6	5	6
Dean-graduate	7	6	7
Chairmen	8	9	8
Students	9	13	14
Legislators	10	8	5
Federal government	11	10	10
State government	12	11	11
Alumni	13	14	13
Grants	14	12	12
Citizens	15	15	15
Parents	16	16	16

TABLE 41 Perceptions of university power structure (bottom-level prestige universities)	Rankings		
	Higher administrators	Lower administrators	Faculty
President	1	1	2
Regents	2	2	1
Vice-presidents	3	3	3
Faculty	4	8	10
Dean-professional	5	5	5
Dean-liberal arts	6	6	7
Dean-graduate	7	7	6
Legislators	8	4	4
Chairmen	9	10	11
Students	10	12	14
State government	11	9	8
Federal government	12	11	9
Alumni	13	14	13
Grants	14	13	12
Citizens	15	15	15
Parents	16	16	16

higher administrators would hardly overestimate. (That is, they would realize that they tend to "overperceive" student power because they must adapt to it to a greater extent than do lower administrators and faculty.)

VARIATIONS IN GOAL PREFERENCES
Even though persons may see reality in much the same way, it is of course entirely possible that their values will differ. We approach this comparison with the feeling that if any differences exist at all between faculty and administrators, they must show up here. As was the case with the goals analysis above, in 1964 a method employing gamma produced very sparse results. In 1971 we used a simpler method for presenting our data, with no attempt at statistical tests. Table 42 presents the differences in goal-preference ranking by the three role groups. As was the case with goals, the differences are again usually small, with very high rank correlations as shown at the bottom of the table. Before considering those goal preferences that are appreciably different, let us see whether the rank correlations hold up under multivariate treatment. In Table 43, we present them for the four prestige levels and the two types of university control. The correlations remain very high. There is a slight tendency for the correlations to be lower in the lower prestige universities, and for those in the public universities to be lower than those in private universities. This tendency was also noted for goals, though it was somewhat stronger. We can say, then, that there is somewhat more variation in goal preference among role groups in lower prestige universities and in public universities. Surely a part of this variation is related to the well-remarked pressure that public universities experience in responding to what are defined as "local needs." So too, one would guess that the wider variation in lower prestige universities is due to their inability to resist pressure to take on a variety of programs which university leaders may feel are necessary for survival. Given that faculty tend to be products of graduate schools which emphasize values associated with research and scholarship, the stage would seem to be set in such institutions for a clash between such faculty and higher administrators.

Yet it is remarkable that even in public universities and those of lower prestige, the correlations are only comparatively lower. In their own right they are very high and bespeak a general consensus on how the goals of the university should be emphasized.

It is worthwhile to look at the few goals in Table 42 which were

TABLE 42 *Differences in goal preference ranking by role groups, 1971*

Goal		Goal as ranked by higher administrators (H)	Rank differences between higher (H) and lower (L) administrators	Rank differences between lower (L) administrators and faculty (F)	Rank differences between higher administrators (H) and faculty (F)
4	Protect academic freedom	1	0	1	0
47	Maintain top quality in important programs	2	−4	−2	−6
15	Keep up to date	3	−2	0	−2
7	Cultivate students' intellect	4	2	0	2
17	Train students for scholarship/ research	5	2	0	2
36	Develop students' objectivity	6	−2	1	−1
10	Dissemination of new ideas	7	0	1	1
22	Maintain top quality in all programs	8	4	0	4
21	Ensure efficient goal attainment	9	0	0	0
27	Reward for contribution to institution	10	−1	−1	−2
46	Protect students' right of inquiry	11	1	0	1
34	Prepare students for citizenship	12	−3	−2	−5
26	Keep costs down	13	−11	−5	−16
29	Produce well-rounded students	14	1	0	1
14	Develop pride in university	15	−5	−7	−12
45	Increase or maintain prestige	16	4	−4	0
6	Develop faculty loyalty in institution	17	−10	−7	−17
43	Involve faculty in university government	18	4	3	7
40	Ensure confidence of contributors	19	−1	−6	−5
8	Develop students' character	20	3	3	6
16	Affect students with great ideas	21	5	−4	1
1	Hold staff in face of inducements	22	3	−6	−3
18	Preserve cultural heritage	23	2	−7	−5
25	Carry on pure research	24	2	0	2
37	Prepare students for useful careers	25	−5	−1	−6
39	Carry on applied research	26	0	0	0

TABLE 42 *(continued)*

Goal	Goal as ranked by higher administrators (H)	Rank differences between higher (H) and lower (L) administrators	Rank differences between lower (L) administrators and faculty (F)	Rank differences between higher administrators (H) and faculty (F)
38 *Provide community cultural leadership*	27	−1	5	4
33 *Run university democratically*	28	3	10	13
5 *Provide special adult training*	29	−6	3	−3
30 *Assist citizens through extension programs*	30	−2	−1	−3
41 *Reward for contribution to profession*	31	8	5	13
31 *Ensure favor of validating bodies*	32	−2	−1	−3
13 *Give faculty maximum opportunity to pursue careers*	33	2	12	14
19 *Satisfy area needs*	34	−2	0	−2
2 *Let will of faculty prevail*	35	6	8	14
24 *Prepare students for status/ leadership*	36	−1	−2	−3
11 *Educate to utmost high school graduates*	37	−2	2	0
20 *Involve students in university government*	38	−2	2	0
32 *Maintain balanced quality in all programs*	39	6	3	9
44 *Provide student activities*	40	2	−3	−1
42 *Emphasize undergraduate instruction*	41	−1	2	1
3 *Encourage graduate work*	42	1	−2	−1
12 *Keep harmony*	43	−1	2	1
35 *Accept good students only*	44	1	−2	−1
28 *Protect students' right of action*	45	0	1	0
9 *Cultivate student's taste*	46	0	0	0
23 *Preserve institutional character*	47	0	0	0

NOTE: *Rank correlation* $r_{HL} = .965$
$r_{LF} = .959$
$r_{HF} = .807$

H = Deans and higher administrators
L = Directors and chairmen
F = Faculty

	Prestige level				Type of control	
	1 (top)	2	3	4	Private	Public
High administrators related to low administrators	.968	.941	.961	.949	.957	.961
Low administrators related to faculty	.959	.967	.941	.955	.962	.953
High administrators related to faculty	.905	.922	.876	.783	.913	.872

TABLE 43 *Rank correlations among role groups in goal preferences, by university prestige and type of control*

ranked appreciably differently by different role groups. Adopting again the procedure of calling a variation of nine or more positions "substantial," the following goals were ranked substantially differently by faculty and administrators. Administrators gave higher ranking than faculty to the following goal preferences:

26 Keep Costs Down

14 Develop Pride in University

6 Develop Faculty Loyalty in Institution

In turn, faculty gave higher ranking than administrators to the following goal preferences:

33 Run University Democratically

13 Give Faculty Maximum Opportunity to Pursue Careers

2 Let Will of Faculty Prevail

There was some variation from the situation in 1964. In that year, the goal Develop Students' Character was found to distinguish the role groups and to be emphasized more by faculty, whereas Cultivate Students' Taste and Ensure Efficient Goal Attainment, while present in 1971 (though with only small rank differences), were not present in 1964. None of these showed large differences among the role groups.

The only goal with a large rank difference which was new in 1971 was Keep Costs Down, which administrators valued more than did faculty. In looking at the short list of goal preferences which distinguish the role groups, there are no surprises. Administrators would be expected to value more keeping costs down, maintaining pride in the university, and the importance of faculty loyalty.

In turn, the faculty would predictably value a democratically run university (provided it was also one where the will of the full-time faculty would prevail—a nice contradiction which did not seem to bother the faculty), and a university in which they had maximum opportunity to pursue their careers.

In both 1964 and 1971, then, the agreements between faculty and administrators are far more impressive than the differences. If anything, the two groups seem to be closer together on perceptions and values. When we remember our conclusion in Chapter 4 that insiders were ranged against outsiders, the closeness of the faculty and administrators on goals and values suggests something of a closing of ranks in the face of—whatever comes.

WHAT DIFFERENCE DOES IT MAKE? To discover that faculty and administrators share similar perceptions of the goals and power structure of the university and share many value judgments about the goals is not to create a picture of harmony between the two role groups. Such congruence of perspective and values does suggest that when differences arise, there is enough basis for at least amicable negotiation on the rules of the game. Yet a willingness to negotiate is far from sufficient to guarantee an enduring relationship or even one in which persons will be around long enough to carry out the terms of whatever is agreed upon. For that to happen, persons must exhibit a commitment to the university itself as a desirable place of employment, a place which offers important satisfactions or opportunities which cannot be secured elsewhere. We asked two questions that enable us to assess such attachment. On the question of commitment to the university as a place of employment, we asked persons[4] whether they would agree or disagree with the following two questions: "It would take some very strong inducements to get me to leave this university for a position elsewhere" and, "It would take some very strong inducements to get me to accept a position at any place *other than* an institution of higher learning." The responses on these questions are presented in Tables 44 and 45. The similarity of response among our three role groups is striking.

[4] Since we sought to tap commitment to the university, we felt that including junior faculty who hardly had time to develop such a commitment would not be appropriate. This is especially important because we are comparing faculty to administrators, many of whom are somewhat older and have been on their jobs longer than the average faculty member. To make the comparison fair, we restricted the comparison to senior faculty only.

	Strongly agree	Agree	Undecided	Disagree and strongly disagree	Total
Higher administrators					
Number	327	306	103	78	814
Percent	40.1	37.5	12.6	8.3	
Lower administrators					
Number	588	710	201	215	1,714
Percent	34.3	41.4	11.7	12.5	
Senior faculty					
Number	169	216	65	79	529
Percent	32.1	40.7	12.2	14.8	

TABLE 44 *Role groups compared in response to question: "It would take some very strong inducements to get me to leave this university for a position elsewhere."*

Close to three-fourths of each role group agree or agree strongly that they would require strong inducements to leave their present university (Table 44). The percentage of those who disagree is, however, somewhat higher for the faculty than for either group of administrators. Still more interesting are the results in Table 45, for here we ask about the willingness of academics to leave the area of higher learning altogether. Such a question, we hoped, would tap not simply dissatisfaction with the present job but the degree of alienation from the higher academic enterprise. What comes through is an even stronger commitment, with over 80 percent of all three role groups agreeing that it would take strong in-

	Strongly agree	Agree	Undecided	Disagree and strongly disagree	Total
Higher administrators					
Number	399	263	77	65	804
Percent	49.6	32.7	9.5	8.0	
Lower administrators					
Number	888	522	133	174	1,717
Percent	51.7	30.4	7.7	10.1	
Senior faculty					
Number	256	158	32	64	510
Percent	50.1	30.9	6.2	12.5	

TABLE 45 *Role groups compared on answer to question: "It would take some very strong inducements to get me to accept a position at any place other than an institution of higher learning."*

ducements to get them to leave higher academia—some 50 percent agreeing strongly. On the other hand, the percentage who disagree, while preserving the small differential among the role groups, is practically identical with the percentage who disagreed in answer to the previous question. Those who disagreed with either question may represent a hard core of disaffected persons who are both unhappy with the university at which they are presently employed and quite alienated from the university system as a whole. Although this group averages around 10 percent for the whole population, and is higher for the senior faculty than for administrators, it should not obscure the more impressive finding that more than three-fourths would require strong inducements to leave their present university and over 80 percent to leave university life altogether. In the main, then, there are no large differences among role groups, and faculty are as strongly committed to the higher education enterprise as are administrators. There is, however, a slightly higher percentage of alienated and unhappy persons among the faculty.

We get some further clues about the sources of this alienation by looking at the replies to another question, which was asked as a general indicator of morale. The question was stated:

On the line below indicate with a check the approximate amount of power you feel you have to get the things done that you would like to get done in connection with your university role.

A great deal  No power at all

We also asked the following question:

How would you have answered the above question seven or eight years ago? If not in office at that time, how do you think your predecessor would have answered it?

A great deal  No power at all

This second question was aimed primarily at administrators, but the faculty replies are of interest. The replies of all respondents are presented in Tables 46 and 47.

As can be seen in Table 46, there are role group differences which, while not as large as we have become accustomed to in this study, are still evident. The gamma for this table is .280— which is well above the five percent significance level (that is, well

	A great deal	Quite a lot	Medium amount	Little or no power	Total
TABLE 46 *Role groups compared on "The power I have to get things done required by my university role."*					
Higher administrators					
Number	126	406	244	112	888
Percent	14.2	45.7	28.6	12.7	
Lower administrators					
Number	169	629	564	481	1,843
Percent	9.1	34.1	30.6	20.6	
Senior faculty					
Number	29	139	167	210	545
Percent	5.5	25.5	30.6	38.5	

within the bounds of chance), but still worth noting because of its potential importance for the alienation issue. The extent to which persons feel powerless has been considered an important dimension of alienation (see Blauner, 1964). Hence it is worth noting that close to 40 percent of the senior faculty at American universities indicated that they had little or no power to do the things required by their university role, a percentage which is double that for lower administrators and three times that for higher administrators. At the other end of the scale, higher administrators were more than twice as likely to check a response close to a "great deal of power" as were senior faculty. Further, when we look at Table 47, we see some tendency for the sense of powerlessness

	A great deal	Quite a lot	Medium amount	Little or no power	Total
TABLE 47 *Role groups compared on "The power I had seven or eight years ago."*					
Higher administrators					
Number	128	293	233	216	870
Percent	14.7	33.6	26.7	24.8	
Lower administrators					
Number	180	452	566	618	1,816
Percent	9.8	24.8	31.1	34.0	
Senior faculty					
Number	147	165	155	71	538
Percent	27.3	30.8	28.8	13.3	

to have increased over the last seven or eight years (for example, 13.3 percent of the senior faculty check the lower end of the scale in reply, compared to 38.5 percent for the power at present). Considered in isolation, this finding might well cause alarm. After all, these are not idealistic youth whose view of the possible will become tempered by their experience with reality as they grow older. They are senior faculty who provide the major support for the values of the university and who carry out its major tasks. But the report of their apparent alienation must be considered in context. First, it comes through with a quite low gamma and may well then be a chance occurrence, one which could vanish with a different sample. But even if we assume it is a reliable finding, it must be set down alongside the information in Tables 44 and 45 which showed that well over 75 percent of the faculty (and the other role groups) would require very strong inducements to leave higher education. Now, whatever may be said about alienation, it becomes significant as a motivator when persons act on it. What we seem to have, then, is a relatively large proportion of the senior faculty who feel relatively powerless, but who are strongly committed to remaining in higher academia and at their present university. Perhaps this may be a result of lack of alternatives for many, but whatever the reason, they do not see themselves as leaving. When an alienated group finds itself in a situation which it does not contemplate leaving, one would speculate that its sense of powerlessness will be expressed in one of two ways: (1) withdrawal from involvement in the central goals of the university and a concentration on one's immediate job or (2) attempting to modify the university environment in such a way that the alienated group may gain greater control. It is impossible to say which course such senior faculty might adopt, but their strong professional commitments would seem to make the option of withdrawal somewhat less likely.

We must also recall that the faculty was one power group perceived by others as having *increased* its power since 1964 (Chapter 4, p. 131). Of course that was simply the faculty as a whole, which included junior faculty. Even allowing for the general tendency of persons to underestimate their own organizational power, that finding suggests still another interpretation of the sense of powerlessness of senior faculty. It is possible that a sense of powerlessness is *precisely* what happens when a group unaccustomed to power finds its own power increasing. Faculty have found, over the past seven years, that they have been called upon to take stands on universitywide issues which many had simply not thought much about before. Such stands were often outside their own area of specialization. Physicists were challenged by students to take a stand on the social effects of nuclear warfare; medical school instructors were asked to make their studies more relevant to the problems of the poor; and political scientists were asked about the implications of their research for "counter-insurgency" policies of the federal government. And more senior faculty were turned to by administrators for help in defending the legitimacy of the university itself. With increased student participation in university governance, there also went increased faculty participation. Although senior faculty members have always been called upon to head major committees, many became more directly involved in time-consuming administrative duties, revolving about such problems as the firing of a popular instructor, the establishment of a set of rules to ensure due process in other disputed cases, suits by students against university-inspired injustices, and even more complex matters. Their training as scientists or scholars did not prepare them for these roles, and many experienced a strong sense of frustration as they discovered that administration, far from being something that could be sneered at or ignored, was a complex, enervating activity in which success might not be achieved, no matter how hard one worked. A sense of powerlessness would not then be so surprising.

ADMINISTRA-TORS AND FACULTY: ALLIED AND IN CONFLICT   The title of this section is a paraphrase of one used by Lipset (1972) as a chapter title: "Faculty and Students: Allied and in Conflict," and it seems equally fitting. Lipset suggests that faculty, as scientists and intellectuals, find a critical stance vis-à-vis the establishment a natural one. In that sense they find they are allied with the critical and rebellious students. But the same critical tendency on the part of faculty leads them to look with suspicion at student-proposed solutions for complex social problems. Their own training as scientists and scholars sensitizes them to complexity and to the problems and costs of change. The activist students desire support, not analysis, and so faculty and students begin to split, and hostilities develop. So too, the administrators and faculty find themselves allied when facing the external power holders that we discussed in the previous chapter. Attacks from legislators, regents, and threats of withdrawal of funds force a closing of ranks, or at least a willingness to come together. As persons come together, they develop (if they did not have it before) common perceptions of goals and a more realistic (and truer) perception of the power structure. In time, their values about those goals also come closer together, perhaps because some persons with different values leave. Yet faculty take poorly to the task of becoming part-time administrators, of serving in important policy-making and policy-execution jobs on their campuses. The more they participate, the more they feel powerless, like fish out of water. They might withdraw, teach their classes, and spend more time on leisure activities, but their training as professionals has affected too many of them with a strong sense of duty and, as we saw, the overwhelming majority do not contemplate leaving the university. So they find themselves in uneasy harness with administrators, forced to do things for which they were not trained, resenting the amount of time that those things consume, yet not considering seriously any alternative. As they spend more and more time with administrators, the conflict with them is bound to increase precisely because much of that increased interaction is not voluntary. A situation of continuous conflict is not one that anyone regards with pleasure, but as time goes on, the conflicts become resolved, even though they are soon replaced by new conflicts. And both administrators and faculty seem too attached to the university to want seriously to consider any other alternative.

6. The Shape of Social Change in American Universities

Our research was designed to examine the impact of the events of the 1960s on the goals and power structure of American universities. As it happened, we had made a study of the goals and power structure of American universities in 1964 as part of a desire to contribute a scientifically based study to the literature on higher education. The original motivation for that study was an interest in the university as a social organization. To that end, then, we selected a set of universities in the "full" sense—that is, those which included not only a graduate school, but those in which work was not heavily concentrated in one or two major areas, but spread across the humanities, the physical, biological, and social sciences, as well as offering work in at least three professional schools. We required also that there should be a fully functioning undergraduate liberal arts college. There turned out to be 79 universities that met those criteria, of which we concentrated on a nondenominational group of 68.[1]

We took considerable care in developing an organizational model which was appropriate to universities. We felt that neither the classical bureaucratic model nor the conception of the university as a community were directly applicable. Instead, we developed a model in which the university was conceived of as a relatively loose structure of units which was increasingly being coordinated to the point where we could begin to speak of the university as a complex organization. As such, we could assume that it was a social system which had definable goals and persons and agencies directing it toward those goals, that is, a power structure. Yet those power holders were several in number (we allowed for 16 persons and

---

[1] As we noted in Chapter 1, there were actually nine denominational universities, but we also excluded the University of Washington and the University of Minnesota because these were the home institutions of the investigators.

agencies, though the major power holders were closer to the figure 7 or 8), hence allowing for a relatively diffuse sharing of power, and along with that sharing, a relatively large number of goals (47), including some that were contradictory. The existence of such contradiction is by no means strange and in fact is assumed to be "normal," even in tightly coordinated bureaucracies.

For respondents, we defined a population of all academic administrators and 10 percent of the faculty, a number which came to approximately 15,500. Our response rate was just under one-half, or about 7,500 persons (usable replies). Although concerned with representativeness, we took the view that our respondents were closer to being informants than the target of study. We had, in other words, approximately 75 persons on each campus whom we asked to serve as our eyes, to report to us what the goals of the university were (as they saw them), and the shape of the power structure (as they saw it). The results of the study were reported in Gross and Grambsch (1968).

At the time we did the study, we had no idea that 1964 was to be the year of the Free Speech uprising at the Berkeley campus of the University of California, or of what was to come in the later years of the 1960s. We need do no more than list the familiar campus events of those years: the uprising at Columbia University in 1968, troubles at the University of Chicago and other universities over involvement with the Institute for Defense Analysis, the many other campus protests in 1969, the repeated criticisms of the structure of the university as an educational institution (large classes, impersonal teaching, lack of interest in students, over-emphasis on research), the attacks on the university as a racist and sexist institution, and, of course, the strikes that followed the extensions of the Vietnam War to Laos and Cambodia. The university played various roles in these events—as a staging platform for attempts to alter the broader society or activate social changes in other parts of the world, as a forum for the deliberation of alternative ideologies, and as a target of planned social change. Indeed, as a major societal institution, the university could hardly escape getting caught up in those events. As a consequence, since we had done our study in 1964, it was thought that a replication in 1971 might shed light on whether the university structure had changed in the seven-year period.

In 1971 we sent a somewhat shortened form of our original questionnaire to a population similar to the one we had contacted in

1964, though a shortage of funds forced us to curtail its size. We sent questionnaires to all administrators at the rank of dean or higher, to at least one-fourth of all chairmen and research directors, and to approximately 3 percent of the faculty, coming to a total of around 9,000 persons. Our response rate was somewhat higher than it had been in 1964, for this time we received about 50 percent — or approximately 4,500 usable replies.

MAJOR FINDINGS Our major findings were these: The top goals of American universities revolved about support functions, led by the goal of protecting the academic freedom of the faculty, as well as related goals having to do with the careers of the faculty. Students and teaching of undergraduates were generally assigned places near the bottom of the list of 47 goals. The overall findings suggested that output goals in universities were being taken for granted and that attention was being given to institutionalizing the internal operations of the organization. When respondents were asked which goals they felt should be emphasized, students and teaching occupied higher positions, suggesting a guilty conscience, a conclusion supported by feelings about "sins of omission." There was a feeling that students deserved more attention, that there should be more loyalty to the institution on the part of the faculty, and less emphasis on cosmopolitan values.

When we compared the findings of 1971 to 1964, we were struck with the fact that there was practically no change in the rank ordering of goals or goal preferences. If the major events of the 1960s had had an effect on universities, the effect did not show up in the goals — that is, the direction in which universities were moving — or in the values associated with those directions. Respondents felt that universities were moving in the directions in which they should be. There was, however, a drop in the average emphasis on goals, suggesting a withdrawal of universities from instrumental pressure to attain goals of any kind. We interpreted this finding to suggest that universities were less aggressive, perhaps simply more realistic, in recognizing their own limitations, perhaps becoming increasingly willing to give up functions to other institutions of higher education such as community and comprehensive colleges.

We made a systematic comparison of goals and goal preferences, examining the extent to which they were congruent with one another, with the important finding that such congruence had increased strikingly since 1964. The data allowed us to make two interpretations of that increased congruence: (1) Universities were becoming more distinctly stratified, with different strata adopting very different sets of goals and goal preferences from other strata and (2) there was very strong evidence that faculty and administrators had come to feel that the goals at their universities were emphasized to the extent that they should be. The events of the sixties had, it seemed, produced not so much a shaking up, as a shaking down, with strong signs of internal stability in our 68 universities. Although this hardly meant the end of campus protest, it did suggest at least that the faculty and administrators, who were in the best position to report on these matters, felt that those most likely to lead such protests had either changed their minds or gone elsewhere; if disputes had not been solved, then dispute-settlement mechanisms had developed, and universities were perceived to be able to govern themselves.

The findings thus far were averages over the whole set of 68 universities. We next turned to internal variations. When we compared public and private institutions, we found a considerable increase in the number of findings since 1964, particularly in private universities, and for the case in which a goal within a university was compared to other goals at the same university. The increase we interpreted as evidence that private and public universities were becoming increasingly different (rather than alike, as some observers have claimed). The private universities emphasized goals which suggested elitism, an emphasis on the liberal arts, pure research, and a concern with preservation of the cultural heritage. The public universities were characterized by a strong egalitarianism, applied research, a concern with serving the population in the immediate area, and other service activities.

When universities of differing amount of productivity were compared to one another, clear differences were again found. Places of high productivity emphasized pure research, graduate work, faculty professional careers, a continuing concern with top quality in all programs, the protection of academic freedom, and the retention of staff in the face of inducements from other universities. They were places in which there was an actual de-emphasis on concern with the "well-rounded student," on loyalty to the institution (rather than to professional careers), and to the needs of the immediate geographic area. The differences among universities by productivity added up to a strong case that productivity has real costs. Further, the gap between high- and low-productivity institutions was wider than it had been in 1964.

When universities of different prestige levels were compared, we found a similar set of large differences, with some evidence that universities at the bottom of the prestige ladder were giving up the battle and settling for a different kind of university. Such universities were showing concern for the student as a consumer, for the well-rounded student, building student character, and providing local community cultural leadership. Rather than simply doing less successfully what high prestige places were doing, they were beginning to value doing things that prestige universities did not consider worth doing at all. All things considered, the data on type of control (private versus public control), productivity, and prestige offered very strong support for the claim that universities were becoming increasingly differentiated, even fragmented.

The above constituted the main "descriptive" findings. We turned next to the dynamic aspect of universities—namely, the kinds of power holders and structures that were responsible for (or at least accompanied) the goals and goal preferences. Our first finding was that the power structure of 1971 was unchanged from that in 1964. The president, regents, and vice-presidents were still on top (in that order); parents, citizens, alumni, and grant sources were still at the bottom; faculty were in the middle, above chairmen. Legislators and state government were, predictably, still high up in public institutions, and grant donors higher in private universities than in state universities (though not much higher).

Yet when we asked persons whether they thought power had changed or not, a strikingly different picture emerged. Practically everyone (with the exception of chairmen) was perceived to have increased his power over what it had been in 1964. This increase is not paradoxical, but indicative of an increasing ability of persons to control the resources and facilities, as well as to enlist the help and organizational cooperation necessary to attain their ends. There was, however, an important split in the extent of increase in power. "Outsiders" (legislators, state and federal government) plus students and faculty showed the largest increase, whereas administrators had stayed about the same (a slight increase actually), and chairmen had lost power. Most interesting was the perceived increase in student power, when the picture of the overall power structure showed students in 1971 to be just slightly above where they had been in 1964 (that is, not far from the bottom). Apparently the slight increase in student power was considered so surprising as to be worthy of special comment. The rise in perceived power of the faculty was related to their frequent riding of the student bandwagon, together with their increasing involvement in administration and concern for the university as a whole, a position they were forced to take when the university came under attack.

The power structure was found to pit insiders (administrators, faculty, students) against outsiders (regents, legislators, state and federal government, citizens). Such power was not zero-sum—that is, powerful deans were not associated with weak chairmen, for example, but with powerful chairmen; just as powerful legislators were found associated with powerful regents (and weak ones with weak ones). A strong association between power and goals was found. External power holders were found associated with practical, land-grant goals, in contrast to internal power holders who supported liberal arts goals and those associated with faculty careers. But when we compared 1971 to 1964, we found that it looked as if it was more difficult for power holders to accumulate power by identifying themselves with any given set of goals. This seemed to be due to the fact that goals had become more complex, that they required greater resources and much greater expertise than they ever had.

There was also evidence that the power struggle had shifted from the national to the local level. Those external power holders with their base at the local level (legislators, local citizens, regents) appeared to have increased their ability to affect goals at the local university, whereas internal power holders (the faculty, administration) were found to require more power (usually at the national level) to affect local goals. These findings provided further evidence of the fragmenting of universities—the breakup of the university system—than we had noticed in comparing universities by type of control and levels of prestige.

The finding that power holders clustered in the form of internal and external sets led us finally to examine the much celebrated split between two of those internal groups. namely, the faculty and administrators. We found that there were no appreciable differences between the two groups in how they perceived the goals of universities or how they perceived the power structure. If differences exist, the two groups are able to overcome the limitations of their different positions in the university and perceive "reality" in much the same way. The same was true for their values with reference to goals, though there were small differences. These differences, however, were quite predictable and not suggestive of any important value differences between the two groups. Such a finding was not surprising, since most academic administrators are former faculty and many members are likely to return to faculty duties.

Both the faculty and administrators were found to be strongly attached to the university as a place of employment, but a higher proportion of the faculty showed signs of a sense of powerlessness. We speculated that this finding does not necessarily suggest alienation, but follows from their increase in faculty power (however small), to the point where faculty members were forced not "up against the wall," but on top of the wall to help man it. They were thrust increasingly into decision-making and policy-making positions, and those, for most, were far from their trained specialties. A sense of powerlessness was, perhaps, only to be expected until their negotiating and political skills increased, and they became able to handle their new duties more effectively.

SOCIAL CHANGE IN UNIVERSITIES What then can we say about social change in universities since 1964? Before assessing our findings, it is worth noting that universities have been accused of offering resistance to change. Yet over a large enough time span, there is no question that they have changed. In a tongue-in-cheeck tour de force, Hefferlin (1969, pp. 27–28) writes:

If you had been John Bowden or another of the dozen or so freshmen attending little King's College in New York City—the predecessor of Columbia—two hundred years ago, you would have been required to start the day with Chapel and then spend from nine o'clock to noon translating and reciting from Caesar's *Commentaries,* Ovid's *Metamorphoses,* The *History* of Sallust, Vergil's pastoral poems, the *Ecloques,* Cornelius Nepos' *Vitae Excellontium Imperatorum,* Aesop's *Fables,* Groitius' *The Truth of the Christian Religion,* and—in Greek—the *Dialogues* of Lucian and the New Testament. You would have taken dinner at noon with the two professors, Samuel Clossy and Myles Cooper (who was also president). You would have studied during the afternoon until six, when called to required prayers. After supper (consisting, according to college rules, of bread, butter, and cheese "or the remainder of the Dinner") you would have been on your own, as long as you were inside the college fence by nine o'clock.

A hundred years later, if you had been Robert Arnold or another of forty freshmen in Columbia's "academic department," during the morning you would have also attended morning prayers, studied geometry and algebra, translated from Herodotus, Homer, and the odes of Horace, recited from textbooks on the history and customs of ancient Greece and Rome, memorized the intricacies of their grammar, and done exercises in punctuation, simile, paraphrasing, abridging and criticism from Quackenbow's *Course of Composition and Rhetoric.* You might have access to the college library between one and three in the afternoon, if President Barnard had so authorized you. You would not, however, have had to go to evening chapel, which had been dropped by 1817, or to Saturday morning prayers, which had been discontinued in 1844.

In 1968, if you were one of the seven hundred members of Columbia's Class of 1972, you would more than likely still have been reading Homer and Herodotus, Vergil and the Bible—but all in English, and only as four selections among some twenty-six classics ranging from the *Illiad* to Dostoyevsky in humanities and from an equal number ranging from Machiavelli to Keynes and Schumpeter in contemporary civilization. In college composition you would have received "intensive training in the composition of expository and argumentative essays." You would have taken either astronomy, biological sciences, chemistry, geography-geology, mathematics, or physics, and one of eleven foreign languages. If exempted from these courses by an achievement test, you could have elected a course from among some forty open to freshmen, including elementary geophysics, history of science, university orchestra, etching and engraving, introduction to the study of religion, systematic sociological theories or—if you desired a commission in the Naval Officer Reserve Corps—naval history and sea power to 1815. Depending on your predilection you could have attended morning prayers at 8:40, a Roman Catholic mass at noon, Episcopal Eucharist on Wednesday evening, or at anytime stopped by the office of the Counselor to Jewish Students. Athletics, however, would have replaced religion as a compulsory exercise: you would have been expected to participate in one of nine team sports and one of eight individual or combative sports in physical education.

Perhaps any attempt to find large changes, or any change at all, in so short a time as seven years (1964–71) is expecting too much. Yet the accusation of lack of ability to change seems contradictory to the equally frequent criticism that universities change all too much. Here the complaint has been that universities are much *too* responsive to pressures from government to do classified research or from local citizens to help them in their everyday problems, including the business task of marketing agricultural products, and hence all too readily abandoning their classic commitments to liberal arts education (see Nisbet, 1971). The resolution of this contradiction can be sought in a recognition that those who accuse the university of resistance to change actually mean that the university is resistant to the sort of change these critics would like to see. We often face conflicting demands for change, with the proponents of each side claiming that the obstacle is inertia or stubborn campus conservatism.

Yet there are solid grounds for the claim that universities do change slowly. Universities are organizations, and organizations in general change slowly. Organizations are, after all, set up to attain ends corresponding to some presumed need or want. If they are successful and if the needs or wants persist, then the organization will go on, preserving the form it has found successful. In particular, if the organization is a voluntary one, then it will tend to attract to it persons who accept its goals and are not inclined to change them. The classic tendency is for organizations to become institutionalized over time, partly because they develop investments in their current social structure. For example, organizations provide jobs for many persons who then develop a stake in the continuation of the organization. Even when the organization attains its goals and *should* go out of existence, those with investments in it will try to think up new goals to enable the organization to continue.[2]

In addition to those tendencies—which apply to all organizations —universities have a set of forces of their own which slows down attempts to change them. One of the major goals of universities is to conserve and transmit the wisdom of the ages. As such, they tend to celebrate conservatism in the classic Burkean sense, out of recognition that knowledge and wisdom are a slowly increasing mass which admits few revolutionary changes. Then too, the very age of universities often gives them a privileged position in the community, and even the police hesitate before coming onto campus. Internally, there is the loose, near-feudal structure, with control over academic matters resting with the department, a tendency particularly marked in the more prestigious universities. Making any large-scale change requires consultation at "the bottom," with that bottom being quite capable of sabotaging any change

---

[2] The generalizations in this paragraph are derivable from the burgeoning research on formal or complex organizations in recent years. Standard works include Blau and Scott (1962), Caplow (1964), Etzioni (1961), Perrow (1970), Thompson (1967).

imposed against its will. After all, the faculty carry out the major activities of the university. And the faculty, as many have noted (see Fashing & Deutsch, 1971, pp. 20–21 and 260–261), consists of independent professionals (and often entrepreneurs), with a powerful sense of trade union concern for the protection of their rights and privileges.

The forces resisting change seem formidable indeed, adding up to a quite dismal prospect for those who seek change. Thus it is not surprising that Fashing and Deutsch (1971, pp. 258 ff.), in a study of change at six institutions,[3] conclude that students are the major source of change in those institutions, that administrators may be associated with change, though often as mediators, whereas faculty are either opposed to change or do not assist it. Similarly, Hefferlin (1969, p. 146), after a study of 110 institutions, concludes that "Outsiders initiate; institutions react."

THE PROSPECTS FOR CHANGE

What then do our findings suggest about the ability of universities to change? There are two things which have not changed. First, the goals of universities remain substantially what they were in 1964. Universities continue to emphasize those goals which assist faculty in the pursuit of successful professional careers; doing pure research is still emphasized; and goals associated with students, especially undergraduate teaching, are assigned a low priority. Second, the power structure of the university is substantially unchanged: The president and regents remain at the top; the faculty are in the middle; and students are near the bottom.

If one stopped here, one might easily conclude that universities were indeed slow to change, that the powerful forces of resistance we listed above continue to do their work. But our findings also show some striking changes, of which the most important are the following. First, within universities there has been an increased meeting of the minds on the proper goals of the university. Conflict has given way to substantial consensus that the present goals of the university are desirable and that the emphasis they receive is about what it should be. Such goal congruence was evident to a strong extent on fully 39 out of the 47 goals. This does not add up to an end to conflict, but rather to some degree of maturation in the ability to handle conflict. It also suggests that universities have taken

[3] University of California at Berkeley, San Francisco State College, University of Oregon, Western Washington State College, University of California at Los Angeles, and Stanford University.

a more realistic view of their objectives, yielding some to state colleges and community colleges and expecting less of other objectives. As such, students may find they have more options open to them, that community colleges and other institutions are not simply inferior universities, but organizations with substantially differing goals not in competition with universities. Surely some of the problems of universities followed from their attempts to be all things to all men. With the decline of this tendency, problems, if not fewer, may be easier to resolve or at least may yield to approaches other than open confrontation.

Second, universities have become distinctly more stratified. The sets of goals exhibiting congruence across universities show distinct differences and clustering. Goals and goal preferences are found to divide sharply in private as compared to public universities, in highly productive as compared to less productive universities, and in top prestige as compared to bottom prestige universities. This stratification has reached the point where one might more appropriately speak of it as fragmentation, for stratification does imply that the universities are part of the same system. If anything, some universities (most strikingly those of low prestige) appear to be seeking wholly new objectives which do not compete with those of more prestigious universities. This tendency suggests a breakup of the system itself, with still further options for students of different interests and talents. The university system may then become less of a monolith, better adapted to the enormously diversified student body that now finds attendance at an institution of higher learning not simply an advantage but an obligation.

Third, with some exceptions, all the role groups (faculty, deans, students, etc.) are believed to have increased their power, pointing to a situation of reduced alienation, of greater ability to enlist the help of others in the achievement of one's own ends. External power holders, such as regents and legislators, are able to exert more power on the internal goals of universities than ever, however, though their ability to increase their power by pushing for goals they favor has been reduced. This latter effect seems to be due to the growing complexity of goals themselves, to the fact that their attainment is much more a process requiring expert knowledge and cooperation of all role groups.

Fourth, this increased potential power of the external power groups has, however, been matched by an apparent closing of ranks among the internal power holders — the faculty, administrators, and students. Such a conclusion is reinforced by our finding that administrators and faculty see eye to eye on the goals and goal preferences of the university and see the power structure in much the same way as well.

Fifth, and last, the increased faculty involvement in administration and policy making over the last seven years has forced many faculty members into roles which they find unfamiliar and which they have usually tried to avoid. Instead of "putting down" administrators as "lackeys," they find these tasks are not only time consuming, but highly complex, demanding an expertise of their own. Not being well prepared for those tasks (they are, after all, trained as physicists, psychologists, or biologists), they feel a sense of powerlessness, which we believe is temporary until their policy-making and negotiating skills improve.

But what of student unrest? We found that though the tendency now was for student unrest to be endemic to the university scene and no longer more characteristic of any one type of university than another, still universities with differing amounts of unrest were distinguishable by the kinds of goals they exhibited. Places of high unrest were those emphasizing the dissemination of new ideas, maintenance of top quality in all programs, the students' right of inquiry, pure research, and holding onto staff in the face of inducements from other universities. That is, they were places emphasizing pure research, maintaining a high level of quality and originality and a searching intellectual climate for students as well as faculty. Such places would be oriented to change and therefore attract radicals, both students and faculty, and they would also be places that would attract the more distinguished scientists and scholars. Hence, such places would predictably be both sources of criticism and continuous re-examination of university goals and practices, as well as sources of original research and high productivity. But they turn out also to be places where both faculty and administration feel that a low priority should be assigned to student needs and undergraduate teaching. This attitude would seem to add up to a kind of arrogance which promises continued conflict between faculty and administration and students. With our earlier comments on the fragmentation of the university system, such conflict may well be concentrated only on certain campuses, as students grow weary of spending their energies on fighting and shift to campuses manifesting greater concern for students and undergraduate teaching. But even when conflict occurs, we would expect that the faculty, more involved in administration and policy making at the broad university level, will be in much better position to negotiate and help resolve the conflict.

Our research suggests, then, that universities have indeed changed in the last seven years. They have become more stable, better able to handle conflict in a rational, problem-solving manner, and more differentiated in ways adapted to the diverse student body. Moreover, faculty and administration have come together more closely than ever. In part, this closer association is a matter of closing ranks against attacks from hostile legislatures and citizens, but part of it is a maturing of the faculty who, without sacrificing their primary commitment to professional excellence, have become more seriously involved citizens of the university.

References

Aiken, Michael, and Paul E. Mott: *The Structure of Community Power,* Random House, Inc., New York, 1970.

Anderson, G. Lester: "The Organizational Character of American Colleges and Universities," in Terry F. Lunsford (ed.), *The Study of Academic Administration,* Western Interstate Commission for Higher Education, Boulder, Colo., October 1963.

Ashby, Eric: *Any Person, Any Study,* McGraw-Hill Book Company, New York, 1971.

Astin, Alexander W., and Calvin B. T. Lee: *The Invisible Colleges,* McGraw-Hill Book Company, New York, 1972.

Bachrach, P., and M. Baratz: "The Two Faces of Power," *American Political Science Review,* vol. 56, pp. 947–952, 1962.

Baldridge, J. Victor: *Power and Conflict in the University,* John Wiley & Sons, Inc., New York, 1971*a*.

Baldridge, J. Victor: *Academic Governance,* McCutchan Publishing Corporation, Berkeley, Calif., 1971*b*.

Bales, Robert F.: "Task Roles and Social Roles in Problem Solving Groups," in Eleanor F. Maccoby, Theodore M. Newcomb, and Eugene L. Hartley (eds.), *Readings in Social Psychology,* pp. 437–447, Henry Holt and Company, Inc., New York, 1958.

Ben-David, Joseph: "Universities," in *International Encyclopedia of the Social Sciences,* vol. 16, pp. 191–199, 1968.

Ben-David, Joseph: *The Scientist's Role in Society,* Prentice-Hall, Inc., Englewood Cliffs, N.J., 1971.

Ben-David, Joseph: *American Higher Education,* McGraw-Hill Book Company, New York, 1972.

Berger, P. K., and A. J. Grimes: "Cosmopolitan-Local: A Factor Analysis of the Construct," *Administrative Science Quarterly,* vol. 18, pp. 223–235, June 1973.

Berliner, Joseph: "A Problem in Soviet Business Administration," *Administrative Science Quarterly,* vol. 1, pp. 86–101, June 1956.

Blalock, Hubert M., Jr.: *Causal Inferences in Nonexperimental Research,* University of North Carolina Press, Chapel Hill, 1964.

Blau, Peter M., and W. Richard Scott: *Formal Organizations,* Chandler Publishing Company, San Francisco, 1962.

Blauner, Robert: *Alienation and Freedom,* The University of Chicago Press, Chicago, 1964.

Bottomore, T. B.: *Elites and Society,* Basic Books, Inc., Publishers, New York, 1964.

Burn, Barbara B., Philip G. Altbach, Clark Kerr, and James A. Perkins: *Higher Education in Nine Countries,* McGraw-Hill Book Company, New York, 1971.

Caplow, Theodore: *Principles of Organization,* Harcourt, Brace & World, Inc., New York, 1964.

Caplow, Theodore: Foreword to Reece McGee, *Academic Janus,* Jossey-Bass, San Francisco, 1971.

Carnegie Commission on Higher Education: *New Students and New Places,* McGraw-Hill Book Company, New York, 1971.

Carnegie Commission on Higher Education: *Reform on Campus,* McGraw-Hill Book Company, New York, 1972.

Cartter, Allan M.: *An Assessment of Quality in Graduate Education,* American Council on Education, Washington, 1966.

Cartwright, Dorwin, and Alvin Zander (eds.): *Group Dynamics,* Row, Peterson & Company, Evanston, Ill., 1953.

Clark, Burton R.: *The Distinctive College: Antioch, Reed and Swarthmore,* Aldine Publishing Company, Chicago, 1970.

Cole, S., and J. Cole: "Scientific Output and Recognition: A Study in the Operation of the Reward System in Science," *American Sociological Review,* vol. 32, pp. 397–413, June 1967.

Collins, John N.: "Student Participation in University Administration and Campus Disorder," paper prepared for delivery at 1970 Annual Meeting of American Political Science Association, 1970.

Corson, John J.: *Governance of Colleges and Universities,* McGraw-Hill Book Company, New York, 1960.

Costner, Herbert A.: "Criteria for Measures of Association," *American Sociological Review,* vol. 30, pp. 431–453, June 1965.

Costner, Herbert L., and Robert K. Leik: "Deductions from 'Axiomatic

Theory,'" *American Sociological Review,* vol. 29, pp. 819–835, December 1964.

Crane, Diana: "Scientists at Major and Minor Universities: A Study of Productivity and Recognition," *American Sociological Review,* vol. 30, pp. 699–714, October 1965.

Crane, Diana: "The Academic Marketplace Revisited: A Study of Faculty Mobility Using the Cartter Ratings," *American Journal of Sociology,* vol. 75, pp. 953–964, May 1970.

Cyert, Richard, and James G. March: *A Behavioral Theory of the Firm,* Prentice-Hall, Inc., Englewood Cliffs, N.J., 1963.

Dahl, Robert A.: *Who Governs?* Yale University Press, New Haven, Conn., 1961.

Demerath, Nicholas J., Richard W. Stephens, and Robb R. Taylor: *Power, Presidents, and Professors,* Basic Books, Inc., Publishers, New York, 1967.

Dodds, Harold W.: *The Academic President—Educator or Caretaker?* McGraw-Hill Book Company, New York, 1962.

Douglas, Jack D. (ed.): *Understanding Everyday Life,* Aldine Publishing Company, Chicago, 1970.

Dreitzel, Hans Peter (ed.): *Recent Sociology No. 2: Patterns of Communicative Behavior,* The Macmillan Company, New York, 1970.

Eckert, Ruth E.: "The Share of the Teaching Faculty in University Policy-Making," *Bulletin of the American Association of University Professors,* vol, 45, pp. 346–351, Autum 1959.

Eells, Walter Crosby, and Ernest V. Hollis: *The College Presidency: 1900–1960,* Office of Education, U.S. Department of Health, Education and Welfare, Washington, 1961.

Etzioni, Amitai: *A Comparative Analysis of Complex Organizations,* The Free Press of Glencoe, Inc., New York, 1961.

Etzioni, Amitai: *Modern Organizations,* Prentice-Hall, Inc., Englewood Cliffs, N.J., 1964.

Fashing, Joseph, and Steven E. Deutsch: *Academics in Retreat,* University of New Mexico Press, Albuquerque, 1971.

Federal Support to Universities, Colleges and Selected Nonprofit Institutions, Fiscal Year 1969, U.S. Government Printing Office, Washington, 1970.

Folger, John J., Helen S. Astin, and Alan E. Bayer: *Human Resources and Higher Education,* Russell Sage Foundation, New York, 1970.

Friedrich, Carl J.: *Man and His Government*, McGraw-Hill Book Company, New York, 1963.

Gans, Herbert: *The Urban Villagers*, The Free Press of Glencoe, Inc., New York, 1962.

Goodman, Leo A., and William H. Kruskal: "Measures of Association for Cross Classifications," *Journal of the American Statistical Association*, vol. 49, pp. 732–764, December 1954.

Goodman, Leo A., and William H. Kruskal: "Measures of Association for Cross Classifications: III. Approximate Sampling Theory," *Journal of the American Statistical Association*, vol. 58, pp. 310–364, June 1963.

Goodman, Paul: *The Community of Scholars*, Random House, Inc., New York, 1962.

Gouldner, Alvin W.: "Theoretical Requirements of the Applied Social Sciences," *American Sociological Review*, vol. 22, pp. 92–102, February 1957.

Gouldner, Alvin W.: "Organizational Analysis," chap. 18 in Robert K. Merton et al. (eds.), *Sociology Today*, Basic Books, Inc., Publishers, New York, 1959.

Gouldner, Alvin W.: "Metaphysical Pathos and the Theory of Bureaucracy," in Amitai Etzioni (ed.), *Complex Organizations*, pp. 71–82, Holt, Rinehart and Winston, Inc. New York, 1961.

Grambsch, Paul V.: "Academic Administrators and University Goals," *Academy of Management Annual Proceedings*, pp. 64–73, December 1966.

Grambsch, Paul V.: "Conflicts and Priorities," in G. Kerry Smith (ed.), *The Troubled Campus*, pp. 101–107, Jossey-Bass, San Francisco, 1970.

Greeley Andrew M.: *From Backwater to Mainstream: A Profile of Catholic Higher Education*, McGraw-Hill Book Company, New York, 1969.

Grimes, Andrew J., and Philip K. Berger: "Cosmopolitan-Local: Evaluation of the Concept," *Administrative Science Quarterly*, vol. 15, pp. 407–416, December 1970.

Gross, Edward: "Universities as Organizations: A Research Approach," *American Sociological Review*, vol. 33, pp. 518–544, August 1968.

Gross, Edward, and Paul V. Grambsch: *University Goals and Academic Power*, American Council on Education, Washington, 1968.

Hansen, Morris, William N. Hurwitz, and William G. Madow: *Sample Survey Methods and Theory*, John Wiley & Sons, Inc., New York, 1953.

Hefferlin, J B Lon: *Dynamics of Academic Reform,* Jossey-Bass, San Francisco, 1969.

Helmstadter, G. C.: *Research Concepts in Human Behavior,* Appleton-Century-Crofts, Inc., New York, 1970.

Hodgkinson, Harold L.: *Institutions in Transition,* McGraw-Hill Book Company, New York, 1971.

Hooper, Mary Evans: *Earned Degrees Conferred: 1969–70,* Institutional Data, U.S. Government Printing Office, Washington, 1970.

Kaysen, Carl: *Higher Learning, The Universities and the Public,* Princeton University Press, Princeton, N.J., 1969.

Kerr, Clark: "Governance and Functions," *Daedalus,* vol. 99, pp. 108–121, Winter 1970.

Knudsen, D. D., and T. R. Vaughn: "Quality in Graduate Education: A Re-evaluation of the Rankings of Sociology Departments in the Cartter Report," *American Sociologist,* vol. 4, pp. 12–19, February 1969.

Lazarsfeld, Paul F.: "Interpretation of Statistical Relationships as a Research Operation," in Paul Lazarsfeld and M. Rosenberg (eds.). *The Language of Social Research,* pp. 115–125, The Free Press of Glencoe, Inc., New York, 1955.

Lazarsfeld, Paul F., and Herbert Menzel: "On the Relation Between Individual and Collective Properties," in Amitai Etzioni (ed.), *A Sociological Reader on Complex Organizations,* pp. 499–516, Holt, Rinehart, and Winston, Inc., New York, 1969. (This paper originally appeared in the 1961 edition of this reader.)

Lewis, Lionel S.: "On Subjective and Objective Rankings of Sociology Departments," *American Sociologist,* vol. 3, pp. 129–131, May 1968.

Lipset, Seymour Martin, and Philip G. Altbach (eds.): *Students in Revolt,* Houghton Mifflin Company, Boston, 1969.

Lipset, Seymour Martin: *Rebellion in the University,* Little, Brown and Company, Boston, 1972.

Lunsford, Terry: *The Official Perspective in Academe,* Center for Research and Development in Higher Education, Berkeley, Calif., 1970.

MacIver, R. M.: *Community,* Macmillan & Co., Ltd., London, 1936.

March, James G., and Herbert Simon: *Organizations,* John Wiley & Sons, Inc., New York, 1958.

Mayo, Elton: *The Human Problems of an Industrial Civilization,* The Macmillan Company, New York, 1933.

McGee, Reece: *Academic Janus,* Jossey-Bass, San Francisco, 1971.

Merton, Robert K.: "Bureaucratic Structure and Personality," in *Social Theory and Social Structure,* pp. 195–206, The Free Press of Glencoe, Ill., Chicago, 1957.

Meyer, Marshall W.: "Size and Structure of Organizations: A Causal Analysis," *American Sociological Review,* vol. 37, pp. 434–440, August 1972.

Moser, C. A.: *Survey Methods in Social Investigation,* William Heinemann, Ltd., London, 1961.

Mueller, John H., Karl F. Schuessler, and Herbert L. Costner: *Statistical Reasoning in Sociology,* Houghton Mifflin Company, Boston, 1970.

Nisbet, Robert: *The Degradation of the Academic Dogma,* Basic Books, Inc., Publishers, New York, 1971.

Orlans, Harold: *Effects of Federal Programs on Higher Education,* The Brookings Institution, Washington, 1962.

Parry, Geraint: *Political Elites,* Frederick A. Praeger, Inc., New York, 1969.

Parsons, Talcott: "A Sociological Approach to the Theory of Formal Organizations," *Structure and Process in Modern Societies,* The Free Press of Glencoe, Inc., New York, 1960.

Parsons, Talcott, et al., (eds.): *Theories of Society,* The Free Press of Glencoe, Inc., New York, 1961.

Parsons, Talcott, and Gerald M. Platt: "Considerations of the American Academic System," *Minerva,* vol. 6, pp. 497–523, Summer 1968.

Parten, Mildred: *Surveys, Polls, and Samples,* Harper & Brothers, New York, 1950.

Perrow, Charles: "The Analysis of Goals in Complex Organizations," *American Sociological Review,* vol. 26, pp. 854–866, December 1961.

Perrow, Charles: *Organizational Analysis: A Sociological View,* Wadsworth Publishing Company, Inc., Belmont, Calif. 1970.

Presthus, Robert: *Men at the Top,* Oxford University Press, New York, 1964.

Riesman, David: "Predicaments in the Career of the College President," in Carlos E. Kruytbosch and Sheldon L. Messinger (eds.), *The State of the University.* Sage Publications, Beverly Hills, Calif., 1970.

Roose, Kenneth D., and Charles J. Andersen: *A Rating of Graduate Programs,* American Council on Education, Washington, 1970.

Rose, Arnold M.: *The Power Structure,* Oxford University Press, New York, 1967.

Rourke, Francis E., and Glenn E. Brooks: "The Managerial Revolution in

Higher Education," *Administrative Science Quarterly,* vol. 9, pp. 154–181, September 1964.

Rudolph, Frederick: *The American College and University,* Alfred A. Knopf, Inc., New York, 1962.

Schumpeter, Joseph: *Capitalism, Socialism and Democracy,* Harper & Row, Publishers, Incorporated, New York, 1950.

Scott, Joseph W., and Mohamed El-Assal: "Multiversity, University Size, University Quality and Student Protest: An Empirical Study, *American Sociological Review,* vol. 34, pp. 702–709, October 1969.

Selznick, Philip: *TVA and the Grass Roots,* University of California Press, Berkeley, 1953.

Semas, Philip W.: "Students 'Satisfied' with Education, Most of Them and Teachers Agree," *The Chronicle of Higher Education,* vol. 5. no. 1, Jan. 18, 1971.

Shamblin, Don H.: "Prestige and the Sociology Establishment," *American Sociologist,* vol. 5, pp. 154–156, May 1970.

Shils, Edward: "Observations on the American University," *Universities Quarterly,* vol. 17, pp. 182–193, March 1963.

Shils, Edward: "The American Private University," *Minerva,* vol. 11, pp. 6–29, January 1973.

Sills, David L.: *The Volunteers,* The Free Press of Glencoe, Inc., New York, 1957.

Simon, Herbert: "On the Concept of Organizational Goal," *Administrative Science Quarterly,* vol. 8, pp. 1–22, 1964.

Smith, Virginia B.: "More for Less: Higher Education's New Priority," in *Universal Higher Education: Costs and Benefits,* pp. 123–142, American Council on Education, Washington, 1971.

Stoke, Harold W.: *The American College President,* Harper & Brothers, New York, 1959.

Strauss, George: "Some Notes on Power Equalization," in Harold J. Leavitt (ed.), *The Social Science of Organizations,* pp. 39–84, Prentice-Hall, Inc., Englewood Cliffs, N.J., 1963.

Stroup, Herbert: *Bureaucracy in Higher Education,* The Free Press, New York, 1966.

Tannenbaum, Arnold S.: *Control in Organizations,* McGraw-Hill Book Company, New York, 1968.

Thompson, James D., and William J. McEwen: "Organization Goals and Environment," *American Sociological Review,* vol. 23, pp. 23–50, 1958.

Thompson, James D.: *Organizations in Action,* McGraw-Hill Book Company, New York, 1967.

Trow, Martin: "The Democratization of Higher Education in America," *European Journal of Sociology,* vol. 3, pp. 231–262, 1962.

Trow, Martin: "Reflections on the Transition from Mass to Universal Higher Education," *Daedalus,* vol. 99, pp. 1–42, Winter 1970.

Trow, Martin: "The Expansion and Transformation of Higher Education," *International Review of Education,* vol. 18, no. 1, 1972.

United States Senate: *Staff Study of Campus Riots and Disorders, October 1967–May 1969,* U.S. Government Printing Office, Washington, 1969.

Veysey, Laurence: *The Emergence of the American University,* The University of Chicago Press, Chicago, 1965.

Wriston, Henry W.: *Academic Procession,* Columbia University Press, New York, 1959.

Wynn, Sheila C.: *University Administrative Style and Student Protest,* unpublished M.A. thesis, University of Washington, Seattle, 1970.

Zuckerman, Harriet A.: "Nobel Laureates in Science: Patterns of Productivity, Collaboration, and Authorship," *American Sociological Review,* vol. 32, pp. 391–403, June 1967.

Appendix A: Comments

Unlike 1964, we made provisions in the 1971 questionnaire for invited comments. Approximately one-fifth of the respondents availed themselves of our invitation and wrote either specific comments dealing with the questionnaire itself or more general statements about administration in universities and educational philosophy. The comments ranged from serious dissertations to facetious remarks, from anger and despair to optimism and contentment.

Comments were received from respondents in every university in the study with only one exception. In general, there was a remarkable uniformity of response of approximately 20 percent of the respondents from each university.

The comments were for the most part written in by hand, and occasionally, a portion of a comment was undecipherable. Some of the illegible comments came from medical faculty and administrators, but in no bigger proportion than that of other members of the academic community. Medical doctors do not have a monopoly on illegibility of handwriting.

Because of the large number of comments, we thought at one time of drawing on them liberally in the body of our discussion in the book. But in the end we drew away from such a practice because it proved all too easy to "remember" comments that happened to support a point we sought to make. We also considered a systematic analysis of comments, to parallel our analysis in the book. But such an analysis — for example, classifying comments by the position of the person making the comment — seemed to represent dubious research practice. Comments, after all, do not represent a "sample" of any definable population. They are simply remarks made by persons who felt like making them. One might argue that disgruntled persons are more likely to make comments, as some studies of letters to congressmen seem to show. But we simply have no such data on our respondents and would be unable to make statistical analyses with any confidence.

In spite of these problems, we felt that the comments were definitely worth reporting. We had clearly touched a nerve when so many persons chose to write extended comments after taking the trouble to fill out a long questionnaire. Evidently, the experience stimulated our respondents to think about other matters, in some cases related to the theme of our questionnaire, in other cases on quite unrelated subjects. Hence we felt we could most truly reflect the content of the comments by grouping them under broad headings.

We were pleased to have a number of congratulations expressed in various responses, plus comments to the effect that the questionnaire was interesting and penetrating. We have also noted the brickbats and the unfavorable reactions. We assume that some of the nonrespondents are also those who have criticisms, and they have chosen the "discard" method of expressing them.

The major comments clustered around several major themes. One we have entitled "The Crisis in Higher Education." The second is "Management of Universities," and the third is entitled "Basic Conflicts." Under each of these headings a large number of comments might be used. It must be reiterated that we have only selected a very few which seem to us to be representative.

The Crisis in Higher Education Most of the respondents assume that the university is an ongoing institution and that it is not seriously threatened with extinction. A large number of the people making comments believe that the university is seriously changing. In a few cases the view was expressed that the university career was no longer to be preferred and that the university was no longer a "fun place" to be, especially from a teaching standpoint. In general, the comments emphasized that excellence in scholarship seems to be crumbling under the pressure of forces no longer under control. Some respondents lash out rather bitterly at administration, trustees, and legislatures. Others believe that the overwhelming pressure comes from the students and their insistence upon "relevance," rather than upon scholarship and knowledge for its own sake. The result of all the pressures, many respondents believe, is a breakdown in public confidence so that universities are now viewed with suspicion. The comment of an administrator from a Western state university sums up this point.

The top priority goal of all U.S. universities is regaining public confidence which was recently lost when several administrations and faculties were overwhelmed by recent guerilla tactics employed by student radicals. In some parts of the country our privilege of adventurous thinking and planning is lost.

This individual is longing for the good old days. He believes the universities have lost something. He attributes the cause to the student radicals; he seems to imply that the prescription for "finding ourselves" is to get rid of the student radicals.

Another respondent, this time from a Midwestern state university, expresses something of the same view, but attributes the cause to the university administration and others who speak with authority for the university. He says:

The university has lost track of the citizens to whom it is ultimately responsible. It has been arrogant in its feelings with the middle-class voters who no longer respect the university as a place of reason, objectivity, moderation, and sound information. Such a loss is very serious and could take years to recover.

The comment of a third respondent is directed at the idea of returning to a former state. He believes that the responsibility of the fall from grace rests upon all who are part of the academic institution but, especially, those directly involved in teaching and research, namely the faculty. He is a faculty member at a well-known Southern state university.

We must reestablish the desire for excellence for our own sake and reestablish in students the respect for those who achieve excellence. The students must be stimulated to pursue interests energetically and rationally, building on a sound foundation of basic information gained in earlier academic years. We must counter the ever-expanding wave of skepticism and mistrust and the psychoneurotic personality deterioration that has become stylish in recent years under the guise "liberated thinking" or "pseudo-intellectualism."

He is speaking for many members of the academic community who look with disfavor upon many of the trends they observe around them.

Another respondent assigns the blame for our difficulties in universities to our poorly defined goals. He says:

American universities are in serious difficulty due in large part to poor administration structure and operating procedures. Goals are very hazy; answers do not come as a result of basic philosophical beliefs undergirding the goals of the institution, but as a matter of expediency.

A number of respondents have expressed the same view in different words. Many believe that universities have allowed themselves to become overextended and on the basis of expediency have become all things to all people. Not all of them are pessimistic. Indeed, one detects that a great number of respondents believe that new institutions will emerge because the old ones cannot cope with the problems and that the academic institutions will be stronger in the long run. This is a return to the earlier viewpoint that most respondents believe that the academic community will survive, although there will be changes in the institutional forms.

In recent years there have been serious attempts to thrust the university, as an institution, into the political arena. The university senates and other governing bodies such as regents or trustees were asked to take a stand on everything from the Vietnam War to the banning of automobiles as instruments of pollution. Has this been a factor in the crisis in higher education? In the comment of many respondents this certainly looms very large. One of the more extreme comments, which is from a person serving in a large Midwestern state university, is as follows:

I feel rather strongly that the American university should not be diverted from its proper academic goals by feverish and enthusiastic pleas for community involvement. The university should be reasonably responsive to the needs of the immediate localities but national universities should not try to become (in the name of relevance) amateur social-work institutions devoted to solving social ills.

Another comment indicates that the crisis is due, in part, to our descending from the ivory tower. Our respondent writes:

In general the total effect of the transition from university to multiversity has been negative to disastrous. Even God cannot be all things to all men and a university should not try. At the risk of ridicule and misunderstanding, I believe this university or any university should recover what it once aspired to be, a repository of learning and a disseminator of it. Armored against the huckster, the special pleader—not aloof, but, I would hope, a bit above the storms of life—always benignly a part of the whole but always too wise and knowing to drift with the currents of the moment.

A substantial number of respondents have expressed themselves on the subject of making a severe change in their career plans because of the changes in the university. Whether they are serious or not depends on a number of different factors, including the economic outlook and additional changes at their particular institution.

Management of Universities The role of management is far from settled in American universities. Some of our respondents tell us that management is overemphasized, overbureaucratized and, in general, overwhelming. For example, one private Eastern university respondent writes:

If this university is any indication of what higher education is becoming and I believe it is, then we are in serious trouble. My impressions are that universities are becoming big business and like this one increasing the top administration (from one vice-president to seven vice-presidents in two years) at the expense of the academic purpose and goals of the university. This university administration not only wishes to run the academic part of the university but is trying to pressure the faculty into recruiting students and funds to keep themselves in a position of power and affluence.

There are a number of comments which amplify this point, namely, that administration has become overwhelming. A respondent from a Midwestern state university writes:

I think that my university suffers from an excess of middle managerial avoirdupois. There are swarms of assistant deans, directors, assistant directors, etc., whose principal activity is to attend meetings and conferences with each other. I suspect this condition exists, not only in academe, but also throughout commerce, industry, and government. It calls for a Thorstein Veblen to sort it out.

There are other pithy comments about university bureaucracy. One respondent believes that university administration could be cut by 50 percent and efficiency improved. Still another believes that universities are doomed because they have allowed bureaucracy to set in and to dominate all university life.

On the other hand, there are a good many comments to the effect that administration is regarded as an important and necessary function which needs to be performed in a better fashion. A number of respondents believe that there has been entirely too much dabbling by faculty in administration and that, in general, universities should be run by professionals. For example, a comment from an Eastern state university respondent is as follows:

I feel that it should be taken as a given that administrating a university is an impossible task, particularly for academicians. It would probably improve things to professionalize this task.

A respondent from a Southern private university makes the following comment:

My observation is that extensive faculty participation in university governments is detrimental to both the faculty and the university. The faculty needs to retain the strength to survive a few years of bad administration and to force changes in the administrative appointments, but should delegate most of the day-to-day running of the university to administrators.

Whether in specific situations these comments would hold for matters of action remains to be seen. In general, however, respondents seem to be more tolerant of administration, as long as it performs well. We suspect, however, that performing well is, in part, a question of definition. There are some administrations which have become very "hard line" and authoritarian. These are looked on favorably by the population generally but not necessarily by the academic community itself. On the other hand, those administrations that are too democratic or involve too much consultation or participation are oftentimes looked on with favor in the academic community but not by outsiders.

There seems to be general agreement that administrative power should be decentralized. In part, this is coupled with ideas about size and the need for greater decentralization as an expediting device. On the other hand, some respondents believe that decentralization is necessary in order to solve organizational problems. For example, a respondent from a Midwestern state university writes:

In my opinion large, complex universities are attempting incorrectly to solve organizational problems through increasingly unresponsive and monolithic central administrative mechanisms. More responsibility and authority should be directed back down to the college level.

Another respondent puts it more succinctly:

> Universities are too big; departments too specialized; administrative over-
> head too big and opaque. A goal should be to decentralize power.

One final comment is representative of a rather large number of those who believe that an academic career is not necessarily the best preparation for university administration. A respondent from a Mountain States university observes as follows:

> Universities should be operated on a business-like basis by administrators
> who have not spent their entire productive lives under the sheltered in-
> fluence of an academic community. Our product is an educated individual
> and he should be produced by a system that utilizes responsible manage-
> ment procedures.

This subject is of more than mere academic interest to a great many boards of trustees and other administrators. In professional schools the selection committee for a new dean and, in some cases, a department chairman has to make a basic decision as to whether to consider people not presently connected with an academic in-stitution. There is less consideration of this kind at the vice-presi-dent and presidential level, although some of the data we have gathered have suggested that career patterns of higher administra-tion oftentimes reveal nonacademic backgrounds.

Basic Conflicts *(1) The ivory tower versus the university in the "real" world* Cer-tainly one of the most talked about issues of our times concerns this particular conflict. There are many facets to this issue, some dealing with the question of relevance in courses in teaching, others dealing with general university involvement in local and contem-porary issues, while still others deal with the responsibility to per-form services under the influence of the legislature or other ruling bodies. There are a great number of comments on each one of these facets with a substantial number of respondents coming down on either side of an issue.

An official from a Western state university illustrates one point of view expressed by a number of respondents when he says:

> In my view a great university compromises itself when it becomes involved
> in the local and the contemporary. We need to return to some of the ivory

tower concepts. University governments should be the minimum necessary but they should command loyalty. A university is not a democracy. Student control is a danger. Politicalization is a danger.

On the other side of the coin, a respondent from a Midwestern state university says:

Universities should be less traditional; more responsive to societal needs in the current era; retain quality but make knowledge meaningful and useful for people attending them today. Increased recognition and greater rewards should be extended to faculty members who provide superior, even good performance, in extension and public-service programs of university achievement level.

There is considerable discussion around the issues of outside influence, particularly repondents from state universities. Some people regard outside influence as sinister and detrimental to the university. Other people are more concerned with the influence that outsiders have upon the nature and extent of university programs. For example, one hears the phrase "all things to all people" as universities try to placate all interest groups and fulfill all obligations. As illustrative of this point of view quotes from several respondents are appropriate.

An institution cannot be all things to all people but should do well that which it chooses. Some graduates will have a vocation. Some will need graduate work to have a vocation.

Another respondent writes:

I feel that some American universities have expanded their programs far beyond their abilities to support all of these programs adequately in terms of library resources and services. This seems especially so in the humanities and social sciences.

Another respondent says:

I feel that our universities should select one or two major areas, such as agriculture, engineering, education, etc., and finance these areas well and allow them to become high-quality programs. Our present programs seem to be directed towards "being all things to all people" — something that cannot be accomplished on a severely restricted budget.

(2) Conflicts over power relationships   The tendency of faculty to "dabble" in administration is a subject of many of the comments. In some ways this is where true feelings about administration may surface. The basic conflict appears to be the difficulty in drawing a fine line between administrative functions that should be left to administrators and administrative functions that ought to be conducted by faculty. One respondent from a private Eastern university sums up the issues very well in his comment. He says:

I firmly believe that faculty should have a great deal to say about the aims and purposes of our universities and practically total control over curriculum, giving thoughtful attention to the more thoughtful student opinions on this subject. On the other hand, twentieth century universities are highly complex, corporate enterprises requiring capable management personnel and middle- and top-level managerial positions. Only too frequently the responsibilities of these positions are not matched by the requisite authority. Management is now a full-time occupation and should properly be left to managers. The efforts to interfere unnecessarily with management are more extensive than is desirable. The primary responsibility of faculty is research and instruction, not business management. I feel strongly about this.

Another power conflict arises from the growth of student power. A number of respondents have indicated that they view with alarm the growth of student power, while others tend to accept it and in several cases believe that it is long overdue. One of the most extreme statements is from a respondent from a private Eastern university who says:

Recent student revolution has given students the real control. The only acceptable attitudes are those of students. One can no longer speak or discuss freely because of accusations and counteraction of students. Universities in the U.S. are degenerating into high schools. Instead of the creation of new knowledge as the main goal, pleasure (not usually community oriented) is the main point. Within the teaching picture academic standards are dropping disastrously. Student performance is way down. Professors are afraid to grade accordingly because they fear students will call them bad teachers.

Although this is an extreme statement, there are others who voice similar concerns. There are some other observations regarding the growth of student power. A Midwestern state university respondent summed it up quite nicely:

Students in U.S. colleges and universities have achieved their present position of power by persuading the faculties to share their power with them. The prospective effect of this in the long run is going to be to reduce the faculty power vis-à-vis administration. The responsible administrators and boards of trustees are not going to be bound by decisions run by such a coalition, a good portion of which is ignorant and inexperienced in matters of higher education. The coalition will gradually lose its credibility and its long-run effect will be to increase the power of administrators at the expense of the power of faculties.

A number of other respondents do not look at the long-run picture but are obviously expressing concern over the same questions. On the more pragmatic level an observation regarding student government is very much to the point. A respondent from a Western state university notes:

One goal universities should strive toward is true student government representation. Eight hundred students out of a total full-time enrollment of twenty-five thousand who vote in student elections does not make for a very representative student government.

It appears that this person along with several others has generally accepted the idea that student power should remain, but he is advocating that we learn how to make it a more adequate student voice. Whether over time student power will develop in such a manner that it is taken for granted is still a question for discussion. It would appear that in those universities that place strong emphasis upon democratic measures student participation in decision making is likely to grow. In other universities, however, student power is going to be viewed suspiciously and organization structures will evolve that will lessen its impact.

(3) Conflicts between teaching and research   This issue has been thoroughly discussed on a number of occasions, but it is interesting to note that many of the same kinds of questions keep coming up. In our study there were a number of comments that appear on the research side of the issue. For example, a Midwestern state university respondent says:

Much of the research accomplished today is done by teams. These teams, however, are difficult to build and maintain and many administrations make it their policy to destroy all teams. It seems to me that at some universities, such as this one, research teams should be encouraged.

Another person from a private Southern university says:

There can be little doubt that any advance in medicine will be made by dedicated scientists doing basic research and I am in complete support of this. However, when laboratory investigation becomes the sole means by which professional recognition is obtained in professional societies or granting agencies an alternative system rewarding teachers, counselors, and clinicians must be developed. Although such recognition for teachers versus researchers has received support from many quarters the "publish or perish" approach continues to be the major impetus to younger faculty members.

This seems to reflect a very representative view of many of our respondents. Variations on this theme appear in a large number of comments. In general, our respondents believe that teaching is not rewarded as highly as research, and they believe that devices must be developed so that teaching is measured and rewarded to a much higher degree. On the other hand, there are some respondents who have indicated that they do not believe research is properly rewarded. The following quote, for example, from a state university respondent in the Mountain States:

I am particularly concerned that this university does not reward appreciably those who are successful at research funding, often using its research revenues through use charges to go into the general funds. The university is poor but this is no way to foster sponsored research, maintain faculty who obtain sponsored research, or, for that matter, increase university revenues from sponsored research.

It seems to be evident that this conflict is still with us and will remain as long as universities have to choose between one reward system and another.

Conclusions   The comments section of the questionnaire has provided us with additional insight into the feelings and aspirations of administrators and faculty in universities. Occasionally, the comment indicated that some members of the academic community believe that academic persons take themselves too seriously. We were reminded that there are other important institutions in society and that educators may have exaggerated their place in the scheme of things. Taken together, the comments represent an outpouring of spirited and very human views of the university. Some have seriously tried to evaluate the university itself; still others wanted to express their own philosophy.

Two of the comments seem to be appropriate in summing up matters. In one case a person from an Eastern private university said:

I know that this is really important but here it is 11:00 P.M. and I haven't really finished yesterday's work so you don't have very good answers here.

The other, in many ways, typified our feelings, as well as those of everyone in universities.

I have been in university work for 15 years and every day I ask myself the question: What is the goal of a university? If you find out, please let me know.

$\mathcal{A}ppendix$ $\mathcal{B}$: $\mathcal{D}etails$ of $\mathcal{S}tatistical$ $\mathcal{C}alculations$

Assumptions and Procedures in Gamma Calculations
The most widely used measure of association in this research was Goodman and Kruskal's gamma (Goodman & Kruskal, 1954, 1963). This measure is appropriate for ordinal variables and was well-adapted to this study. As noted in several places in the book, we did not feel confident that the accuracy of scores was sufficiently stable to warrant assumptions of an interval scale, but used scores to generate ranks. For example, in measuring prestige of universities (discussed below), we felt that universities could, at best, be divided into four levels of prestige and that further divisions were not defensible in view of the crudity of instruments of measurement.

However, the main advantage of gamma was that it is one of the group that Costner (1965) has called "proportional reduction in error measures." A familiar example is r^2 which ". . . is a measure of proportional improvement in the accuracy of estimation, that is, the proportional reduction in the error of estimation obtained by using a specified 'independent' variable to estimate a given 'dependent' variable by a specified linear prediction formula" (Costner, 1965, p. 343). Gamma admits of a similar interpretation, and is, as noted, directly applicable to ordinal data.

Gamma involves a prediction of the order of pairs of cases. For example, in the case of two sets of ordered classes, one set representing the X variable and the other the Y variable, pairs of cases (say, case A and case B) may be concordant (C, where the ordering of A and B is the same on both variables, e.g., $X_A > X_B$ and $Y_A > Y_B$), discordant (D, the order of A and B is reversed on the two variables, e.g., $X_A > X_B$ and $Y_B > Y_B$), or tied on one or the other or both variables. Goodman and Kruskal's (symmetric) gamma is then computed by the following formula:

$$\text{Gamma} = \frac{C - D}{C + D}$$

This involves ignoring ties on the rationale that they result from crude measurement.

Mueller, Schuessler, and Costner (1970, p. 288) offer the following interpretation of gamma:

The numerical value of gamma, disregarding sign, gives the percentage of guessing errors eliminated by using knowledge of a second variable to predict order. The sign of gamma indicates which of two possible predictions of order is more accurate: a positive sign indicates that a prediction of *same* order on the predicted variable, as on the predictor variable, is more accurate, while a negative sign indicates that a prediction of *reverse* order is more accurate.

In a 2 $\times$ 2 table, gamma is identical to Q. If the number of ties is large, the sampling variability for gamma increases. Skewness in the marginals increases the number of ties and hence reduces the number of pairs on which the gamma is based. Also, zero cell frequencies produce certain anomalies. We have inspected all tables and in most cases, eliminated any "findings" in which zero cells generate misleading inferences, or in which skewness results in gammas based on very small numbers of nontied pairs. In some cases, we did retain the finding but have reproduced the table to make a comment on it.

Goodman and Kruskal (1963) offer formulas for computing the sampling variability of gamma. We made use of the measure based on the upper bound for the variance of the sampling distribution which provides a conservative test of significance. The formula utilized was

$$z = G \sqrt{\frac{C + D}{N(1 - G^2)}}$$

As noted, we report only results where z was greater than 1.96; that is, exceeding the 5 percent level of significance.

Calculation of University Prestige Scores

Calculation of prestige scores for the universities in 1964 is described in Gross and Grambsch (1968, pp. 128–132). For 1971, prestige scores were recalculated using the more recent ratings available in Roose and Andersen (1970). For the previous set of scores (from Cartter, 1966), ratings of the quality of the graduate faculty were available for up to 29 departments; for this set, a university may have been rated in as many as 36 departments.

In the more recent study, no specific scores are presented. The group scoring above 3.0 is presented in ranked order, whereas the two other groups (2.5–2.9 and 2.0–2.4) are each presented in alphabetical order.

Calculation of final prestige scores was carried out in a method similar to that for the previous set of scores. The method is detailed here:

1 For each university,[1] the number of departments rated in each of the three groups was established. Since no specific scores were available, weights given to each category were the midpoints of each interval.

Category	Interval	Weighting factor
1	3.0–5.0	4.0
2	2.5–2.9	2.75
3	2.0–2.4	2.25

2 Three scores were then calculated for each university:

$$\text{weighted sum:} \quad X = 4N_1 + 2.75N_2 + 2.25N_3$$

$$\text{Score I}: \quad \bar{X} = \frac{X}{N} \text{ (weighted mean)}$$

$$\text{Score II}: \quad \bar{X} + X$$

$$\text{Score III}: \quad \bar{X} + N$$

where

$$N_i = \text{number of departments rated in category } i, \ 1 \leq i \leq 3$$
$$N = \Sigma N_i$$

Prestige Levels

3 Each set of scores was then arranged in descending order. The top ten universities in each set were assigned a 1; the next ten, a 2; the next 22, a 3; and all remaining were assigned a 4.[2]

4 These three scores (rounded) were averaged for each university — this average becoming the prestige level.

[1] Ratings for three universities did not exist.

[2] The three unrated universities were assigned to level 4.

Appendix C: The Questionnaire

ACADEMIC ADMINISTRATORS AND UNIVERSITY GOALS

A Project of the
CENTER FOR ACADEMIC ADMINISTRATION RESEARCH
UNIVERSITY OF MINNESOTA

Conducted by
EDWARD GROSS
PROFESSOR OF SOCIOLOGY
University of Washington

and

PAUL V. GRAMBSCH
PROFESSOR OF MANAGEMENT
University of Minnesota

This questionnaire is being given to all presidents, vice-presidents, deans, and directors, plus a carefully selected sample of department chairmen and faculty at 80 major universities in the United States. It will provide us with a comprehensive picture of how administrators view the university, and how they differ in their influence on university policy.

The success of the study depends completely upon the kindness and generosity of each respondent. We hope the results will be of value to you in your university. They will appear in the form of published articles and monographs.

Responses to any and all questions are entirely voluntary, of course, and failure or unwillingness to participate will be accepted without comment or interpretation on our part.

This research has been funded by a grant from the Ford Foundation.

The questionnaire is completely confidential. No one will see it except the members of the research staff. Nevertheless for purposes of control of returns, we need your name to serve as a double check on the accuracy of our number control system. After the sample check has been made, we will destroy the sheet.

Name _____

CONTROL NUMBER _____

235

1. THE GOALS OF THIS UNIVERSITY

One of the great issues in American education has to do with the proper aims or goals of the university. The question is: What are we trying to accomplish? Are we trying to prepare people for jobs, to broaden them intellectually, or what? Below we have listed a large number of the more commonly claimed aims, intentions or goals of a university. We would like you to react to each of these in two different ways:

(1) How important *is* each aim at this university?

(2) How important *should* the aim be at this university?

	of absolutely top importance	of great importance	of medium importance	of little importance	of no importance	don't know or can't say
EXAMPLE: to serve as substitute parents **is**	☐	☐	☒	☐	☐	☐
should be	☐	☐	☐	☐	☒	☐

A person who had checked the alternatives in the manner shown above would be expressing his perception that the aim, intention or goal, "to serve as substitute parents," *is* of medium importance at his university but that he believes it *should be of no importance* as an aim, intention, or goal of his university.

NOTE: "of absolutely top importance" should only be checked if the aim is *so* important that, if it were to be removed, the university would be shaken to its very roots and its character changed in a fundamental way.

ALL QUESTIONS ARE ABOUT *THIS* UNIVERSITY, that is, THE ONE AT WHICH YOU ARE PRESENTLY EMPLOYED.

A. THE GOALS OF THIS UNIVERSITY

		of absolutely top importance	of great importance	of medium importance	of little importance	of no importance	don't know or can't say
1.	hold our staff in the face of inducements offered by other universities						
	is	☐	☐	☐	☐	☐	☐
	should be	☐	☐	☐	☐	☐	☐
2.	make sure that on *all* important issues (not only curriculum), the will of the full-time faculty shall prevail						
	is	☐	☐	☐	☐	☐	☐
	should be	☐	☐	☐	☐	☐	☐
3.	encourage students to go into graduate work						
	is	☐	☐	☐	☐	☐	☐
	should be	☐	☐	☐	☐	☐	☐
4.	protect the faculty's right to academic freedom						
	is	☐	☐	☐	☐	☐	☐
	should be	☐	☐	☐	☐	☐	☐
5.	provide special training for part-time adult students, through extension courses, special short courses, correspondence courses, etc.						
	is	☐	☐	☐	☐	☐	☐
	should be	☐	☐	☐	☐	☐	☐

GOALS (cont.)

	of absolutely top importance	of great importance	of medium importance	of little importance	of no importance	don't know or can't say
6. develop loyalty on the part of the faculty and staff to the university, rather than only to their own jobs or professional concerns						
is	☐	☐	☐	☐	☐	☐
should be	☐	☐	☐	☐	☐	☐
7. produce a student who, whatever else may be done to him, has had his intellect cultivated to the maximum						
is	☐	☐	☐	☐	☐	☐
should be	☐	☐	☐	☐	☐	☐
8. develop the inner character of students so that they can make sound, correct moral choices						
is	☐	☐	☐	☐	☐	☐
should be	☐	☐	☐	☐	☐	☐
9. make a good consumer of the student—a person who is elevated culturally, has good taste, and can make good consumer choices						
is	☐	☐	☐	☐	☐	☐
should be	☐	☐	☐	☐	☐	☐
10. serve as a center for the dissemination of new ideas that will change the society, whether those ideas are in science, literature, the arts, or politics						
is	☐	☐	☐	☐	☐	☐
should be	☐	☐	☐	☐	☐	☐
11. educate to his utmost capacities every high school graduate who meets basic legal requirements for admission						
is	☐	☐	☐	☐	☐	☐
should be	☐	☐	☐	☐	☐	☐

The table consists of rows of checkboxes for each item, with "is" and "should be" response rows.

12. keep harmony between departments or divisions of the university when such departments or divisions do not see eye to eye on important matters

is   □ □ □ □ □ □ □ □ □ □ □ □

should be   □ □ □ □ □ □ □ □ □ □ □ □

13. make this a place in which faculty have maximum opportunity to pursue their careers in a manner satisfactory to them by their own criteria

is   □ □ □ □ □ □ □ □ □ □ □ □

should be   □ □ □ □ □ □ □ □ □ □ □ □

14. develop greater pride on the part of faculty, staff and students in their university and the things it stands for

is   □ □ □ □ □ □ □ □ □ □ □ □

should be   □ □ □ □ □ □ □ □ □ □ □ □

15. keep up to date and responsive

is   □ □ □ □ □ □ □ □ □ □ □ □

should be   □ □ □ □ □ □ □ □ □ □ □ □

16. make sure the student is permanently affected (in mind and spirit) by the great ideas of the great minds of history

is   □ □ □ □ □ □ □ □ □ □ □ □

should be   □ □ □ □ □ □ □ □ □ □ □ □

17. train students in methods of scholarship and/or scientific research, and/or creative endeavor

is   □ □ □ □ □ □ □ □ □ □ □ □

should be   □ □ □ □ □ □ □ □ □ □ □ □

GOALS (cont.)

	of absolutely top importance	of great importance	of medium importance	of little importance	of no importance	don't know or can't say
18. serve as a center for the preservation of the cultural heritage	is ☐	☐	☐	☐	☐	☐
	should be ☐	☐	☐	☐	☐	☐
19. orient ourselves to the satisfaction of the special needs and problems of the immediate geographical region	is ☐	☐	☐	☐	☐	☐
	should be ☐	☐	☐	☐	☐	☐
20. involve students in the government of the university	is ☐	☐	☐	☐	☐	☐
	should be ☐	☐	☐	☐	☐	☐
21. make sure the university is run by those selected according to their ability to attain the goals of the university in the most efficient manner possible.	is ☐	☐	☐	☐	☐	☐
	should be ☐	☐	☐	☐	☐	☐
22. maintain top quality in all programs we engage in	is ☐	☐	☐	☐	☐	☐
	should be ☐	☐	☐	☐	☐	☐
23. keep this place from becoming something different from what it is now; that is, preserve its peculiar emphases and point of view, its "character"	is ☐	☐	☐	☐	☐	☐
	should be ☐	☐	☐	☐	☐	☐

24. provide the **student** with skills, attitudes, contacts, and experiences which maximize the likelihood of his occupying a high status in life and a position of leadership in society

    is

    should be

25. carry on pure research

    is

    should be

26. keep costs down as low as possible through more efficient utilization of time, and space, reduction of course duplication, etc.

    is

    should be

27. make sure that salaries, teaching assignments, perquisites, and privileges always reflect the contribution that the person involved is making to the functioning of this university

    is

    should be

28. protect and facilitate the students' right to advocate direct action of a political or social kind, and any attempts on their part to organize efforts to attain political or social goals

    is

    should be

29. produce a well-rounded student, that is one whose physical, social, moral, intellectual and esthetic potentialities have all been cultivated

    is

    should be

241

GOALS (cont.)

	of absolutely top importance	of great importance	of medium importance	of little importance	of no importance	don't know or can't say
30. assist citizens directly through extension programs, advice, consultation, and the provision of useful or needed facilities and services other than through teaching — is	☐	☐	☐	☐	☐	☐
should be	☐	☐	☐	☐	☐	☐
31. ensure the favorable appraisal of those who validate the quality of the programs we offer (validating groups include accrediting bodies, professional societies, scholarly peers at other universities, and respected persons in intellectual or artistic circles) — is	☐	☐	☐	☐	☐	☐
should be	☐	☐	☐	☐	☐	☐
32. maintain a balanced level of quality across the whole range of programs we engage in — is	☐	☐	☐	☐	☐	☐
should be	☐	☐	☐	☐	☐	☐
33. make sure the university is run democratically insofar as that is feasible — is	☐	☐	☐	☐	☐	☐
should be	☐	☐	☐	☐	☐	☐
34. produce a student who is able to perform his citizenship responsibilities effectively — is	☐	☐	☐	☐	☐	☐
should be	☐	☐	☐	☐	☐	☐
35. accommodate only students of high potential in terms of the specific strengths and emphases of this university — is	☐	☐	☐	☐	☐	☐
should be	☐	☐	☐	☐	☐	☐

☐	☐	☐	☐	☐	☐	☐	☐	☐	☐	☐	☐
☐	☐	☐	☐	☐	☐	☐	☐	☐	☐	☐	☐
☐	☐	☐	☐	☐	☐	☐	☐	☐	☐	☐	☐
☐	☐	☐	☐	☐	☐	☐	☐	☐	☐	☐	☐
☐	☐	☐	☐	☐	☐	☐	☐	☐	☐	☐	☐
☐	☐	☐	☐	☐	☐	☐	☐	☐	☐	☐	☐

is / **should be**

36. assist students to develop objectivity about themselves and their beliefs and hence examine those beliefs critically

is / **should be**

37. prepare students specifically for useful careers

is / **should be**

38. provide cultural leadership for the community through university-sponsored programs in the arts, public lectures by distinguished persons, athletic events, and other performances, displays or celebrations which present the best of culture, popular or not

is / **should be**

39. carry on applied research

is / **should be**

40. ensure the continued confidence and hence support of those who contribute substantially (other than students and recipients of services) to the finances and other material resource needs of the university

is / **should be**

41. make sure that salaries, teaching assignments, perquisites, and privileges always reflect the contribution that the person involved is making to *his own profession or discipline*

GOALS (cont.)

		of absolutely top importance	of great importance	of medium importance	of little importance	of no importance	don't know or can't say
42. emphasize undergraduate instruction even at the expense of the graduate program	is	☐	☐	☐	☐	☐	☐
	should be	☐	☐	☐	☐	☐	☐
43. involve faculty in the government of the university	is	☐	☐	☐	☐	☐	☐
	should be	☐	☐	☐	☐	☐	☐
44. provide a full round of student activities	is	☐	☐	☐	☐	☐	☐
	should be	☐	☐	☐	☐	☐	☐
45. increase the prestige of the university or, if you believe it is already extremely high, ensure maintenance of that prestige	is	☐	☐	☐	☐	☐	☐
	should be	☐	☐	☐	☐	☐	☐
46. protect and facilitate the students' right to inquire into, investigate, and examine critically any idea or program that they might get interested in	is	☐	☐	☐	☐	☐	☐
	should be	☐	☐	☐	☐	☐	☐
47. maintain top quality in those programs we feel to be especially important (other programs being, of course, up to acceptable standards)	is	☐	☐	☐	☐	☐	☐
	should be	☐	☐	☐	☐	☐	☐

In spite of the length of the above list, it is entirely possible that we have not included aims or goals which are important at this university, or we may have badly stated such an aim or goal; if so, please take this opportunity to correct us by writing them in below.

GOAL		of absolutely top importance	of great importance	of medium importance	of little importance	of no importance	don't know or can't say
48. _____	is	☐	☐	☐	☐	☐	☐
_____	should be	☐	☐	☐	☐	☐	☐
49. _____	is	☐	☐	☐	☐	☐	☐
_____	should be	☐	☐	☐	☐	☐	☐

B. WHO MAKE THE BIG DECISIONS?

1. Think again of the kind of place this university is; that is, what its major goals or distinctive emphases are. Below are listed a number of positions and agencies. In each case, indicate by a check mark in the appropriate space *how much say* you believe persons in those positions have in affecting the major goals of the university. Note we are asking only about the *university as a whole*. A man might have a lot of say in his own department, but not in the university as a whole.

	a great deal of say	quite a bit of say	some say	very little say	no say at all
The regents (or trustees)	☐	☐	☐	☐	☐
Legislators	☐	☐	☐	☐	☐
Sources of large private grants or endowments	☐	☐	☐	☐	☐
Federal government agencies or offices	☐	☐	☐	☐	☐
State government agencies or offices	☐	☐	☐	☐	☐
The President	☐	☐	☐	☐	☐
The vice-presidents (or provosts)	☐	☐	☐	☐	☐
Dean of the graduate school	☐	☐	☐	☐	☐
Dean of liberal arts	☐	☐	☐	☐	☐
Deans of professional schools as a group	☐	☐	☐	☐	☐
Chairmen of departments, considered as a group	☐	☐	☐	☐	☐
The faculty, as a group	☐	☐	☐	☐	☐
The students, as a group	☐	☐	☐	☐	☐
Parents of students, as a group	☐	☐	☐	☐	☐
The citizens of the state, as a group	☐	☐	☐	☐	☐
Alumni, as a group	☐	☐	☐	☐	☐

2. In reviewing the above list of positions and agencies how has the influence of each on major university policies changed during the past *seven* or *eight* years? Has it increased, decreased or remained about the same?

	increased markedly	increased moderately	remained about the same	decreased moderately	decreased markedly
The regents (or trustees)	☐	☐	☐	☐	☐
Legislators	☐	☐	☐	☐	☐
Sources of large private grants or endowments	☐	☐	☐	☐	☐
Federal government agencies or offices	☐	☐	☐	☐	☐
State government agencies or offices	☐	☐	☐	☐	☐
The President	☐	☐	☐	☐	☐
The vice-presidents (or provosts)	☐	☐	☐	☐	☐
Dean of the graduate school	☐	☐	☐	☐	☐
Dean of liberal arts	☐	☐	☐	☐	☐
Deans of professional schools as a group	☐	☐	☐	☐	☐
Chairmen of departments, considered as a group	☐	☐	☐	☐	☐
The faculty, as a group	☐	☐	☐	☐	☐
The students, as a group	☐	☐	☐	☐	☐
Parents of students, as a group	☐	☐	☐	☐	☐
The citizens of the state, as a group	☐	☐	☐	☐	☐
Alumni, as a group	☐	☐	☐	☐	☐

C. THE POWER I HAVE

1. On the line below indicate with a check the approximate amount of power you feel you have to get the things done that you would like to get done in connection with your university role.

A great deal |_____|_____|_____| No power at all

2. How would you have answered the above question seven or eight years ago? If not in office at that time, how do you think your predecessor would have answered it?

A great deal |_____|_____|_____| No power at all

3. If your answers to numbers 1 and 2 are different, how would you describe the difference in power?

Markedly greater (now) |_____|_____|_____| much less (now)

D. SOME OF YOUR IDEAS ABOUT YOURSELF AND YOUR WORK

1. It would take some very strong inducements to get me to leave this university for a position elsewhere.

strongly agree	agree	undecided	disagree	strongly disagree
☐	☐	☐	☐	☐

2. It would take some very strong inducements to get me to accept a position at any place *other than* an academic institution of higher learning.

strongly agree	agree	undecided	disagree	strongly disagree
☐	☐	☐	☐	☐

3. How do you feel about your administrative job(s) at the university?

☐ (1) excellent. I can ask for nothing better

☐ (2) good.

☐ (3) fair.

☐ (4) poor. I hope to make a change

4. What are your plans for the future so far as your work is concerned?

☐ Continue in my present position, or one much like it

☐ Move up to a higher administrative position, or one like my present one at a more prestigious university, if an opportunity comes up

If so, what would represent the culmination of your ambition in administration? _____

_____

☐ Get into, or return to, teaching or research in this, or another university

☐ Leave university work altogether and go into some other kind of institution

E. LASTLY, ABOUT YOURSELF

1. Present age _____

2. Sex _____

3. Marital Status _____

4. Number of Children _____

5. Race _____

6. Place of Birth _____

7. Father's education _____ (Years)

8. Father's occupation during most of adult life _____

9. Mother's education _____ (Years)

10. Your education:

☐ 11 years or less

☐ 12 years

☐ some years of college or university, but no degree received

☐ B.A. (or other bachelor's degree requiring 4 years or more)

   If so, what college or university? _____ Year received _____

   Field of specialization, if any _____

☐ M.A. or M.S., or other Master's degree requiring at least one year beyond the bachelor's degree.

   If so, what university or college? _____ Year received _____

   If so, what field of specialization _____

☐ M.D. If so, what university? _____ Year received _____

☐ Ph.D. If so, what university? _____

    If so, what field of specialization _____

    Year received _____

☐ Other degree than those named.

    What degree? _____ What college or university? _____ What field of

    specialty? _____ Year received _____

11. Title of present position (if more than one is held, please list the other(s): _____

    Department, if any _____

12. In your present position indicate the approximate amount of time spent in each of the following activities:

    Administration   _____ %

    Teaching   _____ %

    Research and Writing   _____ %

    Other   _____ %

13. List below only positions held for 9 months or longer: (please start with *most recent* position)

Kind of Position	Name of Employer	Period of Employment
1.		
2.		
3.		
4.		
5.		
6.		

Comments:

Although a great deal of thought has gone into the construction of this questionnaire, we freely admit that we may have missed items you believe to be important. Please feel free to write in any comments with respect to goals, structure and administration of American universities. We would especially wecome suggestions concerning the analysis of the data assembled through this questionnaire.

_____

_____

_____

_____

_____

_____

_____

_____

_____

_____

_____

Please use the enclosed, self-addressed, reply envelope to return the questionnaire.

Thank you very much.

Index

This book was set in Vladimir by University Graphics, Inc.
It was printed on acid-free, long-life paper and bound by The
Maple Press Company. The designers were Elliot Epstein and
Edward Butler. The editors were Nancy Tressel, Terry Y. Allen,
and Janine Parson for McGraw-Hill Book Company and Verne A.
Stadtman and Sidney J. P. Hollister for the Carnegie Commission
on Higher Education. Milton Heiberg supervised the production.